ALSO BY JEFF GUINN

The Great Santa Search

The Autobiography of Santa Claus

Our Land Before We Die:
The Proud Story of the Seminole Negro

JEREMY P. TARCHER/PENGUIN

a member of Penguin Group (USA) Inc.

New York

How
Mrs. Claus
Saved
Christmas

as told to JEFF GUINN

ILLUSTRATIONS BY MARK HOFFER

JEREMY P. TARCHER/PENGUIN
Published by the Penguin Group
Penguin Group (USA) Inc., 375 Hudson Street, New York, New York 10014, USA •
Penguin Group (Canada), 90 Eglinton Avenue East, Suite 700, Toronto, Ontario M4P 2Y3,
Canada (a division of Pearson Penguin Canada Inc.) • Penguin Books Ltd, 80 Strand, London
WC2R 0RL, England • Penguin Ireland, 25 St Stephen's Green, Dublin 2, Ireland (a division of
Penguin Books Ltd) • Penguin Group (Australia), 250 Camberwell Road, Camberwell, Victoria
3124, Australia (a division of Pearson Australia Group Pty Ltd) • Penguin Books India Pvt Ltd,
11 Community Centre, Panchsheel Park, New Delhi–110 017, India • Penguin Group Ltd (NZ),
Cnr Airborne and Rosedale Roads, Albany, Auckland 1310, New Zealand (a division of Pearson
New Zealand Ltd) • Penguin Books (South Africa) (Pty) Ltd, 24 Sturdee Avenue,
Rosebank, Johannesburg 2196, South Africa • Penguin Books Ltd, Registered Offices:
80 Strand, London WC2R 0RL, England

First trade paperback edition 2006
Copyright © 2005 by 24Words, LLC
Illustrations © 1995 by Mark Hoffer

Most Tarcher/Penguin books are available at special quantity discounts for bulk purchase
for sales promotions, premiums, fund-raising, and educational needs. Special books or book
excerpts also can be created to fit specific needs. For details, write Penguin Group (USA) Inc.
Special Markets, 375 Hudson Street, New York, NY 10014.

The Library of Congress catalogued the hardcover edition as follows:

Guinn, Jeff.
How Mrs. Claus saved Christmas / as told to Jeff Guinn.
p. cm.
ISBN 1-58542-437-4
1. Santa Claus—Fiction. I. Title.
PS3557.U375H69   2005   2005044134
813'.54—dc22
ISBN 1-58542-535-4 (paperback edition)

Printed in the United States of America
3 5 7 9 10 8 6 4 2

This book is printed on acid-free paper. ♾

BOOK DESIGN BY AMANDA DEWEY

The recipes contained in this book are to be followed exactly as written. The publisher is not
responsible for your specific health or allergy needs that may require medical supervision. The
publisher is not responsible for any adverse reactions to the recipes contained in this book.

While the author has made every effort to provide accurate telephone numbers and Internet ad-
dresses at the time of publication, neither the publisher nor the author assumes any responsibility
for errors, or for changes that occur after publication. Further, the publisher does not have any
control over and does not assume any responsibility for author or third-party websites or their
content.

For Sara Carder

Thanks

We had just settled into our seats that evening, each of us enjoying a thick wedge of Candy Cane Pie, a special recipe by a wonderful Norwegian pastry chef named Lars. He makes the most fabulous desserts you can imagine, and many more you can't.

Foreword

WE NEVER STOP WORKING at the North Pole. Though children all over the world only expect to find presents from us on one of three mornings—December 6, December 25, or January 6—we need the rest of the year to design and build their toys. In fact, we work just as hard during the spring, summer, and fall as we do around those wonderful winter holidays of St. Nicholas Day, Christmas, and the Epiphany. Most people, I find, don't realize this. Over the years, I've seen thousands of cartoons about where Santa likes to take his vacations. These are often funny drawings of me on the beach sipping a drink through a straw, or at a baseball game enjoying a hot dog. And it's true I enjoy baseball and hot dogs, but I mostly do so in my den at the North Pole, watching the game on television and eating the hot dog from a tray on my lap. Beaches are less enticing. As someone who is well over seventeen hundred years old and, I admit, perhaps a few pounds overweight, wearing a bathing suit in public is not something I'm eager to do.

Besides, there simply isn't leisure time to spend at the beach. There are no magic North Pole buttons we can push to make toys instantly appear for every deserving girl and boy. I explained in a book I wrote about my life that there is a fair share of magic in what we do, but there's plenty of hard work, too. Everyone living here at the North Pole—and there are hundreds of us—is kept very busy from the time we gather for breakfast each morning, at eight o'clock sharp, until about six or so in the evening, when there's dinner and, afterward, well-deserved relaxation and fellowship until it's time to go to bed.

Designed by the great inventor Leonardo da Vinci, our North Pole home is a complex series of buildings and tunnels mostly underneath the snow, so that no one in planes flying overhead will notice us. The long, well-lighted workshops and assembly lines are separated from everyone's private living quarters by a large dining hall and several other rooms where comfortable chairs and sofas and widescreen televisions and well-stocked bookshelves make it pleasant for friends to gather and chat, read, or watch movies. No one is required to be anywhere doing anything. It's all very informal. Those who want quiet to enjoy their books can have complete peace in one place, while in another, dozens may be happily gathered to watch a hilarious film. Leonardo was careful to make each room soundproof, so that hearty laughter from one room does not disturb companionable silence in another.

Though everyone is free to choose what to do and whom to spend their evenings with, it often happens that one group is comprised of what we call "the old companions"—those of us who have been together longest in this eternal mission of helping everyone celebrate the joy and wonder of the holiday season. I'm never happier than when these very special people are gathered with me—Felix, the Roman slave who became my first companion; Attila, known through the ages as The Hun, and his wife, Dorothea; Arthur, the British war chief who, in legend, became celebrated as a king; St. Francis of Assisi, who wrote some of the first Christmas carols; Willie Skokan, the incomparable craftsman; Leonardo da Vinci and Benjamin Franklin, two great inventors and significant figures in world history; Sarah Kemble Knight, Felix's wife, who wrote the very first book about traveling in America; Teddy Roosevelt, the former president of the United States; Amelia Earhart, the wonderful aviator; and Bill Pickett, the great cowboy who could wrestle any steer to the ground in a matter of seconds. And, of course, there's the person I love and admire most of all, my wife, Layla, whose common sense and courage have inspired us during many challenging times.

Although we've known one another for a very long time, being together remains quite agreeable. Sometimes we don't even get around to watching a movie or reading books at all, because someone tells a favorite story and then everyone else begins reminiscing about wonderful times or places or people. Even though we've heard these same stories hundreds or even thousands of time before, they're still enjoyable. Felix, for instance, loves to tell about how he met George Washington and informed him that the German troops opposing him in the Revolutionary War would be spending Christmas night celebrating rather than guarding their camp. Based on this information, General Washington crossed the Delaware after dark on December 25, 1776, and took the Germans by surprise. Teddy Roosevelt is always ready to jump in and talk about his great adventures, including how he helped create eighteen national monuments. Leonardo might recall painting his masterpiece, the *Mona Lisa*. Every so often, I'm coaxed into recounting my first days of gift-giving, when I was a bishop in the early Christian church and even before that, as a small boy whose dream it was to bring comfort to those in need. Actually, I need very little coaxing.

Everyone always seems to have a story to share, and occasionally that includes Layla. But on most evenings, she prefers sitting quietly and listening to others. It isn't that she's too shy to speak. As Layla has demonstrated throughout the sixteen centuries we've been married, if she feels there is something that ought to be said, she will say it, and always in her pleasant, practical way. Layla is so intelligent, and so perceptive—she was the one back in the 1100s who helped us decide we must give toys to children instead of food, because the food would soon be gone but the toys would be lasting reminders that someone cared enough about them to bring gifts. It was also my wife who suggested that we deliver these gifts on three special nights rather than randomly throughout the year, so that we would have time to properly prepare, but more important, to help keep holiday traditions alive. And it was Layla, in the middle 1640s, who saved Christmas.

That's a story no one but Layla, Arthur, and I really knew until recently, when it came up by accident. We had not deliberately kept it a secret. For more than three and a half centuries, Layla simply didn't feel like talking about these particular Christmas-related events, which have been mostly overlooked by historians. Oh, they get some of the basic facts right—for a while in England, celebrating Christmas was against the law, until finally the people protested and got their beloved holiday back again—but they have no idea of the important part Layla played in it.

None of our other North Pole companions did, either, until the night we sat down to watch a movie about one of history's more controversial figures. I should perhaps explain how we came to watch this particular film. It is our custom to take turns selecting what movie will be watched. If, for instance, Ben Franklin chooses on one night, it will not be his turn again until each of the other "old companions" has had the chance to make a selection. Everyone's choice is always honored, and it's interesting to see who likes to watch what. You would think, for instance, that Bill Pickett would want movies about cowboys, but he loves those colorful films about a boy wizard named Harry Potter.

St. Francis likes the Disney cartoon *Peter Pan*; we've worn out several cassette copies, though the DVD version has lasted longer. Attila would watch *Some Like It Hot* every night, if he could. Christmas-themed movies like *It's a Wonderful Life* and *A Christmas Story* are always popular. None of us like films that contain a great deal of violence. We are people who love peace, not war. But movies based on history are always interesting. After all, some of us might have been there.

We all find it amusing that Arthur enjoys movies about himself. There are so many, most based on the colorful but inaccurate myth that Arthur was a British king who lived in a magical place called Camelot and fought evildoers with the help of a great wizard named Merlin. Arthur always claims to be embarrassed by such embellishment. In fact, he'd been a war chief in the 500s who, for a while, helped hold off Saxon invaders before they finally overran Britain. Layla, Felix, Attila, Dorothea, and I had found him lying wounded in a barn. We nursed him back to health, and he joined us in our gift-giving mission.

But books were written about mythical King Arthur, and poems and songs, too. When movies were invented (by Leonardo, Willie Skokan, and Ben Franklin, though they let others take the credit) there were soon films that also emphasized the Arthur legend rather than real history. We sometimes watch these at the North Pole, always at Arthur's suggestion. He tries to make it seem that he isn't secretly flattered; "Let's watch this new exaggeration," Arthur might say. "How silly it is." But his eyes stay glued to the huge widescreen television on which our movies are played.

One of the better versions, perhaps because of its wonderful songs, is a musical called *Camelot*, based on a fine book, *The Once and Future King*, by T. H. White. The theme of the movie, and the book, is that more is always accomplished by kindness than by violence. An actor named Richard Harris plays King Arthur in the movie. He does it quite well, though he doesn't look exactly like Arthur. He wears a beard in the movie, and Arthur never had a beard.

But a few weeks after we saw *Camelot* for perhaps the twentieth time, when Arthur's turn came around again he suggested we watch Richard Harris in another movie. We had just settled into our seats that evening, each of us enjoying a thick wedge of Candy Cane Pie, a special recipe by a wonderful Norwegian pastry chef named Lars. He makes the most fabulous desserts you can imagine, and many more you can't. We were thrilled when he agreed to join us at the North Pole. And, afterward, some of us began to put on a bit of additional weight, me perhaps most of all.

"This movie has more real history than *Camelot*," Arthur explained, setting down his plate of pie. "It's called *Cromwell*, and it's about the British Civil War in the 1640s."

"You were in England during that time, weren't you?" asked Sarah Kemble Knight. Sarah hadn't joined us until 1727, so she often requested such clarification.

"I was, along with Layla and Leonardo," Arthur replied. "That was the same time that Santa and Felix were trying to introduce Christmas to the colonies in America." Before he started the movie, he talked a little about Oliver Cromwell, a leader of the revolution against the British king. Leonardo added a few comments. Layla didn't. I thought she looked rather sad.

Then we lowered the lights and the film began. Richard Harris, playing Cromwell, stormed across the screen, pounding his fist and shouting. He did this in scene after scene, until after one particularly loud episode Layla spoke for the first time.

"He wasn't like that at all," she said. Though her voice was low, everyone instantly paid attention, because it was unusual for Layla to comment during a movie.

"You knew Oliver Cromwell?" Teddy Roosevelt piped up. "I had no idea, Layla. Did you actually speak to him?"

Arthur paused the DVD and reached over to turn on the lights.

"Did Layla ever speak to Cromwell?" he replied. "Why, several times! If you knew the entire story—"

"There's no need to tell it," Layla interrupted. "I'm sorry I said anything. Please, Arthur, start the movie again."

But now everyone was curious. "It surely seems like there's something interesting here," Bill Pickett remarked in his slow drawl. "I'd rather hear about it than watch the movie." Several of our other companions loudly agreed.

Dorothea, who has been one of Layla's closest friends for over fifteen hundred years, quickly said, "If Layla doesn't want to talk about it, she shouldn't have to. Though, of course, I'd be very happy to listen if she does."

Layla frowned. I could tell that there were things she was tempted to say, but for more than three hundred years she had never talked about her time with Cromwell, except to me in 1700 when we reunited back in America. Some memories can be painful as well as happy at the same time, and this, I knew, was one of those instances.

"You hardly ever tell stories, Layla," Amelia Earhart pointed out. "It's usually Felix, or Teddy Roosevelt, or Santa. Please, take a turn now. You say that Cromwell wasn't loud, that he didn't shout like the actor in the movie?"

"No, I never heard him shout," Layla said, choosing her words carefully. "He was a determined man, someone who I completely disagreed with about Christmas. Oliver Cromwell thought Christmas was sinful, and tried to end it forever. But he wasn't *evil*, you see. That was what made it harder when—"

"When what?" Amelia urged.

Layla looked at me, a question in her eyes. I knew she was silently asking whether I thought she should continue. It wasn't a matter of me granting permission. Layla never asks, or needs, my permission to do anything. But she values my opinion, as I always do hers.

"I think this might be a story that should finally be told, Layla," I said, looking around the room. Most of our good, dear friends were perched on the edges of their seats, watching Layla and obviously hoping she would tell whatever the story was about Oliver Cromwell and his attempt to end Christmas. "I've often said that it's wrong for me always to get credit for almost every good thing in Christmas history. Perhaps everyone here should know about your incredible accomplishment, too."

"I really did very little," Layla replied. "It was the others—Elizabeth and Alan Hayes, for instance, and all those brave apprentices in London, and Avery Sabine, though he surely didn't mean to help us. And . . . and—"

"And Sara," Arthur added, his voice very soft.

"And Sara most of all," Layla agreed. She sat quietly for a moment, thinking hard. "All right. I'll tell the story, if everyone wants to hear it."

"Please do," begged Teddy Roosevelt, who usually preferred telling stories to listening. "Who were Elizabeth and Alan Hayes, Layla, and what about apprentices and this Avery fellow? Who was Sara, who seems so special to you? And why haven't you mentioned any of this before?"

"Some things are almost too important, and perhaps too painful, to mention," Layla said quietly before drawing a deep breath. "All right, then. In 1645 and again in 1647, the British Parliament voted that celebrating Christmas was against the law. I had spent quite a bit of time with Arthur and Leonardo at our secret toy factory in London, and—"

"Please, Layla, share more than that," Amelia pleaded. "Why were you in England in the 1640s, when Santa was in America?"

"Well, remember, he wasn't called Santa then," Layla reminded. "That name only came fifty or sixty years later. Before that we all called him by his given name, Nicholas. He was in America because we wanted to encourage Christmas celebrations there. I stayed behind since there were still things to do in Europe and England, especially in England. Now, Oliver Cromwell wasn't the only Englishman to oppose Christmas. The story goes back a very long way. There are lots of details. One is even related, in a manner of speaking, to the Candy Cane Pie that Lars baked for us tonight. Are you sure you want to hear it all?"

This time, I answered. "Yes, Layla, tell everything. And start, please, at the very beginning, because I doubt some people here even know very much about your childhood. Don't imagine that we'll be bored. It will be our pleasure to listen."

And so, Layla told her story. It was such a magical evening that the next day I called a writer from Texas who helped me with my autobiography. I asked him to capture Layla's words on paper so that you, too, could enjoy the story of how Mrs. Claus saved Christmas.

—Santa Claus
The North Pole

As I stood as close to the tomb as I could, a strange feeling came over me.
It wasn't sadness, though I felt very bad for the crippled and poor people
and wanted with all my heart to do something to help them.

CHAPTER

One

f I start at the very beginning, we must go back to the year 377 A.D., when I was born in the small farming town of Niobrara in the country then known as Lycia. Its modern-day name is Turkey. With a population of two hundred, Niobrara was, in those days, a medium-sized community. Almost everyone living in my hometown at that time had something to do with growing, grinding, or selling grain, though a few families had groves of dates instead. I know many people today believe most of Turkey is just sand and wind, but there are some very green, fertile places, and Niobrara was in one of them. Most visitors to Niobrara were travelers briefly passing through on their way to bigger, more important cities and ports. And, always, bands of poor nomads would briefly camp on the outskirts of town, hoping to earn a few days' wages by helping harvest crops.

I lived on one of the wheat farms with my Uncle Silas and Aunt

Lodi. They took me in while I was still a baby. My mother was Aunt Lodi's only sister, so when she and my father died unexpectedly of some unnamed disease, it was natural for my aunt and uncle to bring me into their home and raise me as though I were their daughter. There was nothing unusual about this. There were many orphans in those days. People didn't live very long. Even if they were healthy, fifty or sixty was considered great old age. No one knew much about medicine, so if you did get sick the chances were good you would die rather than get better. When I was a child, Aunt Lodi sometimes called me "Layla the Miracle Girl," because I didn't catch whatever disease it was that took my parents. "God must have special plans for you," she would tell me, keeping her voice low so Uncle Silas wouldn't hear.

Aunt Lodi

Like most men of his time, Uncle Silas wouldn't have accepted the possibility that any girl could be special. He loved me, I knew. Childless themselves, he and Aunt Lodi never acted like I was a burden passed on to them because of my parents' bad luck. Uncle Silas often carried me on his shoulders as we passed through town. He told me funny folktales and bought fine soft blankets for my bed and even let me have real leather sandals, a rare treat for a child. But, when I asked, he never let me come into the fields with him to work. Nor was I allowed to go to school to learn to read or write. By tradition, only boys were allowed to do these things, and Uncle Silas was a very traditional man.

"Honor God by knowing your place, little Layla," he would tell me over and over. "Let your Aunt Lodi teach you all the womanly tasks, and learn to be satisfied by them."

Well, I wasn't. By "womanly tasks," Uncle Silas meant I should become expert at cooking gruel and wheat cakes and lamb stew, and at washing clothes in the nearby river and fashioning brooms from river reeds and stout limbs of wood. My aunt did these things with a smile on her face, for she loved Uncle Silas dearly, but sometimes in the evening when he was out talking with his friends she would quietly tell me to not only keep my dreams, but to make them come true if I could.

What were those dreams? Not to settle for a woman's secondary place in a small farming village, for one thing. I had no quarrel with others who wanted nothing more out of life. Each of us should have the right to decide who and what we want to be. But when travelers passed through Niobrara on their way to somewhere else more exciting, I heard them mention Constantinople and Athens and Rome and I yearned to see these places for myself.

I also badly wanted to learn to read and write. We were a Christian community, and there were priests who would gather the boys several days each week for informal lessons. No one had paper and ink to spare back then. The priests would take sharp sticks and scratch letters and numbers into the dusty ground, while their pupils gathered around. When I tried to quietly join them, hanging back at the edge of the group, the priests would eventually notice me and shout that I had to go away immediately. But I kept trying, and each time I might learn a new letter or a new combination of letters that spelled a word before I was ordered to leave. By the time I was ten I was able to read and write quite adequately, though Aunt Lodi and I kept this a secret from Uncle Silas.

It was no secret from him, though, that I could do what in those days we called "sums," adding and subtracting numbers. At night in our hut, Uncle Silas would sit by the fire and try to do the accounts for the farm, adding up the money from the bushels of wheat he'd sold that day, and subtracting the wages he'd paid his nomad helpers to harvest it, then factoring in the cost of new seed. He was a kind man, but not good at math. He would say all the numbers out loud, hoping that would help him get the totals right: "Sixty-four coins for three bushels, plus seventy coins for four more, less sixty-nine coins for the help and forty-four for the seed, and that leaves . . . twenty-two? That doesn't sound right. Sixty-four and seventy, less sixty-nine and forty-four. Twenty-three? Twenty?"

"It leaves twenty-one, Uncle Silas," I said from across the room, where I was already wrapped up in my blankets for the night. Children went to bed quite early then, usually as soon as it was dark.

"What? Are you certain?" Uncle Silas blurted, and he spent the next several minutes muttering various sums until, finally, he saw that I was right. "Layla, how did you know that? Have you sneaked over to the boys' school again while they were studying mathematics?"

"No, Uncle Silas," I said, and it was the truth. That morning, I hadn't sneaked over during their math lessons. They'd been working on reading and spelling instead.

"Then how in the name of heaven are you able to calculate sums so quickly?" my uncle demanded. "It's quite unwomanly, I fear."

"Layla has a natural gift for sums," Aunt Lodi said, looking up from the shirt she was mending. "God-given ability is not unwomanly, I'm sure."

Uncle Silas was less certain, but he still found it convenient to have me help him keep his daily accounts—so long as I did this in the privacy of our home, where no neighbors could observe it. It was pleasing to me to have this special privilege, but I still wanted something more out of life. And, as I grew up, I became more aware of what that was, because of certain stories I kept hearing.

Throughout Lycia, there were tales of a mysterious gift-giver who came to poor people in the night and left them things they needed— cloaks or blankets or sandals. Those who were hungry sometimes awoke to find bread or cheese or dried fruits beside their beds. This was a wonderful, even miraculous thing, because times were hard and most people had all they could do to provide sufficiently for themselves and their own families. Charity was rare.

But this unknown gift-giver, who apparently was ageless since he'd been carrying out his wonderful mission for over ninety years, took charity to previously unthought-of heights. He bestowed his presents in big cities like Myra and smaller towns like Lycia—and Niobrara! Several times during my childhood, some of the nomads camping outside the village came whooping into town, crying out with joy that someone had left new cloaks for their children, or enough bread and cheese to feed their families for a week! Though none of the gifts was ever enough to supply anyone's needs for years or even months, it was the gesture itself that brought such happiness. Someone cared enough about poor people to seek them out and quietly minister to their specific needs.

I don't mean to imply that no one else cared for the poor. At the end of each harvest, after all our bills were paid and enough money set aside for the rest of the year, Uncle Silas was pleased to distribute the remaining grain to the men he'd hired. They, in turn, could sell the grain in other markets and use the money to feed and clothe their wives and children for a little while. This was one public task Uncle Silas gladly shared with me. I loved going with him to the nomad camps and handing the small sacks of grain to the hungry, ragged people there, though afterward I remembered their thin cloaks

Uncle Silas

and thinner bodies and wished I could do even more. Twice, Uncle Silas punished me for giving my nice sandals to nomad girls who were barefoot. My punishment was only being sent to bed without supper. Even when he ordered me to go to my blankets, Uncle Silas added that he understood why I had done it.

"It's a sad thing, Layla, to see the poverty in this world," he said, gently patting my shoulder. "But you must learn, girl, that there's only so much any of us can do to help other people. If they're meant to be hungry or barefoot, that can't be any of our concern."

"Who means them to be hungry or barefoot?" I asked. "If I could, I would spend my whole life bringing gifts to people."

Uncle Silas sighed the way grown-ups often do when children ask difficult questions.

"I suppose God decides who is rich and who is poor," he said. "We must leave these things to him. As for you, girl, no life of gift-giving is possible. Get that thought out of your mind. You're almost twelve now, and in another year or two it will be time for you to take a husband and have a family of your own. Think of that instead."

I *was* thinking of that, when I wasn't dreaming of traveling the world and going out anonymously in the night to give gifts to the poor. All the other girls my age in Niobrara acted obsessed with the idea of marriage. They seemed to believe they would be asked to marry a young man, move into a home with him, have and raise children, and live happily ever after. When they talked about it, they never mentioned the endless chores that made up most of a married woman's life. I didn't mind chores, ever, if I thought they were accomplishing something worthwhile. Planting wheat would have been exciting, had Uncle Silas allowed me to do it, because stalks would grow and grain would be harvested and people would eat. But sweeping a floor just moved dust from one place to another. It seemed to me there was no real accomplishment in that. I had nothing against marriage, either, if I could be an equal partner rather than my husband's servant.

Because Niobrara was a small town, everyone knew everyone else and families often planned from the time of their children's birth who might grow up to marry whom. Though Aunt Lodi understood my dreams of travel and independence, Uncle Silas made a point on too many nights of mentioning various village boys to me, always adding what there might be about them that would make them desirable husbands.

"Have you noticed Hiram's son Matthew lately?" he might ask Aunt Lodi over dinner, pretending to be talking to her but really intending to be heard by me. "He's just turned sixteen, and he's a strapping young fellow, a very good worker. Of course, he's got three older brothers and Hiram's farm isn't big enough to support all the extra families when the four boys marry, but if Matthew married the right girl who inherited her own place, I think he'd be a fine provider."

At twelve, I was not pretty and seemed unlikely ever to become so. My jaw was long, and everyone said my eyes had the unwomanly quality of looking right through people, instead of my gaze being modestly cast down at the ground, which was more proper for a nice girl. No prospective husband was likely to want me for my looks, or for my attitude.

But I was going to inherit Uncle Silas's farm when he and Aunt Lodi passed away, and a very good farm it was. Enough wheat could be grown there to support a family in comfort, if not luxury, and all but the very richest young men in our area were very aware of this possibility. And so, as I became thirteen and then fourteen, boys and even older widowed men began dropping by our home, supposedly to visit my uncle and aunt but really looking over our barn and fields and the niece who would someday own them. When they greeted me, often praising my beauty and charm, I knew they were lying. They thought the farm was beautiful and charming, not me. After each one left, Uncle Silas would ask what I thought of him. My response was never satisfactory.

"Blast it, girl, there must be some man you would like to marry!" Uncle Silas shouted in the spring of 395, raising his voice because he was so frustrated. "I'm not like other men who order girls to marry someone specific. I'm letting you make your own choice. But you must make it soon, Layla! Your aunt and I are getting older, into our fifties, and we could die at any time. You are eighteen, already almost past the prime age for marriage. You must have a husband to take over the farm and care for you!"

"Why must I have a husband at all?" I asked for the hundredth, or perhaps the thousandth, time. "I could run the farm. I can certainly take care of myself, too."

Uncle Silas shook his head. "Young women must have husbands, Layla. That's all there is to it. Talk to the girl, Lodi! See if you can get her to see the sense of what I'm saying."

Aunt Lodi was gentler than Uncle Silas, but she was concerned about me, too.

"I want you to be happy, Layla," she said as we carried a basket of clothes down to the river to wash them. "You are intelligent, and warm-hearted, and I understand all your dreams to travel and help the poor. But you must be practical, too. It is hard, even impossible, for a woman to make her way alone in the world. Perhaps you could find a husband who wanted to do the same things."

"There's no one like that in Niobrara," I said gloomily. "When any man here looks at me, he sees the farm instead of Layla. And if I can't travel away from here, how can I meet a man who would love me for who I am, rather than what I'm going to inherit?"

"We'll pray about this, you and I," Aunt Lodi replied. "You are too special for your dreams not to somehow come true."

A few days later, Aunt Lodi suggested to Uncle Silas that the three of us make the forty-mile trip to Myra.

"We all need new clothes, and I've heard so much about the wonderful tomb there that I'm eager to see it," she said. Of course, my uncle and I both knew about the tomb to which she referred. For many years, Myra and its surrounding towns had been blessed by the presence of Bishop Nicholas, by all accounts a wonderful man who loved everyone and who encouraged generosity of spirit. It had been during his lifetime that the mysterious gift-giver began leaving his presents, and there had been some rumors that Nicholas was the one doing it. But in 343 he died quietly in the night. The community responded by building a splendid new church in his honor, and his body was placed in an elaborate tomb. Almost immediately, sick people began coming to the tomb to pray for cures, and some of them claimed they had miraculously been healed. And when the gift-giver continued coming quietly by night and leaving food or clothing to those in need, everyone knew it couldn't have been Bishop Nicholas after all—which is when the stories really took on new, fantastic tones. Now people whispered that the mysterious person had magical powers—he could turn himself into the wind, perhaps, and whistle into houses through cracks under doors.

So, a trip to Myra was exciting in several ways. The possibility of new clothes meant little to me. I never really cared what I wore. But I did want to see the wonderful tomb, and any time I could be somewhere different than my old familiar hometown, I was ready to go. Though I had been taken by my uncle and aunt to small communities near Niobrara, I had never traveled so far before, or to such a big city. If going to Myra wasn't quite the adventure of which I'd been dreaming, it was still closer to that dream than anything I'd previously experienced.

It took several days to prepare for the journey. Uncle Silas had to rent a cart, and a mule to pull it. Aunt Lodi and I baked extra loaves of bread and bought some dried fruit in the town market. Going forty miles would take at least two days. We needed food to eat on the way. There were no paved roads between Niobrara and Myra, just well-worn paths where dust swirled a little less because the dirt was so hard-packed by generations of feet, hooves, and wheels.

I loved the trip to Myra, though it also frustrated me. It was wonderful to watch other travelers, many of them wearing exotic-looking robes. We passed caravans of heavily-laden camels and could smell the aroma of the rare spices they were transporting. But the trip took so long! When the wheel of our cart caught in a rut, it took an hour for my uncle, sweating, to wrench it out. I wanted to help, but as a woman I was required to stand quietly to the side, the hood of my robe pulled modestly around my face. How boring!

But there was nothing boring about Myra, which had so many buildings you could actually see them hundreds of yards ahead before you even entered the city! People milled about, and animals added moos and bleats to the general cacophony, and the market in the center of the city must have had a hundred different stalls. Uncle Silas left Aunt Lodi and me at the market, telling us to look around for good bargains on new cloaks while he found a stable for the mule and an inn for us to sleep in that night—we would be staying for several days. Aunt Lodi was eager to begin shopping, but I wanted to do something else.

"Please, let's go right away to see the tomb of Bishop Nicholas," I pleaded. "The cloaks will still be for sale in the morning."

"The tomb will be there in the morning, too," Aunt Lodi replied. "Why are you so anxious to see it?"

I didn't know. I just felt I had to go there. It took several minutes, but I convinced my aunt that it would be all right for me to find the tomb by myself while she shopped. Aunt Lodi made me promise that I would take only a brief look at the tomb, then rejoin her at the market.

"You and Silas and I can go take a long look at it tomorrow," she said. "Be certain you meet me right back here by sunset. I don't want you walking the streets of a strange city all alone after dark."

I promised I would, and hurried off. It wasn't hard to find the tomb. The first woman I asked knew exactly where it was, though she warned me I might not be able to get a very good look at it.

"The cripples, you know, gather around it before dawn and spend all day praying to be healed," she said. "Bishop Nicholas, of course, is given credit for granting such miracles, and perhaps he does. My hands get very swollen and sore sometimes; I'm thinking of going to the tomb and praying to him myself."

And she was right. The tomb was actually inside the church, and a magnificent thing it was, higher all by itself than any structure I had ever seen before, with the date of Bishop Nicholas's death carved into the stone—December 6, 343, it was—as well as his likeness. He had been, apparently, a striking-looking man, with long hair and a beard. He appeared a bit stouter than most, but then bishops also ate better (and, apparently, more) than the rest of us. I wanted to look closer at the carving of the bishop, but dozens of cripples surrounded the tomb and I didn't want to push them aside. Some were blind, others couldn't walk, and their crutches lay beside them as they prayed, silently or out loud, to be healed. As I stood behind them, I also noticed in the shadows to the side of the tomb a number of other people, all ragged and hungry looking, quietly waiting, though I had no idea for what.

"Who are they?" I asked a reasonably well-dressed man who was standing beside me.

"It's an odd thing," he said. "Ever since this tomb was built, poor people passing through Myra seem to get comfort from just being near it."

As I stood as close to the tomb as I could, a strange feeling came over me. It wasn't sadness, though I felt very badly for the crippled and poor people, and wanted with all my heart to do something to help them. And it wasn't exactly excitement, either, though I was thrilled to be in a large city for the first time in my life. If I had to describe it, I would say I felt inspired. My eyes moved from the poor people to the carving of Bishop Nicholas's kind face, back and forth between them while time passed and I didn't notice the afternoon shadows growing long and deep. Finally, as night fell, everyone began to leave. I felt as though I was being jostled awake from a wonderful dream. Then I realized it was nighttime, and I remembered Aunt Lodi waiting back at the market.

She was very angry with me when I finally returned, a bit out of breath because I'd run all the way from the tomb.

"If Silas knew you'd been out gallivanting until after dark, he'd pack up the cart and have us back on the road to Niobrara at dawn.

What was there about the bishop's tomb that made you forget your promise to come right back?"

I don't recall my answer, though I do remember she didn't tell Uncle Silas about how I had disobeyed. The three of us stayed in Myra for four days. We bought clothes and ate wonderful food and wandered around the city marveling at its size and all the people who lived there. Twice, we went to see the bishop's tomb. Both times, I was overcome by the same sense of inspiration. I did not tell my uncle and aunt about it, but afterward when we were back home in Niobrara I found myself having the same dream almost every night. I would be in a different place in each dream, but in the company of the same man. He was older than me and somewhat overweight. His hair and beard were white. No one who looked like him lived in Niobrara, yet his face was very familiar.

The first dog kept barking, and several more joined in the thunderous chorus. There was nothing for me to do but turn and run. As I did, I dropped the loaves of bread, which were long and thin, and then I lost my grip on the blankets as I dashed madly through the darkness back toward the city.

TWO

was twenty-four when first my aunt, and then my uncle, passed away. Though I mourned them, it was hardly a surprise when they died. Aunt Lodi was fifty-seven, and Uncle Silas was fifty-nine. By the standards of the day, each had reached great old age. And, in a way, it was merciful that Uncle Silas quickly followed Aunt Lodi to heaven, because in the days after she was gone he was simply lost without her. The wheat in his fields remained unharvested. He sat in our hut staring into the fire, saying very little. I did the best I could to comfort him, but it soon became obvious he was not long for life, either.

"Marry, Layla," he said during our last conversation. His voice was quite weak. "Find a good husband."

"I promise," I replied, and felt somehow I was telling the truth, even though I was no more willing than ever to marry a man from Niobrara and become a farmer's wife.

Uncle Silas's death created a very difficult situation for me. As his only heir, his farm became mine. But no woman in Niobrara, or anywhere else that anyone in Niobrara knew of, lived alone and managed a farm by herself. This was supposed to be done on her behalf by a husband or son or uncle or cousin, or at least a close male friend. I had none of these.

"Choose a man and get on with your life," people told me over and over. When I tried to hire workers to harvest the grain, they all refused to work for a woman. A year after my uncle had passed I was still unmarried, and even the other women in the village began to act uncomfortable around me. Once, several of them pulled me aside and told me I was acting "unnatural."

I knew better. I had spent the year making plans. Never forgetting Aunt Lodi's words, I was not only keeping my dreams, I was going to try to make them come true.

Layla

Besides the farm, which was worth something itself, Uncle Silas had bequeathed me some money. It wasn't a fortune by any means, but the small pile of coins he'd accumulated over the years amounted to enough for what I needed—a sum sufficient to keep me in simple food and clothing for a long time, with quite a bit left over. And I knew what I wanted to do with the money that was left.

The mysterious gift-giver of local legend might be magical, or might not. I could not be that person—I certainly had no special powers—but I could do some of the same things. I would take my money and use it to buy blankets and cloaks and food for people in need. During the year between my uncle's death and the time I left Niobrara, I thought long and hard about how best to do this. Gradually, I realized several things.

First, as a giver I, too, must remain anonymous. Even the very poorest people still had pride and might be insulted by a strange woman simply handing them gifts. The legendary gift-giver, whoever that was or might have been, was right to leave presents at night and in secret.

Second, I must distribute my gifts as widely as possible. There were poor, deserving people everywhere. To stay in one place for too long would also cause another problem. After a while, people in the area would begin to stay awake at night in the hope that they could find out who the gift-giver might be. Besides, I wanted badly to travel.

Third, it would be impossible to give anyone in need all that he or she might require. If I helped a few in a substantial way, all my money would soon be gone and I would have nothing left for anyone else. But if I did something small but important for each one, then hundreds, perhaps even thousands, of good if impoverished men, women, and children would at least know that, in a hard world, someone had cared enough about them to leave tokens of respect and assistance. In a very real sense, my gift to them would be hope.

There was, of course, another inevitable dilemma. Even if I was very frugal regarding my own needs, and kept the gifts I gave small and inexpensive, the money I had would only last for so long. In seven or eight years, ten at the most, it would all be gone. I had only one farm to sell, only one accumulation of coins to spend. When they were used up, I would have no way to get any more. It was possible, even probable, that when my final gifts were given I would then become exactly the same as those I'd done my best to help—an impoverished person who would have to depend on the charity of others. Starvation might be my eventual fate.

I accepted this. It didn't frighten me, perhaps because I did not expect something like that to happen. I believed—somehow, actually, I *knew*—my future held something different, something wonderful. At night I still dreamed of being in many places with the white-bearded man, and the inspiration I felt that first afternoon at the tomb of St. Nicholas had remained with me ever since.

So it was just after my twenty-fifth birthday that I walked into Niobrara and announced to the men gathered near the well there that I was selling my uncle's farm. Did anyone want to buy it at a fair price?

Oh, the men made a fuss, and told me I shouldn't sell, that I should marry and let my husband run the farm instead, but I knew that they were already making calculations in their heads. What was the lowest price they could offer to a woman who, by reason of her gender, certainly wouldn't have the intelligence to recognize the amount wasn't nearly enough? So over the next few days, one by one they came to my hut and made their bids, and every time went home shaking their heads and muttering about this extremely unfeminine woman who drove such a hard bargain. But it was a good farm, certainly a profitable one, and after a week or so I made a very fine sale indeed. I collected the money, got together the few belongings I wanted to take with me, and prepared to leave Niobrara and embark on my great adventure.

This was when I began to understand the extent of my challenge.

I had a good-sized pouch of coins strapped inside my cloak, with cotton mixed in with the coins to keep them from jingling. I hadn't yet been out much in the world, but I knew well enough that thieves lurked everywhere, and any of them would be eager to rob a female traveler with money. Still, I could afford to rent a cart and mule—my plan was to return to Myra, pray at Bishop Nicholas's tomb myself, and then begin my own gift-giving mission wherever whim and fate might take me.

But no one in Niobrara would rent me a mule and cart. Everyone said it was simply too dangerous for a woman to travel to Myra all by herself. I was certain I would be safe, so long as I was careful, but no one would hear of it. When I said I would walk to Myra instead, they said they could not allow it and would restrain me if necessary. I had to wait impatiently for almost three days before a farm family from town set off to Myra, and allowed me to ride along with them in their wagon. It was a very frustrating trip. The whole way, the husband and wife kept telling me how foolish I was to be leaving such a nice, safe place—surely I would rather marry and settle down instead of risking my life on some dangerous, lonely trip.

They dropped me off in the market at Myra with many final recommendations that I should come to my senses. I managed not to reply that I was being quite sensible, thank you very much. Then I found that things would be just as difficult for me in Myra as they were in Niobrara, if not more so.

Since I planned to stay for several days, buying and then distributing gifts to the very poorest people in Myra I could find, I first needed to take a room at an inn. I wanted the inn to be clean but inexpensive. Every coin I spent on my own comfort would be one less I had for gifts. But I must have gone to a dozen inns where I was turned away. In the big cities, it seemed, unmarried adult women traveling by themselves were assumed to be of very bad character. How could they be otherwise, if no men were willing to marry them? It was almost dark when I finally found a place to stay. The innkeeper grudgingly took my money and warned me to behave myself.

"I run a nice place here," he said, waving a hand at a very dirty collection of bug-ridden rooms.

"And a very expensive place, too," I replied, handing over more coins than I'd intended to pay for a few nights' shelter.

"If you don't like the price, feel free to go elsewhere," he said, his tone quite insulting. "My guess is, no one would have you, and you'd have to sleep in the street."

"Is this the same price you would charge a single man for a room?"

"It's what I'm charging *you*."

I hoped that he would be unique in my travels, but, sadly, he wasn't. No matter where I went, people always seemed to look with disdain on me for being a woman who traveled alone, and I knew I was often

charged more than what was fair for rooms. And, as I would soon discover, unfair costs of lodging were to be among the very least of my
problems.

Still, that night in Myra I could hardly sleep, as much for being excited as for the nasty bedbugs that crawled everywhere along the floor
and walls. In the morning I would visit Bishop Nicholas's tomb, pray,
and then make my way to the market. There I would buy bread and
dried fruit and some blankets, and spend much of the next few nights
quietly distributing them by the sleeping mats of the poor.

Only the first part of my plan went as expected. I was up with the
sun and hurried to the tomb, which was already surrounded by cripples and other pilgrims. That was all right. I simply bowed my head
and asked God to bless me as I tried to do good works. I raised my
head and found myself looking again at the carving of Bishop
Nicholas, focusing on his strong, kind face. Though I knew it was impossible, it seemed as though his eyes, carved in stone to look straight
ahead, somehow briefly turned to gaze at me—and did that stone
mouth momentarily widen into a *smile*? How odd!

But I had no time to spare on further speculation. Before leaving the
inn, I had carefully removed several coins from the pouch sewed into
the lining of my cloak—enough money to buy a dozen loaves of
bread, some containers of dried dates, and several blankets. At the
market, I lined up and bought these things, only to find that I had too
much to comfortably carry. I had to leave some of my purchases in the
stalls where I bought them, promising to retrieve them the next day.
Even so, it was an awkward walk back to the inn with bread loaves
tucked under my arms, and the blankets I was balancing on one shoulder spilling over in front of my face. Several people I passed pointed at
me and laughed.

After making a simple supper from a bit of the bread and two of the
dates, I waited impatiently in my nasty little room for night to come.
During the day, I had seen several ragged nomads in the city. I knew

some of them were camped just outside Myra; I'd noticed their patched tents set up by the side of the road when I arrived with the farm family in their wagon. These wanderers, surely, were just like the ones I'd known back in Niobrara—poor, honest families who had no permanent homes because they could not afford them. Instead, they moved from place to place, finding temporary work and never certain which nights there would be food for themselves and their children.

Finally it got dark. I put on my cloak and gathered up some bread, fruit, and two blankets. I was just able to carry everything. My heart pounded as I slipped out into the street, where I immediately realized I had no idea how to find the nomad tents outside town. There were no streetlights. There were many more buildings than I was used to. Clouds kept me from seeing the stars, which would at least have let me figure out north and south. It took several hours of wrong turns and unexpected dead ends before I finally stumbled out of the city and into the countryside, where I found myself on a road that might or might not have been the one to Niobrara.

No matter; the clouds shifted and there was enough moonlight for me to see tents, tattered ones, and I knew the people sleeping in them must be desperately poor. Stealthily, I approached the nomad camp. My gift-giving was about to begin!

Then a dog started barking. I'd forgotten that many of these wanderers kept canine pets, as much for protection as for companionship. This dog had caught my scent, and, of course, did not understand I was coming to give his owners presents rather than rob them. People who'd been sleeping in the tents jumped up, many of them shouting. The first dog kept barking, and several more joined in the thunderous chorus. There was nothing for me to do but turn and run. As I did, I dropped the loaves of bread, which were long and thin, and then I lost my grip on the blankets as I dashed madly through the darkness back toward the city. I arrived at the inn without the gifts I had meant to deliver, and without the satisfaction of actually giving them. My sleep during the few hours left before dawn, though, was curiously refresh-ing. The bearded man I had been dreaming about—how familiar his features seemed; *where* had I seen him before?—appeared to me again, and this time he winked and said, "You'll learn, and it will get better."

Well, my dream-friend was right about that. I had learned how im-portant it was to scout out during the day those places where I planned to leave my gifts at night. It was, for instance, important to know where watchdogs might prowl. So on my second day in Myra I spent the morning locating another nomad camp just outside the city, mak-ing certain no one in that group had a dog, and carefully studying the best route between the camp and the inn, so I would know my way even in the pitch dark.

My reconnaissance yielded other useful information. I counted five children in the group. All were barefoot, a painful state in a time when roads were strewn with rocks. I returned to the market to claim the bread, dried fruit, and blankets I hadn't been able to carry the day before—they still comprised quite an armful—but I also added five child-sized pairs of sandals to the load.

That night, I went out again, and this time things went smoothly. I found the camp, quietly made my way to the tents, and left bread and fruit by the sleeping mats of the snoring adults. Two of the older ones shivered in the cool night air, because they had nothing to cover them-selves with. I left a blanket for each. Finally, I left a pair of sandals by the side of each sleeping child. I took a moment to study their faces, which were streaked with dirt. How hard their lives must be, I thought, constantly moving from place to place, often required to do the same hard fieldwork as grown-ups, always worried about whether, at night, there would be any supper at all. Well, they would have one very special morning, at least.

I made my empty-handed way back to the inn and lay down, but I simply couldn't sleep. I was too excited. As soon as it was dawn, I hurried back toward the nomad camp, and there by the light of the still-rising sun I saw five little figures dancing with glee, twirling in the dust on their new, treasured sandals even as their parents called for them to come to the fire and enjoy a tasty, nourishing breakfast of bread and fruit.

It was a wonderful moment for me, too, and in the next years I was blessed to have many, many more of them. We learn in the Bible that it is better to give than to receive, and I was reminded of the truth in this every time I did my gift-giving. The satisfaction I felt, and the joy that washed over me, when I left food or clothing or blankets for those in need more than made up for the frustrations that continued to plague me.

The main problem was that each wonderful moment of gift-giving required whole days and weeks of preparation. I had known from the start that I would have to keep moving about, traveling as far as I could between the places where I left the gifts. To stay in one place too long would be to invite discovery of who I was and what I was doing. My intention had been to divide my time between big cities and small villages, enjoying diversity in my happy task. There were plenty of poor folk everywhere. But I discovered it was difficult to make my way to country villages and impossible to properly carry out my mission once I was in them. In small towns, strange single women were objects of scorn, pity, or a combination of both. There was no way for me to quietly blend into the population, watching to learn where the poorest people lived, what food or clothing they needed most, and then purchasing these things before quietly leaving them beside the right sleeping mats during the night. Just the act of a lone woman buying many loaves of bread or pairs of sandals would set all the residents of small towns to gossiping, and when these very same things were left in the night for the poorest people in the village to enjoy, well, it would be no mystery who had done the gift-giving. A few times I tried buying these things in big cities, then transporting them with me to the country communities, but that proved much too difficult. If anything drew more attention than a lone woman arriving in a hamlet, it was a lone woman arriving with great packs of provisions and clothing.

That was one reason I mostly had to keep to the cities. The other involved transportation. It might take me several weeks just to find some way to get from one place to another, let alone make the journey. I didn't mind walking, but, as my former Niobrara neighbors had told me, that was too dangerous. Bandits lurked along every road, waiting to prey on travelers foolish enough to be on their own. I thought about buying a mule and wagon, but their price would have substantially reduced the money I had to purchase gifts. The only economical, and safe, way for me to get from one place to the next was to find caravans heading to the same places I wished to go. Usually, it would not cost much for me to rent a place on one of the wagons or carts in the caravan. Then, along with dozens or even hundreds of others I would make my slow, bumpy way to another major city. At the very least, every trip would take days, and some took weeks. If roads were bad or wagons broke down, the caravan might make only a few miles' progress between dawn and dark.

Upon arriving in the new city, I would then have to find a place to stay for a few days, and that was never easy. As was the case in Myra, most innkeepers did not want to rent rooms to a single woman. Those who would always wanted more money than the rooms were worth, but most of the time I had no choice but to pay whatever was being asked. After that, it took more time to scout out everything, to find where the poorest people lived or camped, and which camps had dogs or were too well-guarded. I would estimate that I spent two weeks traveling and planning for each night that I was actually able to leave gifts.

I don't mean to make it seem as though I was generally unhappy. During those moments that I crept up to campfires, laid down bread or fruit or blankets or clothing, and then stealthily disappeared back into the night, I felt a joy that warmed me even during the most frustrating times in between. No life is perfect, and no dream is realized exactly as it was imagined. Unless we accept the unwelcome parts of our lives instead of resenting them, we can't completely enjoy all the good things that come to us. I grumbled sometimes, but I would not allow myself to brood. As the years passed, I was able to look on my problems as challenges, situations to be overcome if only I had enough common sense and determination. If I let certain things discourage rather than inspire me, it would be more my own fault than anyone else's. Realizing this, I was able to maintain a positive attitude.

Even so, the time came in the year 412 when the coins I carried were so few that I no longer needed to keep them in a pouch hidden under my cloak. I could drop them in a pocket of my robe instead. The fact I had managed to stretch my inheritance for ten years of gift-giving gave me great satisfaction. The additional fact that I'd be penniless within days was also something I had to consider.

I was staying at an inn in Constantinople, by far the largest city I'd visited during my decade of journeys. I found myself there quite often during the years. The larger the place, the more poor people in and around it, of course; because the population of Constantinople was so immense, more than three hundred thousand by some counts, no one took much notice of a woman on her own. There were even a few inns that specifically offered shelter to those like me, and for a reasonable cost. It was a relief not to be stared at, and to be treated with respect instead of insolence.

In my room, which was, for a change, clean and bug-free, I sat on the sleeping mat provided and took out the few coins that remained to me. I had paid in advance for one week's lodging, because that left me just enough to buy supplies for about that many nights of gift-giving. When the week was up, so, apparently, would be my wonderful mission. I had just passed my thirty-fifth birthday. By the standards of the day, I was in my late middle age. I still felt healthy and strong. Somehow I'd avoided the common diseases that claimed lives so regularly.

By God's grace I had all my teeth, and my hair remained brown instead of gray. But old age had to be well on its way. I'd been lucky my money and health had lasted so long.

After I spent these last coins and passed my last night at this Constantinople inn, I wondered what would become of me. In such large cities, there were usually places where unmarried women could live and work in the Christian church. That was a possibility; I certainly believed in and loved the Lord. Otherwise, I could become a nomad, perhaps joining with some band or another that would take me in and give me a place in a torn tent at night. While I had any strength left, I had no intention of becoming a street beggar. Well, for these last few days I would simply go on as I had been, and let fate or divine grace determine what happened next.

Reminding myself that self-pity is the worst disease of all, I stood up, put the coins I had left in the pocket of my robe, and made my way to one of Constantinople's many marketplaces. The day before, I had spied a nomad camp on the outskirts of the city, one with many ragged children and hungry-looking old people huddled around tiny fires. They were wrapped in thin, dirty blankets, which was sad, but they seemed to have nothing at all to eat, which was worse. I counted almost twenty people.

Now, in the market, I took out my few coins and estimated how much would buy just enough food to fill all twenty of their stomachs for a few days. While that wouldn't permanently improve their lives, at least it would give them a chance to gain some strength and, perhaps, some hope, because they would know someone cared about them. So I bought bread, and dried fruit, and some blocks of cheese. It was certainly plain fare, but it was nourishing and cheap enough for me to buy quite a lot. Over my ten years of gift-giving I had learned better how to carry large loads. My robes and cloak had many deep pockets.

As I stood in front of one vendor's stall, shoving cheese and fruit into those pockets, I happened to glance at another stall nearby. Bread was being sold there to a pair of customers who were putting the loaves into large pockets in their robes, too. The first thing I noticed about these men was that they were, to say it kindly, both somewhat stout. Because their robes were so wrinkled and stained with dust, I suspected they, too, must be travelers. Their backs were turned to me as they tried to pack away all the bread they had purchased—why would two men need so many loaves? Then, chatting away to each other like old, beloved friends, they walked past me and I was able to see their faces. The fellow on the left looked to be about forty. His hair was mostly brown but streaked with gray. He had no beard, unusual for the time, and he squinted his eyes a little. Like many people before glasses were invented, this was an obvious sign he was nearsighted. He seemed in every way to be a pleasant, even kindly person, but it was his companion who drew my attention.

I could have sworn I recognized that long white hair and beard, and that smile, which was at once warm and welcoming. Other people automatically smiled back as they stepped aside to let him pass. There was about him a unique sense of *goodness*, if that isn't too strange a description. Very briefly, our eyes met, and when they did I nearly gasped, because I realized this was the man from my dreams. As a sensible person I knew this had to be impossible, yet here he was! I wanted to say something, I meant to reach out and pull at his arm and speak to him, but the shock I was feeling left me too confused to move, and by the time I recovered myself he and his companion had been swallowed up in the marketplace crowd.

Still stunned, I slowly made my way back to the inn, trying to make sense of what had happened. Surely I'd just been granted a sign—but of what? Should I now do nothing else but search every street in Constantinople until I found this man again? And, if I did, what should I say to him? He might be repulsed by a strange woman saying to him that she knew him from many years of dreams. But beyond the dreams, I had the sense that I had seen him somewhere else, too.

As night fell, my only instinct was to go ahead and bring my gifts out to the nomad camp. After all, because I had spent the last of my money, this would be one of my last moments of gift-giving, too. I would take most of the provisions I had just purchased. The few things remaining I would bring to others in need, and when the final loaf and dried fig and bit of cheese were distributed, the next part of my life would begin. I wondered, perhaps even allowed myself to hope, that the man with the white beard and wonderful smile might be involved.

"At least let me see who you are," he said, gently tugging my hood away from my face. My long hair tumbled out, and as the light coming through the windows of the inn fell upon my face, I knew it was clear I was certainly not a man.

Three

here were four tents in the nomad camp, with two small fires burning nearby. I always found it easier to leave gifts when tents were involved rather than proper huts or houses, which usually had doors. Though door locks weren't yet in use, sometimes families would block their doors from the inside by placing heavy objects against them, since, particularly in cities, there were thieves who might try to sneak in. I, of course, was also sneaking in, but to leave things rather than take them. Tents only had entryway flaps, and these were easily pushed aside.

I approached the camp carefully, as I always did, trying to be certain no one else was around. On this night, I couldn't escape the feeling that someone was lurking nearby, but after an extra half hour of waiting and watching I decided to get on with my task. The camp was about a half mile outside Constantinople, but it was beside a good-sized road, and someone might ride or walk by at any time. At least there were hills all around. Even if that made it easier for others to hide from my sight, this meant in case of emergency I, too, would have a good chance of getting away.

I quietly walked toward the nearest tent. I knew from my scouting earlier in the day that a mother and father and their two children would be sleeping there. Just before I eased aside the flap to go inside, I reached into the deep pocket of my cloak and put my hand on a long, thick loaf of bread. In those days, a loaf might be the entire dinner for a family of four or six or even ten, so they were quite substantial. Think of how long a modern-day baseball bat usually is, and that was about the length of a loaf in 412, only the loaf was easily twice as thick as the bat. Years of practice made what I would do next completely automatic. The pockets inside my cloak were quite long, from my waist all the way down to the hem around my ankles. I could put several loaves into them at once, along with other smaller items of food or clothing. On this particular night, I would begin by entering this first tent, pulling out one loaf, and placing it gently by the side of one of the sleeping mats. Then I would take out smaller things, in this case some dried fruit and cheese, and put these items by the other mats, so that each sleeper would find something when he or she woke up. I didn't want anyone to feel ignored. After that, I'd leave gifts in each of the other tents, in turn. So my hand was on the bread as I slipped into the closest tent, but almost instantly I recoiled in near panic, because someone very large was standing inside, and he was holding a heavy-looking club.

Now, I had nearly been caught many times over the years by someone who hadn't been able to get to sleep, or else I bumped into something and made a noise, but I had always been able to make a quick escape. I'd never come into a tent to find someone not only wide awake, but on his feet and armed. At least he seemed as astonished to see me as I was to see him; we both peered at each other in the darkness for several seconds, and then, since he didn't call out a warning to anyone else, I realized he must be a thief who was cruel enough to want to rob these poor people of the very few things they had. Anger boiled up in me, and before he could swat me with his nasty club I yanked the long loaf of bread from my cloak and waved it in front of his face, though I couldn't clearly make out his features. In the dark, I hoped he would think I had a club, too, and apparently he did, because after shaking his own club at me for a few moments he gestured for me to follow him and exited the tent through a flap on the other side.

Here was a real dilemma. If I went with him, this hulking fellow might just hit me over the head with his club and rob me, too. But if I didn't go, he might shout out an alarm and send all the nomads running after me, while he made his own escape in the opposite direction. Well, I was a woman, perhaps, but I still could fight if it came to that. More than once in my ten years of traveling, I'd had to defend myself with a punch or a kick. I could do it again.

So I followed the man out of the tent and a few dozen yards beyond the nomad camp. There, in the first swell of hills, another man was waiting. That was when I knew I should turn and run, since I was outnumbered, but the second man, who was large, too, stepped forward quickly and I couldn't get away. Showing signs of fear would only make me a more inviting victim, so I tugged the hood of my cloak tightly around my face, hoping they would not realize I was a woman.

The man I'd followed out of the tent hissed, "You thief, why can't you leave those poor people alone? They don't have anything for you to steal!"

That made me furious rather than frightened. I still couldn't see his face clearly, but his mean words were certainly uncalled for.

"Don't accuse me," I whispered back. "You're the robber. Well, if the two of you want to fight, I'm ready!" I'd put my long loaf back in my robe pocket as I'd left the tent, but now I reached to pull it out again. But the second man, moving quickly for someone so large, was faster. He reached into my pocket first and pulled out bread instead of a cudgel. Then he reached back in and rummaged about a little before whispering, "There's only food here, bread and fruit."

"Well, go ahead and steal it," I whispered, still keeping my tone harsh and, I hoped, masculine-sounding. "Eat it while those poor people starve, and may you get bellyaches afterward, you fat fiends."

"We're not going to steal this food, and don't call me fat," whispered the first man. My eyes were adjusting to the darkness, and I could see him better. But, like me, he and the other man had the hoods of their cloaks pulled around their faces, too, so I still had no idea what they might look like. "Were you going into that tent to *leave* food rather than commit robbery?"

"I've never robbed anyone," I replied, snatching back my bread loaf and returning it to my pocket with as much dignity as I could muster given the strange circumstances. I didn't want to lose the bread. After all, I had so very few things left to give before my mission was over. "Where have you put your club? Are you going to hit me with it?"

He chuckled, and pushed into my hand another long loaf, which I had obviously mistaken for a weapon. "Neither of us seems to be a robber, my friend. I think I want to know you better. My companion and I have a warm, clean room back in the city. Join us there; we'll eat and drink and talk."

Well, I certainly couldn't accept this invitation. I still wasn't sure I could trust these men, and if they were somehow bad and they discovered I was a woman, my situation would only become worse. So I suggested we first distribute food to the poor nomads in their tents instead, hoping that in the process I would have a chance to run away. But while the second man waited outside the camp, the first one I'd stumbled into stayed right by my side as we left bread and fruit and cheese. When the last item was placed by the final sleeping mat, the man gently took my arm and led me back to where his friend was waiting. I was caught.

As we walked back into the city, the first man let go of me, but I noticed he and his companion walked on either side of me, perhaps so I couldn't get away. They began to talk in their normal voices. I kept whispering. My cloak was baggy, its long empty pockets flapping since the food I'd stored in them was gone. Apparently, these two still thought I was a man.

We arrived at the inn where they were staying, and they invited me to come up for something to eat and drink. Sensing my chance, I simply shook my head and turned to walk away, but the man who'd waited outside the nomad camp caught me and said somewhat impatiently, "What's the matter with you? You know now we're not thieves. If you don't have a place to stay, you can even sleep with us."

"I have to leave," I whispered. "Good night." I meant to go. I would have, but then the first man reached out toward me. I could have avoided his touch. But somehow I was frozen in place.

"At least let me see who you are," he said, gently tugging my hood away from my face. My long hair tumbled out, and as the light coming through the windows of the inn fell upon my face, I knew it was clear I was certainly not a man.

"Let me go. I can fight if I have to," I said with as much force as I could summon.

"You don't have to," he said reassuringly. "Please, my good woman, don't be afraid we'd harm you."

I couldn't be sure of that. The two men were standing close together, staring at my newly revealed face. Impulsively, I reached out and, one after the other, pulled their hoods away from their faces. At least if I was attacked by them and survived, I might be able to identify them afterward to the city authorities. When I saw the first face I gasped. I recognized this man. He was one of the two men from the market, the beardless one with the nearsighted squint. That must mean the other was— Yes! The man with the long white hair and beard and warm smile, the man I'd dreamed about for so long. I couldn't help staring into his eyes. We must have looked at each other for a full minute or more before he said, "Our offer of something to drink and eat is made in friendship."

Nicholas

I knew I could trust him—why else had he been so long in my dreams?—so I replied, "Then in friendship, I accept."

Up in the room, they produced jars of fruit juice—I very much preferred drinking such healthy stuff rather than wine—and some bread and cheese. Our conversation instantly bubbled over. I had never been someone who liked to talk about herself, but as soon as we sat down on the floor mats I found myself almost babbling as I recounted my childhood in Niobrara with Uncle Silas and Aunt Lodi, and how I decided while still very young that I wanted to be, *would* become, a gift-giver.

"The inspiration came from the old stories, you see," I explained. "In Lycia, people had spoken for a hundred years about a mysterious gift-giver who came silently in the night to give gifts to the very poorest people." The nearsighted man whispered something to the wonderful man with the white hair and beard, who sharply whispered to him to keep quiet. "Well," I continued, "ten years ago when my uncle and aunt died, they left me the farm and some money as my inheritance. Men in my village offered to marry me, but I realized it was the farm they really wanted, not me. I mean, it's obvious I'm not beautiful."

Now the white-bearded man couldn't keep himself from speaking. "You seem beautiful to me," he blurted, and his nearsighted friend laughed and slapped him on the shoulder. For a moment, everything felt quite awkward. I felt myself blushing, and the white-bearded man's cheeks turned bright red, too. I thought I should perhaps feel offended—the remark had been quite forward, as we used to term such a personal comment. But instead I was pleased. Never before had I really cared what any man thought of my appearance. But now I did.

After several silent moments, the white-bearded man composed himself, poured all three of us more fruit juice, and remarked, "Do you know, we've been talking for some time and we haven't even properly introduced ourselves. May I ask your name?"

"Layla," I said.

"Well, Layla, we are honored to meet you. This fat grinning fellow here is Felix. He has been my friend and traveling companion ever since we met in Rome many, many years ago. And my name is—"

Before the word was out of his mouth, I knew. A carved image on a tomb in Myra flashed into my mind.

"Your name is Nicholas," I told him. "I should have known. I recognized you right away, from the likeness on your tomb and from—" I was about to add, "my dreams," but thought better of it.

Nicholas and Felix exchanged a long look. Then Nicholas said carefully, "Well, it's getting quite late. I suggest Felix and I escort you back to your own lodgings. Will you meet us again tomorrow night? We have gifts to give; a very needy family is spending hungry, cold nights hiding in a rich man's barn. You could join us as we help them. Afterward, there are certain things I would like to tell you about."

"It would be my pleasure," I replied. There was a great deal I wanted to ask them, most importantly how a man who had died of old age in 343 still appeared very much alive sixty-nine years later. The odd thing was, though I wondered how it was possible, I never doubted it was true.

Felix lagged a little behind Nicholas and me as we walked back to the inn where I was staying. It wasn't a long walk and only took about ten minutes, but it seemed like much less even than that. Nicholas and I didn't say much to each other, just casual comments about the coolness of the night air and how much more bread and cheese cost in the

Constantinople markets than in Myra. When we reached the inn I found myself wondering, unexpectedly, whether Nicholas was going to kiss me good night, which certainly would have been forward and definitely unacceptable upon such short acquaintance. It was only after he formally shook my hand and turned and walked away with Felix that I realized I'd hoped he would kiss me. I'd sometimes kissed my Uncle Silas on the cheek, but I'd never kissed any man in a romantic way and had never really wanted to before.

Needless to say, that night I slept very little. Perhaps I should have been awake because I was worrying. My money was all gone, I had only a bit of bread and cheese left to distribute, and after that, what would become of me? Instead, I couldn't close my eyes out of sheer pleasure. Nicholas wanted to see me again! Something special was happening.

I was right about that. The next evening, just as the sky turned dark, Nicholas and Felix came to fetch me at the inn. I met them outside the front entrance, my pockets filled with the very last bread and cheese I had. Before I had met them, my intention was to make these things last for several more days of gift-giving. Now, I brought everything that was left. Just to make certain I had been invited as a full contributing partner rather than a welcome but essentially useless companion, I informed them right away that I expected to contribute my share to the night's gifts. Both Nicholas and Felix seemed quite pleased to hear this. They led the way to an extensive property just north of the city. It was a large farm, much bigger than my uncle's. Livestock nestled in wide corrals. The bright moon silhouetted an impressive house fifty yards from a fine barn. Nicholas whispered that sleeping in this barn were a mother and father and their three young children. He and Felix had met the father two days earlier in the Constantinople market when he was begging everyone he passed to hire him for any sort of work so he could buy food for his family.

"His name is Tobias, and he seems to be a very fine fellow,"

Nicholas said. "There are so many men like him—poor due to bad luck, not laziness. He is very talented at threshing wheat and shoeing horses. He learned these trades on a small farm perhaps a hundred miles from here, but when the owner of the farm died a year ago, Tobias and his family were ordered off the property without any sort of explanation. He hasn't been able to find steady work since, and some nights his children cry because they're so hungry."

"Well, they won't be hungry tomorrow morning," Felix added, brandishing a handful of dried fruit and handing it over to Nicholas. "You two go on inside the barn and leave your gifts."

"Aren't you coming, too?" I asked.

Nicholas chuckled. "Felix, here, is a fine fellow with many admirable talents, but stealth isn't one of them. Our custom is for him to stand guard outside while I am inside."

But Nicholas seemed quite glad to have me inside the barn with him. Without any prior plan, we instinctively shared the gift-giving tasks there. He left bread and cheese where the two parents slept on piles of hay. I placed dried fruit by the sides of the sleeping children. Because all five lay in a dark corner of the barn, we knew instinctively the owners of the farm had no idea their barn housed uninvited guests. Probably, the family had been subsisting on a few eggs stolen out from underneath the chickens who perched on the barn's many rafters. Well, for one morning, at least, they'd have a breakfast equal to the one undoubtedly being enjoyed by those living in the fine house a few dozen yards away.

I should have felt sad as Felix, Nicholas, and I walked back into the city. For ten years, I had loved the experience of anonymously leaving gifts, and it was over. If my two new friends now told me it had been wonderful meeting me and good luck in the future, I would be left alone with no real prospects. But I didn't think about this. Instead, I wondered what Nicholas and Felix—all right, mostly Nicholas— wanted to talk about next. It had to be something wonderful.

It certainly was. Back in their room, jars of fruit juice close to hand, Nicholas began by confirming who he was.

"By normal measure, I'm one hundred and thirty-two years old," he said. "I'll certainly understand if you don't believe me."

"Tell me more," I urged, and for several hours he did. I heard about his childhood in Patara, how his parents had died when he was young and he ended up being raised by village priests. How, while still very young, he had felt inspired to use the money he had inherited to help those in need. How his first gift-giving attempts were clumsy and almost ended in disaster. All these things sounded familiar to me, because they were so similar to my own life, ambition, and experiences.

Then came memories of great wonders—how, in the year 343 at age sixty-three, he rode off from Myra in the middle of the night because too many people expected him to work wonders for them, and how, in the years following, he realized two things. First, that he could travel hundreds of miles in the time ordinary people might manage one or two. Second, that he had somehow stopped aging. He had no explanation for how these things had happened, he added. They simply did.

Felix

"And when I met and joined Nicholas a year later, I stopped aging, too!" Felix interrupted. "The magic that graces him is also extended to anyone who joins him, we believe."

I couldn't help shaking my head at the wonder of it all. Nicholas, though, interpreted the head-shaking as a sign I didn't believe what I'd just heard.

"It seems impossible, I know," he said. "Perhaps if you consider it a bit longer before you decide it's not true—"

"Oh, no," I replied. "I believe every word. I mean, I see you here in front of me, and I saw your likeness carved on your tomb, and, of course, I've seen you so long in, well . . ." I was still too embarrassed to admit I'd been dreaming about him for years. I sat up a little straighter on my mat, composed myself, and said briskly, "So it was you all along who did the gift-giving that inspired me to do the same, and now I've met you. How splendid!"

Nicholas seemed both pleased and anxious. "Then you do believe everything I've told you?" he asked.

"Of course I do," I said. "No one could invent a story like that. So now you and your friend Felix, here, will spend eternity doing good, generous things. You're more than lucky—you're blessed!"

"But I'm lonely, sometimes, too," Nicholas said, and I thought Felix, sitting on a mat beside his longtime companion, looked rather offended. "The challenge is so great, and so never-ending," Nicholas continued, his eyes locked on mine. "So many people need so much, and I need your help. Will you join me?" He suddenly remembered Felix. "I mean, will you join us?"

"What exactly do you mean?" I asked. I hoped I knew what he meant, but I wanted to hear him say it.

Nicholas blushed and stammered, so Felix said it for him: "He's asking you to marry him, so I'm going to leave you two alone for a while." He got up and left the room. In the silence that followed, I could hear his heavy feet thumping as he made his way down the hall.

Nicholas remained tongue-tied. It was almost comical to see him try to say something, consider his words, begin to make the first sounds, panic, and have to start all over again. He sputtered for some time, and I finally lost patience.

"Look, are you asking me to marry you or not?" I asked. "It would be nice to know."

He took a deep breath. "Yes, I'm asking you to marry me. I'm sorry to make such a bad job of it. Even though I'm a hundred and thirty-two years old, I've never done this before."

"Are you certain?" I couldn't help asking.

"Oh, yes," Nicholas said. "I've never had such feelings for anyone.

So, will you? Marry me, I mean. I know it's a complicated life I'm offering, and that there's a great difference in our ages. If you're thirty-five, why, I'm ninety-seven years older than you. Someone so youthful might not want to burden herself with someone so, well, senior."

"I don't care how old you are," I replied, feeling rather pleased that someone actually considered me to still be young. "I'll gladly marry you, but there's a condition. You must promise we'll be equal partners, in gift-giving and in marriage. I will always love and respect you. Will you feel the same toward me?"

"I already love and respect you," Nicholas said, and my heart pounded and I found myself smiling so widely that the corners of my mouth hurt. I thought he would now come over and kiss me, but instead he suddenly looked uncertain again.

"What's the matter?" I asked, afraid that he was having second thoughts and might take back his proposal.

"It's just that I'm still learning about special powers and this gift-giving mission," Nicholas said. "I mean, how long will you live, Layla? Felix and I have stopped growing older, but what about you? I couldn't stand it if we married and I lived on forever, only to lose you along the way."

I hadn't considered this. The possibility of living forever, or at least for a much longer time than the average person, seemed almost unimportant compared to marrying Nicholas.

"Maybe, like Felix, I'll stop aging, too," I said. "Maybe I won't. No one can know the future. We'll have enough to do giving gifts. Let's not waste time worrying about something we can't control." Nicholas started to reply. Apparently, he wanted to keep talking. But I was a newly engaged woman and the time for talking was over. "Hush up and come kiss me," I told him—and he did.

Nicholas knew a priest in Constantinople. He married us the next day. Felix was best man. After the short ceremony, the three of us immediately departed for Rome in Italy, a city Nicholas and Felix already knew well and one I had always longed to see. As a wedding present, Nicholas had told me we could go give gifts anywhere in the known world. He and Felix seemed delighted when I asked to go to Rome.

"There are plenty of needy people there," Nicholas told me as we walked arm-in-arm to the dock where we would board a boat and begin the trip. "We're going to be busy. You may regret very soon that you ever married me."

But I never did.

We left those as gifts for poor children in Naples to the south of Rome. The next morning we returned to their neighborhood, and how wonderful it was to see boys and girls shouting with sheer joy as they shot their marbles or played with their dolls or rolled hoops across the meadow.

Four

ou must be wondering when I'll begin telling about Oliver Cromwell. I will, very soon, but first I must explain about how our gift-giving mission gradually changed. Only if you know about how toys and Christmas and America came to be part of what we did can you understand why I happened to be in England without my husband in the 1640s when Oliver Cromwell tried to do away with the holiday, and why I was so determined that he wouldn't succeed. Things that happened as much as twelve centuries earlier had their effect—on me, on Cromwell, and on Christmas itself.

My early days with Nicholas were fascinating. I found it quite different to be traveling and gift-giving in the company of my husband and his friend. As a married woman, I was welcome in any clean, reasonably priced inn; a wife arriving with her husband was not looked on with suspicion in any community. We gave our gifts in small villages as well as large cities. And, of course, I loved traveling formerly impossible distances at equally impossible speeds.

Oh, sometimes we had to make voyages on boats or travel in carts as part of caravans, but most often we simply walked, moving at night, and though there was no sense of hurry we would still find, by sunup, that we had gone eighty or one hundred miles. I was also amazed not to feel at all tired at the end of such lengthy treks. It seemed as though the act of walking refreshed rather than tired us.

I learned that Nicholas and Felix paid for the gifts they gave by carving elaborate wooden covers for books, which were relatively new in the early 400s. Most people still didn't read much, if at all, but those who did now wanted to protect their manuscripts from dust and decay. Every so often, Felix would announce our money was about to run out, and we would purchase a dozen small planks of treated wood. Then he and my husband would spend a few days carving designs on the planks, which were then sold to a friendly merchant they knew named Timothy. He, in turn, would bind the planks around sets of manuscripts, sell the finished books with covers to wealthy customers, and everyone was pleased.

"Though I started my gift-giving with the help of a good inheritance, even that large amount of money had to run out sometime," Nicholas explained. "There was a time I feared my mission would have to end because I had no funds left."

"I know the feeling," I replied, and told him how we had met at the very moment my own money for gifts was completely spent.

"God's grace is a wonderful thing," he replied before giving me a big hug. As a former priest and bishop in the Christian church, Nicholas never, ever doubted that his special powers came to him directly from the Lord. "Layla, there is truly no coincidence where this mission is concerned. When my money ran out, for instance, was the same moment Felix and I learned that we could carve book covers with the same speed that we could walk great distances. It was true—

is true—of Felix in particular. You will have noticed how I might carve one cover in a night, and, in the same few hours, Felix can carve five or six."

"Felix is amazing," I said, making sure my voice was loud enough for Felix to overhear where he stood a few yards away. My sudden presence was not always easy for him. He'd been used to being Nicholas's only companion for almost seventy years, and now he had to share his friend with someone else. Though Felix and I were very cordial to each other, I sensed sometimes that he felt uncomfortable, if not resentful, now that Nicholas had a wife who received so much of his attention. So I went out of my way to make sure Felix understood how special he was to my husband, and how I very much wanted us to become good friends, too. I think, over the centuries, we eventually did.

There was another benefit to traveling and working with Nicholas. I stopped aging, too. I know that in the thousand and more years since, many of our later companions took this for granted from the start, but they had the benefit of our experience. Then, we had no idea whether the magic would touch me as well, and so for months and even a few years—all right, decades—a day didn't pass without me taking out a disk of polished metal—because we had no glass mirrors then—and peering anxiously at my reflection, looking for lines around my eyes or my first gray hair. They never appeared. By the time I had been with Nicholas for about forty years, making me seventy-five and extremely elderly by the standard of the day, I still looked exactly the same and knew I had stopped aging, too.

Those forty years were full of love and excitement and, I admit, some sadness and frustration. We gloried in our mission, and our ability to range so far across Asia Minor and Europe to give our gifts. We gave thanks for the special powers God had granted to us. But we were always aware that even these powers had their limits. Any time we came near wars, our speed was reduced to that of normal humans.

It seemed, in those years, that all the world we knew of was torn by war. The Roman Empire was gradually crumbling. Tribes with names like Vandals and Visigoths made bloody bids for supremacy. We were able to avoid capture, perhaps even execution, because in those days Christian priests were known to be noncombatants, and so were allowed to wander where they would. Nicholas and Felix were assumed to be priests, and, in the case of my husband, that was close to the truth. Any time we were stopped and questioned, we simply said we were on our way somewhere to minister to the poor—and that, too, was certainly true.

As he had promised, my wonderful husband treated me as an equal partner, both in our marriage and in gift-giving. No decisions were made by Nicholas alone. He always consulted me, and Felix, too. Sometimes Felix or I might suggest where to go next. Of course, in some ways having a woman along was very helpful. In a small village, I could casually join other wives washing clothes in a stream or gossiping by a well. I would hear about local families who were hungry or wearing ragged clothes. More and more, we concentrated on gifts for children. This was not because we didn't care about grown-ups. It was just that there was so much need that we had to set priorities, and, more than anything, we wanted all children to grow up feeling loved and hopeful about their lives. A constant source of frustration was that, no matter how hard we tried, we could never bring gifts to every deserving, needy child. There were so many children, and in so many places!

I had the great pleasure of seeing Rome, and Alexandria, and other famous cities. Gradually I became familiar with hundreds of towns and villages in what we called "the known world." But all three of us never stopped feeling curious about those countries we had yet to visit, and finally in the year 453 we decided it was time to travel to the legendary, mysterious land of Britain. What we knew of the island nation was fascinating. The Romans had conquered some of it for a time, but according to most stories it was still inhabited by wild people who painted themselves blue and lived in trees. It sounded too interesting to resist, so we began making our way there. Under peaceful circumstances we could have made our way from Rome to Britain with three or four nights of magically fast walking, but there were battles all around us and we could only manage about ten miles a day. In particular, a famous Hun war chief named Attila was known to be marching toward Rome. As it happened, we met him, or, I should say, were taken prisoner by him. But after some conversation with Nicholas, Attila admitted he was tired of war. When Nicholas impulsively told him about our special mission, Attila asked to join us, along with Dorothea, his wife.

This was a turning point. Until that moment, we had never even discussed adding to our number. "Do we really *want* a warrior coming along?" Felix asked me, and I believe it was then that he finally accepted me as an equal rather than just as his best friend's wife.

"I think we have to trust Nicholas's instincts, and he wants Attila and Dorothea to join us," I replied. "We'll watch Attila carefully, because he's used to fighting with anyone he meets. And it will be nice for me to have another woman to talk to."

In fact, our two new friends fit in right away. Because he'd had to study so many maps while planning battles, Attila knew his way around better than the rest of us. Dorothea was very kind and, though soft-spoken, quite intelligent. By the time we crossed the channel to England—a monk named Patrick happened to be floating by in a small boat on his way to Ireland and offered us a ride—we were all enjoying one another's company very much, except for Attila and Felix, who constantly argued with each other. But these arguments were entertaining, and kept the rest of us amused as we traveled.

We loved England immediately, for it had the greenest hills and clearest streams any of us had ever seen. Sadly, the lives of the people there did not match the beauty of their land. There was fighting everywhere, with fierce tribes in the north and west constantly assaulting the people of the central and southern regions. At the same time, Saxons from across the sea often sailed over to conduct raids. Why, we kept asking each other, couldn't everyone stop fighting and begin enjoying the wonderful world given to them by God? Then Attila would remind us that too many people measured themselves by how much they could take from others.

"I was like that," he would always point out. "Though I'm pleased to have learned giving gifts is more satisfying than owning things myself, it was a hard-earned lesson. But if I can learn it from you, then others can, too."

Attila

Almost everyone in Britain was desperately poor. Though we'd arrived with plenty of money, very little food or clothing was for sale. What we did find in sad marketplaces were old, stringy vegetables, and sandals and blankets so filthy and tattered that beggars in other parts of the world would have disdained them. So we had to arrange to buy proper gifts like cheeses and dried fruits and well-made blankets from markets in Europe, and have these shipped by boat over to Britain. Then we paid English farmers to let us store these things in their barns. So long as we paid in advance, no one ever asked us why we were doing this. They were just grateful for the few extra coins.

And yet, with the awful fighting and nearly universal poverty, there was still something special about this country. If the people were poor, they were also hopeful, certain that somehow, some way, they would eventually live in peace. Instead of moping in times of trouble, they made up songs and stories about wonderful heroes who would one day come to their rescue. For fifty years we wandered among them, leaving our gifts when we could, trying to avoid battlefields and hoping along with all the ordinary folk that better times for them would soon be coming.

Around the year 500, a British war chief named Arthur won several spectacular victories against Saxon invaders. Many people in Britain be-lieved he must be the longed-for hero who would save the land, but Attila told us that there was no chance Arthur could hold off the Sax-ons for very long.

"There are too many of them," he said, looking rather sad. "This Arthur is a brave man and a great leader, but anyone who fights

Arthur

constantly must eventually lose to someone stronger. This is true now, and will be throughout history. I only hope he escapes with his life."

With our help, Arthur did. One day we found him lying badly wounded in a barn, with his Saxon enemies all around. Obviously, we couldn't leave him there, and he became our sixth member. After he recovered, Arthur proved to be a very good addition to the group. He was brave, as Attila had guessed, and quite resourceful, too. He could carve wood book covers even better than Felix, and his love for his country despite its terrible wars was sincere.

I believe it was because of Arthur that Britain remained so impor-tant to us all. For the next six hundred years we divided our time be-tween that island nation, Europe, and Asia Minor, meeting people and giving gifts and trying always to bring a little joy and comfort to chil-dren who most desperately needed reminding that the world was not entirely a cruel, dangerous place. All of us were happy anywhere we went, but it was during our visits to Britain that Arthur seemed the most content.

"Though battles and invasions continue—the Saxons who con-quered my people are now being challenged in their turn by the Nor-mans sailing in from France—I know that the English people themselves are especially noble in spirit," Arthur said one night as we gathered around a campfire in the hills outside the town of London, which had originally been built by the Romans a thousand years earlier. "If peace ever comes to this land, the rest of the world will look to Britain for inspiration and leadership."

Britain itself often looked to Arthur for inspiration, though the man of its legends had little in common with the war chief who'd joined us. Ordinary people comforted themselves in times of trouble—and, in Britain, it seemed always to be a time of trouble—with tales of Arthur the mythical king, who defeated enemies with the help of a magic sword and the advice of a wizard. There were tall tales about Nicholas and Attila, too, but the stories about Arthur were, at this time, the most widespread. We would tease him about them, always understanding that if they brought some comfort to frightened people, then they were good rather than harmful.

We had great adventures in Britain and everywhere else we went. My husband, Nicholas, wrote about many of these in his own book, so in most cases I won't repeat them here. It was our great good fortune to be befriended by Charlemagne, the king of the Franks who became the leader of the Holy Roman Empire. Thanks to his generosity, we were less dependent on carving and selling wooden book covers to pay for our gifts and travel costs. We studied with great interest events in far-off lands—how a man named Muhammad, for instance, founded the religion of Islam, and how there were rumors that Viking sailors had crossed a great ocean and discovered some vast, fertile new land. Though we could not travel to these places yet—our gift-giving services were so badly needed where we were—Nicholas, Felix, and I declared that someday we would explore them for ourselves. Arthur's main interest was Britain; Attila and Dorothea remained especially devoted to Europe and Asia Minor.

Sometime in the middle of the twelfth century, the nature of our mission changed. We still gave gifts, but of a different sort. As Britain,

Europe, and Asia continued to be torn by war—the latest flare-ups were called "the Crusades," with Christian rulers raising armies to march to Jerusalem and try to take back that holy city from the Muslims—our efforts to bring comfort and happiness to children began to seem almost foolish. If we left food, it was eaten and gone in a day or two. Cloaks and sandals wore out, if the children didn't outgrow them first. The times people of all ages had to live in seemed to be getting worse rather than better. What difference did our gifts of a little food or new clothing make, really?

One night in 1194, Nicholas called us together for a full, honest discussion. We all agreed something had to be done differently. We couldn't do much to lessen the violence of the world, but at least we could find a way to carry out our own mission more effectively. I spoke for a while about the difference between the body and the spirit. Food and clothing were temporarily good for the body, but we needed to give gifts that gave more lasting comfort to the spirit. It was Dorothea, the quietest among us, who eventually made the best suggestion—she thought we should give gifts of toys instead. Now, at this time toys were not something every child, or, indeed, many children,

Dorothea

actually owned. Those that existed were very primitive—marbles made of clay, hoops fashioned from bits of wood, dolls carved from wood or sewn together from rags. But the more we thought about it, the more sense the idea of giving toys made. Bread or fruit would be gone after one meal; children could play with toys for years, and in the process forget, at least for a while, about the dangerous world all around them.

We couldn't purchase toys as we could buy cloaks or loaves of bread. There were no companies that made them, no stalls full of toys in city marketplaces. So we learned to make them ourselves, and it took some time. The first dolls Dorothea and I sewed looked more like socks or mittens than pretend people. Our earliest attempt to make marbles found us using the wrong sort of clay, so they didn't roll straight and then broke on the rare occasions that they actually hit the other marbles at which they were aimed. Still, with some practice we were able to craft toys at the same incredible speed with which we'd been able to carve book covers. We took this as a sign that we should keep trying, and finally we made some that we considered good enough to take to Rome, where we offered them for sale at a market. We sold everything, dolls and marbles and hoops, within minutes, and at a good enough profit to buy materials to make hundreds more. We left those as gifts for poor children in Naples to the south of Rome. The next morning we returned to their neighborhood, and how wonderful it was to see boys and girls shouting with sheer joy as they shot their marbles or played with their dolls or rolled hoops across the meadow.

"Perhaps they're still wearing rags, and too many of them will go to bed hungry tonight," I said. "But for now, they're happy, and tomorrow they'll still have their toys to play with. We must keep on giving gifts of toys."

"Then we have to keep making them," Felix observed. "That's going to be the hardest part. Food and clothing we can buy anywhere and give away the same day. Crafting toys is far more complicated. It will be impossible for us to have some to give away every night, no matter how fast we work."

Though we wouldn't realize it for another three hundred years, the solution to that problem was already in progress. Gradually, people in Britain and Europe were defining specific dates when special gift-giving was most appropriate. Today, many people think that Santa Claus or St. Nicholas or Pere Noel or Father Frost—the name is different in almost every country—simply selected December 6 or 25 or January 6 as the day he brings gifts to children. In fact, those dates were picked for us.

Forget the word *Christmas* for just a moment. Though not known by that name, the date of December 25 became especially holy in the Christian church in the early 300s, when it was arbitrarily selected as the day to celebrate the birth of Jesus. That date was borrowed from other, earlier religions. Mithra, the Persian god of light, supposedly had been born on December 25. The Romans traditionally enjoyed a weeklong celebration called Saturnalia from December 17 through 24. They had parties and ate special food and gave each other little gifts. When Christianity became the official religion of Rome in the 300s, people still wanted their holiday. In 350, just seven years after my husband supposedly died in Myra, Pope Julius I used December 25 as Jesus' birthday on the new Roman calendar. Of course, the holiday was intended from the start as a special time to give thanks to God for sending Jesus, and not everyone carried over the old Saturnalia tradition of giving gifts on that date. But many people did. In some places, grown-ups began giving small presents to children on January 6, called Epiphany, and supposedly the day that the three Wise Men arrived in Bethlehem to give their gifts to Baby Jesus.

Going to church on December 25 was something most Christians wanted to do; the service held then was known as a mass. Because this particular mass was devoted to Jesus, it was called Christ's mass. In the year 1038, people in Britain started using the term *Christmas*, combining the two words. Christians in other countries began doing the same, altering the wonderful new word to fit their own languages. In Holland, for instance, people now looked forward to Kersmis, since the old Dutch word for Christ was *Kerstes*.

We were thrilled with the celebrations of Christmas and Epiphany; not only did they celebrate the birth of Jesus, they also gave common people a better chance to forget their troubles for a little while. Their holiday feasts might be the only time all year that there would be a little meat with their vegetables, or sweet candy for the children afterward. Many villages would hold dances or put on holiday plays. This may not seem very exciting today, when almost every family has a big meal every night and then settles down to watch television or listen to music or play videogames. But in those times, life for adults and children alike mostly consisted of hard work all day, little to eat, and bedtime when the sun went down, since there were no electric lights and candles cost too much to use very often. Perhaps the date of Christmas was based on old pagan beliefs, but why did that have to matter? What counted was that December 25 had become a time to give joyful thanks for Jesus' birth, and the opportunity for everyone, rich or poor, to put aside worries and be happy, even for only a day.

In 1224, one of the people who made these early Christmases so special became the seventh member of our group, and the first new one since Arthur joined us seven centuries earlier. St. Francis of Assisi encouraged poor villagers to create nativity scenes with a manger and animals to remind themselves that Jesus came into the world humble and poor, just as they were. Francis wrote some of the first popular Christmas carols, so common people had special songs to sing and dance to during their holiday celebrations. Francis's contributions to Christmas traditions made people love December 25 more than ever— and only about two hundred years after he joined us, St. Nicholas finally became part of those traditions, too!

Again, this happened *to* us rather than because of anything deliberate we did. By the late 1300s, it again became obvious that the way we did things had to change. It was getting too hard to craft all the toys we needed by campfire light in locations that changed every few days. In order to have the most toys possible, and the ones that were made best, we needed some permanent place to make them—a factory, perhaps, or even two. While Nicholas, Felix, Francis, and I loved traveling most, searching out children who needed gifts and then delivering them in the middle of the night, Arthur much preferred staying in

St. Francis

his beloved Britain, while Attila and Dorothea were happiest in their native country of Germany. So it was decided that Arthur would establish a toy factory in London, while Attila and Dorothea did the same in Nuremberg. Meanwhile, the rest of us would continue traveling and distributing half of the toys made in these factories. The other half would be sold in city markets; Arthur in London and Attila and Dorothea in Nuremberg would use the money to buy materials and pay their employees.

It all worked very well, though we missed our three longtime friends. But every few months we had to replenish our supplies of toys, and so we would go to London or Nuremberg—both large cities for their time, though dirty and small by today's standards—and enjoy reunions there.

I really think it was because of these two toy factories that St. Nicholas and Christmas became linked in the minds of so many people. Arthur, Attila, and Dorothea tried very hard to hire good craftsmen and craftswomen who just wanted to make toys and not gossip about their employers, and mostly they succeeded. One fellow in particular was a very welcome worker who soon was accepted as a full member of our special companions. Willie Skokan was a Bohemian who could take a bit of string, a splinter of wood, and a few drops of paint and combine them into literally any toy he wanted to make. Willie was absolutely marvelous, and we soon couldn't imagine how we'd ever been able to get along without him. He seldom spoke, and when he did he was careful never to reveal our secrets.

But that wasn't true of some others, though I don't believe anyone deliberately tried to expose us. Some of our workers in Britain or Germany just couldn't resist whispering things to their families and friends. By the middle 1400s, stories had spread through Europe and Britain about Nicholas, the ancient Catholic saint who somehow was still around and brought gifts for children at holiday time. In some countries, Germany especially, people began to think that perhaps his special gift-giving time was December 6, the date of Nicholas's "death" in 343.

So now, in addition to our year-round tasks, we were faced with not one but three special days when children particularly hoped to receive our gifts. I finally suggested that we gratefully accept these new obligations as opportunities rather than problems.

"In this way, we can make our night visits three times each year and spend the rest of the time planning our gift-giving and helping Arthur and Attila and Dorothea at the factories," I said. "Why, we can each choose one or two countries for our special individual attention. It will be more efficient, and great fun besides."

So it happened that, each year at holiday time, while Nicholas might roam anywhere, Arthur and his helpers brought gifts in England and all other parts of Britain. Attila and Dorothea took much of Western Europe, while Willie Skokan concentrated on Eastern European countries. Francis led the holiday gift-giving in Spain and Portugal, Felix found Scandinavia to his liking, and no one was surprised when I asked for Italy. The reason, of course, was Befana.

Everywhere else, legend now had it that holiday gifts were brought by a man—St. Nicholas or a similar male gift-giver with another name. But in Italy, children woke up on January 6 hoping for toys or treats from Befana, an old woman. As Italian tradition had it, when the three wise men began their search for the Baby Jesus, they came to Befana's house, asking directions to Bethlehem and inviting her to come with them. She wouldn't give the directions, because she didn't understand who Jesus was. Afterward, when Befana learned Jesus was the savior, she wished she had gone to give presents to him, too, and so ever since she went out before dawn on Epiphany to leave gifts for any child she could find. What fun it was for me to spend that special time leaving dolls and tops and marbles for children all over Italy! Of course, every few years we would switch countries so we could share in all the different traditions. But it's also true Befana and Italy remained especially dear to my heart.

The excitement for us only increased in 1492, when Francis met

Queen Isabella of Aragon in Spain and was able to make a place for himself on the first voyage to the fabled New World by Italian sea captain Christopher Columbus. Francis returned with tales of this wonderful new land, and his enthusiasm was contagious. Everyone, especially Nicholas and Felix, couldn't wait to visit the New World. None of us, though, felt we could leave immediately, for we were still helping build holiday gift-giving traditions in Britain and Europe. Still, I didn't miss the longing in my husband's voice as he talked about crossing the Atlantic Ocean someday. I decided then that it might take fifty years, or a hundred, but as soon as it was practical I would insist that Nicholas get on a boat and travel to that new place he so clearly yearned to see for himself.

About this same time, in 1501 Princess Catherine of Aragon was given in marriage to Prince Arthur of England. Though we didn't know it at the time, this began a series of events that would result in Oliver Cromwell and his Puritans banning Christmas 144 years later.

Nicholas, Felix, and I set off for England the next day. We'd hardly
arrived in London before my husband and his friend disappeared,
hurrying to the docks where Arthur told them the group of
colonists was being recruited for the voyage to America.

Five

ou know you want to visit what they're calling the New World," I said to Nicholas one fine early fall evening in 1620. We were spending a few weeks in Nuremberg with Attila and Dorothea, helping the confectioners at our factory there. When we left our gifts of toys for children, we often added a few pieces of candy, leaving these, when we could, in the stockings that their mothers washed and left hanging by fireplaces to dry overnight. Because the candy was always some kind of hard-boiled sweet, it wouldn't melt from the warmth of the fire. Candy was almost as rare a treat for boys and girls as new toys. We had recently tried something called peppermint candy, which had become available in a few places, and it was very, very good. Attila and Dorothea wanted to be able to make a lot of it at the Nuremberg factory, and quickly—the holidays were only a few months away. But it took time to get the taste just right—too much peppermint flavor made your tongue feel like it was burning instead of pleasantly tingling—and so Attila and Dorothea and Nicholas and I, along with Willie Skokan, who lived in Nuremberg, and Felix, who was also visiting there, were volunteer tasters. The first few attempts were not too agreeable, but as the day passed the peppermint candy tasted better and better, until by late afternoon we thought the confectioners had got it just right.

Afterward, Nicholas and I returned to the nearby inn where we were staying. Attila, Dorothea, and Willie, who worked in Nuremberg full time, lived in a small house. Felix was staying in their extra bedroom. Since that used up all the available space for guests, my husband and I took a room at a clean, modestly priced inn, and very much enjoyed some rare private time together. We loved all our old companions, but it was also pleasant to have an opportunity to concentrate on each other. In particular, I wanted to talk to Nicholas about the New World of English, Dutch, Spanish, and French colonies across the Atlantic Ocean in a vast land unofficially named America on many maps. Ever since Francis had returned from his voyage with Columbus over a century earlier, my husband had clearly longed to see America himself. But there was always a reason he just couldn't go quite yet—new toys to test in London, additional Christmas customs in Germany that we had to learn and adopt, or something else of that nature. So, alone together at the Nuremberg inn, with an hour or so to spare before we joined Attila and Dorothea and the others at their house for supper, I decided Nicholas and I would settle the issue for good. I intended for him to go to America, and soon.

"It would be selfish for me to leave my friends behind," Nicholas said, pacing about our little room while I sat comfortably in a chair before a small, glowing fire. "Everyone here in Nuremberg works so hard, and Arthur has more than he can handle at the factory in London."

"Arthur has Leonardo now," I reminded him. "That's lightened Arthur's load considerably." It was true.

In 1519, we'd added another full-time companion. Leonardo da

Vinci was a brilliant painter and equally imaginative inventor. He colored canvases with extraordinary scenes and filled notebooks with diagrams of machines that could soar through the air like birds or move underwater like fish. Having joined us, he eventually based himself in London with Arthur. There, he did what Willie Skokan did in Nuremberg—inventing new toys was a constant, though delightful, challenge for them both.

"Leonardo is amazing," Nicholas agreed. "But that doesn't change the fact all of us are kept busy every waking minute. Yes, I'd love to visit America, but it wouldn't be fair for me to have a vacation while everyone else had to remain on the job."

"It would hardly be a vacation," I pointed out. "From all the reports, colonists in America are having a terribly hard time. Most of them have little to eat, some of them fight with the natives, and I believe that one British settlement called Roanoke simply disappeared. We've been married for twelve hundred years, Nicholas. I know perfectly well you want to go to America to bring Christmas to the desperate people there whose daily lives consist mostly of hardship. And you should—they deserve Christmas joy, too, and what better way to experience it than to have St. Nicholas among them for the first time?"

"That's true," Nicholas admitted, sitting down in a chair opposite mine. "But we must always be practical, Layla, and though we haven't spoken of it much, these are dangerous times for Christmas in places other than America. That's true in England, especially. My place—our place, I mean—may be with Arthur just now, instead of across the Atlantic Ocean. So many things in England have been confused since 1527, when King Henry VIII decided to divorce Princess Catherine of Aragon."

From the time we first crossed the channel to England in St. Patrick's boat, the country had constantly been ravaged by some sort of upheaval, usually war. When there weren't invaders storming ashore, the English seemed to turn on themselves, fighting each other when there wasn't some enemy from the outside. When the conflict known in history as "the Wars of the Roses" ended in 1485, it seemed for a while as though there might be peace on the beautiful island nation, particularly when King Henry VII married his son Prince Arthur to Princess Catherine of Aragon. But Arthur, who was going to be the next English king, soon died, and his widow Catherine was then married to Arthur's younger brother, Henry. When Henry became king, he and Catherine did not get along very well. Henry met another woman named Anne Boleyn who he wanted for his wife instead, but the Catholic Church would not let him divorce Catherine. Furious, Henry simply left the church, taking his country with him, and established a new Church of England. Catherine, who believed very deeply in the Catholic Church, considered herself still married to Henry and raised their daughter, Mary, as a Catholic. Henry ended up marrying four more times after Anne Boleyn and had two more children, Edward and Elizabeth, who were raised as non-Catholics, or Protestants. And this is where problems for Christmas in England began.

Henry didn't want anything to do with Catholicism left in England. He gave most of the property owned by the Catholic Church to his friends. New, non-Catholic religious leaders weren't comfortable with a Catholic saint named Nicholas bringing presents to English children. The name Father Christmas was substituted, which was fine with us. But even the word *Christmas* became unpopular with the king and his clergy. Some Protestant leaders insisted *Christmas* was just another way of saying "Christ's mass"—which was a fact—and mass was Catholic. To them, anything Catholic was bad. They ordered everyone to say *Christ-tide,* instead. Most people kept saying *Christmas* anyway.

"I have the feeling that the attacks on Christmas in England are just beginning," Nicholas said sadly, staring into the fireplace in our room at the inn. "It might even become dangerous there for Arthur, Leonardo, and our employees at the London toy factory. True, we've mostly been able to keep the existence of the factory there a secret, as we have in Nuremberg, but the wrong people might find out. I simply wouldn't feel right going to America while Arthur was left to deal with such problems."

"Leonardo is there to help Arthur," I said.

Nicholas smiled. "I love and honor Leonardo, but his talent is for art and invention. He's not an especially practical man. We need some-one in England who has a lot of common sense, who can study complicated matters and suggest solutions. Someone like, well, *you*, and you can't help Arthur if we're off in America."

Leonardo

"No one said *we* had to be off in America," I replied. "Nicholas, you and I haven't been apart for twelve centuries. Though we'd cer-tainly miss each other, this may be a time when we each have some-thing important to do in different places. It won't last forever—ten years, maybe twenty. Colonists in America need Christmas desper-ately. Bring it to them. I'll go to London and work with Arthur to help Christmas through difficult times there."

"I think I'd be very lonely in America without you," Nicholas said, sounding mournful and excited at the same time. I knew he would gen-uinely miss me—just as I knew he was thrilled at the thought of bring-ing joyful Christmas traditions to a whole new continent.

"Well, take Felix with you," I suggested. "You two haven't had any adventures on your own since our marriage in Constantinople. Arthur wrote in his last letter that some group is organizing a boatload of colonists to sail to America. They're going to settle near a previous colony called Jamestown. Let's get Felix and go to London; surely the two of you can join that brave band or another one, and soon be on your way. Who knows? America may prove to be so wonderful that in a decade or two you'll send for me, and we can establish a new toy fac-tory there!"

Nicholas grinned, the same warm smile I'd seen in my dreams so many centuries earlier. "But if I go to America, who will help you taste the peppermint candy?" he asked.

I glanced pointedly at his waistline. "It's obvious you've sampled more than enough candy for too many years. I expect that in America

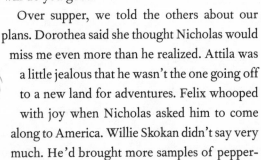

you'll lose a few pounds. From all reports, you'll be lucky to have even a little bread to eat. A diet will do you good."

Over supper, we told the others about our plans. Dorothea said she thought Nicholas would miss me even more than he realized. Attila was a little jealous that he wasn't the one going off to a new land for adventures. Felix whooped with joy when Nicholas asked him to come along to America. Willie Skokan didn't say very much. He'd brought more samples of pepper-

Willie Skokan

mint candy from the factory and sat off in a corner tasting them. Willie took such things very seriously. He wanted our peppermint candy to be the best anywhere.

"I think you should take some of this along with you to London," he said. "Arthur and Leonardo will enjoy it, and I don't think there is a lot of peppermint candy in England yet."

Nicholas, Felix, and I set off for England the next day. We'd hardly arrived in London before my husband and his friend disappeared, hurrying to the docks where Arthur told them the group of colonists was signing on for the voyage to America.

"But there's something you should know about—" Arthur shouted toward their backs as they disappeared down the street.

"What would that be?" I asked, as Arthur helped me carry my bags to the guest room in the cottage he and Leonardo lived in not far from their toy factory. Arthur looked and sounded a bit concerned, and this worried me.

"It's just that the people organizing this colony are, well, rather different," Arthur explained. "Have you heard about the group of Protestants here in England who call themselves the Puritans? No? Well, surely you're aware of how Catholics are quite unpopular with the government and the Church of England. It's all been very confusing for everyone. First King Henry VIII broke the country away from the Catholic Church, then his daughter Queen Mary made Catholicism the religion of the land again, then her sister, Queen Elizabeth, ordered the country to return to Protestantism, and now King James says Catholics may worship as they please, but clearly favors Protestants."

"I've heard of all this," I replied. "As much as possible, we cannot allow it to affect our gift-giving. You know our rule is to always respect the faith of others, even when it is different from our own."

"Of course I know our rule," Arthur said, sounding exasperated. "The problem is not with people like us, but with those who insist the only correct faith is identical to what they themselves believe, and that anyone with any different opinion is automatically evil. Which brings us to the Puritans. They are Protestants who disagree with all but the very simplest forms of worship. They're the ones who are complaining about *Christmas* and insist everyone calls December 25 *Christ-tide* instead. This group Nicholas and Felix want to join is led by Puritans, who say they're going to America so they may worship as they please. I very much fear that in America they will establish a colony where only their religious beliefs are tolerated. By 'religious freedom,' they mean the right to force everyone else to believe as they do."

But Nicholas and Felix returned from the London docks so excited that Arthur and I couldn't bring ourselves to warn them about the people they'd just met. They told us all about it when we sat down for supper. Leonardo joined us. William Brewster, Nicholas said, was the organizer who met with them. Brewster explained he and his friends called themselves the Saints. Within a month, they hoped to have one hundred volunteer colonists, who would sail to America aboard two ships. Upon arrival, they'd start a new community near Jamestown, where everyone would farm and hunt and be happy.

"Only about one-third are actually members of the Saints," Felix said happily. "Everyone else brings some sort of necessary talent—a blacksmith, a doctor, some toolmakers, and so on. I told Mr. Brewster that I was a good craftsman and wood-carver, while my friend Nicholas was a willing worker, if not an especially good one. Do you know what Mr. Brewster replied?"

"We hardly need to mention this, Felix," Nicholas interrupted.

"No, it's funny. Mr. Brewster said he could tell that Nicholas was at least good at eating, and that he'd certainly lose weight in America."

William Brewster

It was obvious Felix and Nicholas had their hearts set on joining the Saints on their voyage, so Arthur and I decided we wouldn't caution them about their new companions. After all, we thought, Nicholas in particular had been successfully bringing Christmas to people around the world for centuries. Even if William Brewster and the Saints didn't cooperate, he was bound to succeed eventually.

In the three weeks between the time we arrived in London and the day the Saints set sail for America, Arthur and I did not bring up our concerns about Christmas in England. Nicholas and Felix were so excited about America that we didn't want to spoil the moment for them. Instead, we talked about what the new colony might be like, and whether it would be cold enough around Jamestown to require them to wear warmer cloaks, and how they would spend their time secretly crafting toys for the children in the new colony to wake up and discover by their beds on Christmas Day.

The Saints sailed aboard the *Mayflower* in September 1620. The 102 colonists were supposed to be divided between two ships, but the second had problems with leaking and William Brewster didn't want to delay the voyage for repairs. So everyone was crammed aboard a single vessel. We learned from Nicholas's letters that things turned sour immediately, with the thirty or so Saints trying to impose their ways on everyone else. In history books, the Saints would be called the Pilgrims, and most of their early squabbles would eventually be forgotten. But when they finally landed on the coast of Plymouth, Massachusetts—hundreds of miles north of Jamestown—Brewster and the other Puritan leaders instantly imposed their religious will on everyone else. Nicholas and Felix weren't surprised in December 1620 when Christmas was hardly mentioned. The new colonists were spending every waking minute trying to build shelters and find food in the harsh winter. But in 1621 the Puritan leaders decreed that Christmas would not be celebrated at all in Plymouth.

"This has made Nicholas and Felix so furious that they've left Plymouth and joined Dutch settlers in their colony of Fort Orange," I told Arthur and Leonardo as I read a letter from my husband that had arrived by ship. "They say that, as awful as it sounds, Christmas has been made completely against the law in Plymouth, and celebrating it will result in severe punishment."

"I'm sorry, but not surprised," Arthur observed. "I suppose, in all their excitement of going to the New World, Nicholas and Felix forgot this has already happened in an entire country. Christmas has been against the law in Scotland since 1583."

This was very sad, but still a fact. In Scotland, a nation separate from England to the north, Puritans were especially anxious to rid themselves of anything to do with the Catholic Church. Christmas, their leaders insisted, was more than just a bad Catholic name for a holiday. In fact, when people celebrated Christmas with singing and dancing and feasting, they violated the way Puritans thought Jesus should be worshipped. They felt people should sit quietly and think about all God's blessings, especially sending his son among us. And choosing December 25 as Jesus' birthday was, to their minds, an insult—Jesus was better than any ordinary person, and only ordinary people had birthdays. They were certainly entitled to these opinions, but they wanted everyone to share them. So the Scottish Puritans and elected leaders made celebrating Christmas a crime. And, as Arthur pointed out, if it happened in Scotland, it could certainly happen in England.

"Our current King James ruled in Scotland before Queen Elizabeth of England died without children in 1603," he reminded me. "So James has allowed Christmas to be banned in one country already. Puritans don't yet control government in England, but they are louder than anyone else, and if they ever are in charge I suspect Christmas will be the first target of their wrath."

"Christmas means too much to too many people in this country," I said firmly. "For poor families in particular, December 25 is the only day of the year when they can feast and dance and sing and forget, for just a little while, how hard they have to work, and how little they have to call their own. It's just a different way of thanking God for Jesus than sitting quietly in a room, thinking. I can't believe the Puritans want to prevent others from having a little holiday happiness."

Arthur's eyes narrowed, and he looked quite grim.

"Layla, we've both lived long enough to realize something," he said. "There are always those who want to control the way everyone else lives, including how, when, and why they are happy."

"Well, the Puritans have picked the wrong place for a fight over Christmas," I replied. "No country celebrates Christmas better than England. Of course, no country needs Christmas more, either." Then, upset at the possibility of the holiday being taken away, I donned my cloak and hurried outside. I walked for hours through the London streets, and everywhere I looked I was reminded why the ordinary people of Britain should not be deprived of their beloved holiday.

The London where Arthur and I fretted about the Puritans and Christmas
almost four hundred years ago was a much dirtier, desperate place, where
most citizens lived in poverty and seldom survived past the age of fifty.

Six

ondon in the 1600s was nothing like the sprawling city we know today. Because some of its very oldest buildings and monuments—Parliament, the Tower of London, some castles and mansions—still stand, many people think the city hasn't changed very much. But it has. The London where Arthur and I fretted about the Puritans and Christmas almost four hundred years ago was a much dirtier, desperate place, where most citizens lived in poverty and seldom survived past the age of fifty. A few rich people enjoyed lives of luxury, living in fine homes and riding everywhere in gilded, horse-drawn carriages. Almost everyone else, including many children, labored for little pay at difficult, physically demanding jobs and went home to dark, damp huts at night with nothing to look forward to but a supper of scraps and then a few hours of sleep before they had to get up and do the same discouraging things all over again.

Four million people lived in England then, and about two hundred and fifty thousand of them were in London, making it by far the largest city in the country. It was one of the oldest, too, originally built as a fort and supply depot by the Romans in 43 A.D. on the south bank of the River Thames, a mighty waterway. When the Romans left four hundred years later, the Saxons gradually took it over, and then the Normans. It became clear that whoever ruled England would do so from London.

That meant the city attracted lots of people, starting with the lords and ladies who made up the royal court. They wanted great houses of stone and later brick to live in, and servants to tend to their needs. Building materials and food and clothing had to be supplied by merchants, who made up a sort of in-between social class. They, in turn, needed people to build their shops and the much more modest homes middle-class families lived in—houses cobbled together from wood and plaster, not more expensive stone. Still others were needed to prepare the food and sew the clothing the merchants sold to the rich, and these workers were paid very small salaries—pennies every week, not every day—and their homes were really tiny huts, often with thatch roofs that would burn far too easily. And so the population of London always grew, with dozens of very poor people added for each rich one.

I walked through London after my conversation with Arthur. It was late November in 1622. Nicholas and Felix had been in America for almost two years. I missed my husband terribly, and, of course, I missed Felix, too. But as I walked, my thoughts were about the people and places I was seeing. What a difference there was between the lives of the rich and poor! Most of London's streets were narrow and dirty. A few avenues were paved with cobblestones, but these were the ones that led directly to the fine mansions. Everyone else walked to and from their homes and jobs on paths of dirt. When it rained, the mud was ankle-deep. During dry weather, dust blew up into everyone's eyes, noses, and mouths. Garbage was everywhere. There were no organized pickups of trash. If you were lucky enough to have an apple to eat and not so hungry that you'd gulp down every bit of it, including the stem and seeds, then you'd toss the core into the street. It would lie there, swarming with flies, until it rotted away, or until it was gobbled by one of the hundreds of pigs that waddled around loose. Stray dogs and cats roamed everywhere, too, fighting beggars and cripples for bits of bread or cheese tossed from passing carriages—not in charity, usually, but by someone riding along in comfort who'd eaten his or her fill and was discarding the leftovers. And rats ate whatever the humans and other animals somehow missed.

As I approached the Thames, I saw that, as usual, its banks were lined with fishermen. The wide river teemed with salmon, trout, perch, and eels. Those who traded in seafood had boats and nets; they could go out in the deepest parts of the river and often haul up a bountiful catch. Common folk who would either catch a fish or go hungry that night often had one poor line to toss in the water, its hook baited with a bit of animal fat. There were at least enough fish in the Thames that they had a good chance of landing their supper. Several times, in fact, whales were spotted, though the last of these was reported in the 1400s.

Food was of constant concern to all but the very rich. Meat came with most meals only in the mansions, where five or six courses might be served as dinner, accompanied by expensive wine. In the small cottages and fragile huts, porridge or bread smeared with lard frequently made up the entire menu. Vegetables grown in tiny garden plots were considered treats. When potatoes were introduced to England and Ireland from Peru in the late 1500s, these became another diet staple. If there was anything besides water to drink, it might be cheap, weak beer, which was shared by children as well as adults. Poor people seldom left their tables feeling comfortably full, only less hungry.

The rich and poor dressed quite differently, too. Wealthy people wore clothing made from cotton and silk, with lots of lace sewn on.

They had plenty of shirts and dresses. These well-to-do men and women often wore elaborate wigs, and their shoes were shiny because they seldom had to step in the dirty streets. Their carriages whisked them wherever they wanted to go. Poor people wore mostly woolen clothes, and didn't change them often because they had no other clothes to put on. And, while the clothing of the rich came in all colors of the rainbow, the poor would try to brighten their drab garments with bright vegetable dyes, and, when it rained, these often ran and stained their arms and legs.

The London I wandered was, quite frankly, a smelly place. This wasn't just caused by the garbage and the animals on its streets. Rich or poor, few people bathed very often. Water was difficult to come by. You could haul buckets of it from the river, but even in the 1600s people realized much of the water there was fouled with garbage. There were places in the city where you could buy barrels of clean water, but this kind of purchase was well beyond the means of most. Water bearers sometimes passed along the streets, selling smaller quantities for a few farthings, but with money needed for food and clothing, buying water for washing was too much of an extravagance. And, though it's not pleasant to think about, there was no indoor plumbing either. Rich people had chamber pots, poor people just plain pots. After they were used, they had to be emptied—often in the same streets where everyone walked.

For entertainment, rich people in London could have parties and dances whenever they liked. They often had country estates where they could ride horses or stroll through flowery meadows if they grew tired of the city crowds and smells. Everyone else had more limited choices. Many poor people couldn't read, and for those who could, books were both rare and expensive. Under the best of circumstances, they might make an occasional visit to a theater. There were plays to see. King James, among others, had encouraged a playwright named William Shakespeare. You could enjoy dramas and comedies for a penny, though at that price you had to stand up the whole time in a crowded area in front of the stage, while those who could afford more expensive tickets sat in nice chairs on elevated platforms. And the working class enjoyed sports, too. Some, like cock-fighting, where roosters were encouraged to attack each other, or bear-baiting, which is exactly what its name describes, were cruel beyond modern belief. But others would be familiar to almost anyone today—football, for instance, which in America is better known as soccer. Football was by far the most popular sport because you didn't need much to play it, just a ball (perhaps a blown-up pig's bladder, or something of that sort), two areas designated as goals, and players with enough energy to run around for a while.

Mostly, though, nine out of every ten people in 1600s London worked hard every day with very little to show for it. Religion, which should have been a comfort, hadn't been much of one since King Henry VIII abruptly left the Catholic Church a century earlier. Ever since, there were confusing, constantly changing rules about how everyone could worship. During the reign of Queen Mary, some Protestants had even been burned at the stake. Now King James supposedly would allow anyone to worship as he or she pleased, but everyone remained afraid that the rules would change again without notice, and they might be in danger because of how they chose to practice their faith. Always, too, there was the threat of war to further complicate things. When England wasn't enduring civil war, its leaders were generally embroiled in battle against foreign foes, most often the French. In matters of daily life, in religion, in national issues, all the poor people of England felt little but stress or even fear. Their opinions didn't count. Nobody powerful really cared what they thought or what they wanted. Their monarch James firmly believed in the divine right of kings—if God allowed someone to be a king, then whatever the king wanted must be God's will, and no one was allowed to disagree. Perhaps the hardest thing for poor people was knowing there was nothing most of them could do to improve their lives. If you weren't born rich, there was little chance you could become wealthy. Property and titles were handed down from one generation to the next. Working-class people had no chance to acquire such things.

But they also had one time each year when all this could be put aside, a time when the most poverty-stricken families could expect that their rich employers would be generous, even thoughtful, to them. That time, of course, was Christmas, and as I walked through London on this early winter evening I smiled as I spied several people already festooning the doors of their humble cottages with holly and green boughs, two popular decorations at holiday time. Of course, the source of this pleasant tradition originally came from earlier, non-Christian faiths—in the winter, primitive people would set out greenery as a sign they believed spring would come again—but now they were just tokens that almost everyone was preparing to celebrate the birth of Jesus.

Certainly they were eager to celebrate by having fun instead of worrying about their next meal! December 25 was a holiday; shops would be closed, so nobody had to go to work. Even well before that special, happy day, common people in England were preparing themselves for a few fine hours when good things would momentarily be part of their lives.

I passed a doorway where two elderly women chattered happily as they tacked a sparse sprig of holly to their front door. I could tell they were desperately poor. Their clothes were ragged and they were painfully thin. And yet, preparing for Christmas, their smiles were very wide.

"A lovely bit of holly, this," one remarked. "Look at the green of the leaves, and the red rosy berry!" There was only one berry on that tiny sprig, but it was enough to bring them holiday joy.

"Nothing like Christmas, I vow," replied her companion. "I can taste the pudding already! Oh, I wish it was the wonderful day right this minute!" When the sprig was properly in place, they stepped back to admire it, their arms around each other's waist.

No one celebrates Christmas better or with more enthusiasm than the English poor, I reminded myself again, tucking my hands under my cloak, since the November winds were already quite cold. Even though Christmas was still a month away, I knew, somewhere groups of singers were rehearsing traditional carols, since music was such an important part of the national festivities. Soon the streets would be filled with *waits*, carolers who would please everyone with their renditions of holiday songs. Originally, waits were night watchmen who would call out the hours, but they gradually evolved into this more festive role. And, as the waits sang, hardworking men and women and children would begin to smile, because Christmas was finally drawing near. They would spend precious pennies for boughs and holly, so their homes would briefly be filled with color and fresh scent. Many saved all year to buy a single scrawny goose; after its bones were picked clean at Christmas dinner, they would be boiled for soup. And goose wouldn't be the only thing served at this special, once-a-year meal. There would be dessert, too, usually a mince pie or plum pudding. Ingredients for these fabulous concoctions were expensive, but on this holiday occasion everyone who could possibly afford to shop for them gladly did so.

Even though St. Nicholas was not welcomed by British rulers and clergy anymore, Father Christmas tried hard to bring little gifts to poor British children while they slept on Christmas Eve. Before he left for America with Felix, my husband very much enjoyed doing this. In his absence, Arthur and Leonardo and I took up the task. Because there were so many deserving boys and girls who had so very little, anything we left was precious to them—a rag doll, perhaps, or a wooden top. One reason we wanted to perfect our peppermint candy was that these children seldom tasted sweets during all the rest of the year. How fine it would be to add to the joy of their Christmas by leaving them such a special treat!

And yet even a visit from Father Christmas was not the highlight of the holiday. That came when everyone was up and dressed.

After church on Christmas Day, working-class people were allowed to call on the very richest people in their neighborhoods. Out in the English countryside, village peasants would gather and happily walk to the manor of whichever lord they served. In city or country, the poor would then serenade their social superiors with loud, happy songs. One that is still sung today captures the spirit of the tradition. Surely you've sung "We Wish You a Merry Christmas," though you may not have sung or even know all the original verses.

Huddled together in the December cold, dressed in their best clothes and with smiles on their faces, the common people would sing:

We wish you a Merry Christmas,
We wish you a Merry Christmas,
We wish you a Merry Christmas
And a happy New Year.

Good tidings we bring,
To you and your king.
Good tidings of Christmas,
And a happy New Year.

You know that part, don't you? But then the singers would continue,

Oh, bring us a figgy pudding,
Oh, bring us a figgy pudding,

Oh, bring us a figgy pudding,
And a cup of good cheer.

We won't go until we get some,
We won't go until we get some,
We won't go until we get some,
So bring some out here.

This, you see, was the custom. On just one annual occasion, rich people would allow poor people into their homes, and they would give them good food, offer something to drink, and, for a little while, treat them as welcome guests, or even equals. Perhaps some of the wealthy class would have preferred not to, but they wouldn't—couldn't—ignore tradition. Of course, afterward they remained in their warm, fine homes, while their visitors had to resume their normal, difficult lives. For rich people, holiday festivities were only beginning on December 25. They would continue enjoying feasts and gifts through Epiphany on January 6—these were the twelve days of Christmas. Poor people went back to work on December 26. But, as Nicholas and the rest of us concluded centuries earlier, at least Christmas Day had brought momentary joy to those who needed it most.

So Christmas on December 25 was, in some ways, all most people in England had to be happy about, and now these Puritans argued that it should be taken away from them. I simply could not imagine why anyone would be so cruel. Though there still weren't that many Puritans in London, there seemed to be a few more every day. As I walked, it was easy to pick them out.

While everyone else, rich or poor, enjoyed wearing clothes of pleasing colors, Puritan men and women generally preferred black, white, or gray. They thought wearing any other colors might encourage pride, and pride was, in their opinion, sinful. Most Puritan men kept their hair clipped short—one nickname for them was Roundheads—and they would stop and glare at anyone acting in ways they considered inappropriate. They considered almost anything inappropriate—dancing, singing anything other than hymns, even laughing out loud. Above all, they hated any form of religion that worshipped God except in the most basic of ways, sitting in an unadorned church listening to a long sermon. They didn't even want music played in church—that, too, was supposedly insulting to God. The only respectful music, to their minds, came solely from the human voice.

Christmas became the focus of their unhappiness because, they said, it reduced gratitude for Jesus being born to an occasion where people got drunk and acted badly. They weren't completely wrong—sometimes that would happen. Though hundreds of thousands of people behaved properly, inevitably a few others would take the opportunity to misbehave. Every Christmas, there would be isolated incidents of someone drinking too much beer and shouting out insults to his upper-class host or of children getting so excited that they became unruly. But the Puritans chose to present these unfortunate moments as typical rather than exceptional—proof, they insisted, that Christmas had become nothing more than an excuse for rowdy, sinful behavior.

Further, they claimed, God was not pleased by so-called Christian celebrations that were simply extensions of pagan ceremonies. Christmas was on December 25 because, prior to Rome embracing Christianity, one of that nation's emperors worshipped the Persian sun gods. Mithra, the Persian god of light, supposedly was born on that date. In 350, it was just changed to be Jesus' birthday, instead. Nobody, the anti-Christmas Puritans argued, really knew the date when Jesus was born, so how could anyone be so presumptuous as to simply pick a day instead?

They hated everything about Christmas, including the custom of exchanging gifts. That, they complained, harkened back to Saturnalia, the weeklong celebration in old Rome that lasted through December 23, when people would give each other little trinkets as part of the celebration. Imitating the way the Wise Men brought gifts to the Baby Jesus had nothing to do with this terrible modern tradition of awful Catholic St. Nicholas bringing gifts to British children, the Puritans insisted. It didn't matter if he was now officially known as Father Christmas. By any name, he was a Catholic saint, and anything remotely connected with Catholicism must be eradicated. Over the years, all of us who traveled and worked with Nicholas had learned everyone has the right to his or her religious beliefs. But we also felt, very passionately, that it is wrong to force your opinions on others who believe differently. I did not dislike the Puritans for what they chose to believe, but I was very offended by their inability to tolerate, let alone respect, the beliefs of others.

"No matter how they try, the Puritans will never be able to take Christmas away from the British people," I insisted to Arthur and Leonardo when I had finally finished my long walk and returned to their house in London for dinner. We were eating a meal that was very middle class, since there was fruit juice to drink and a little meat to go along with cheese and some asparagus that Leonardo had grown in a small garden. Unlike the wealthy, we had only that one course, with no wine or dessert, but unlike the poor, at least we had more than bread, potatoes, and water. "Celebrating the holiday is ingrained in the national spirit. If the Puritans try to take it away, all they'll do is make the common people hate them."

"I wish I felt as certain, Layla," Arthur replied, wiping his mouth with a napkin before he took up his knife and spoon again. We didn't have forks. In 1622, few people did. You picked up your meat on the point of your knife, or else you cut off a tiny slice and used your fingers to transfer the morsel from plate to mouth. "But in our history, too often a few give the orders that must be obeyed by everyone else.

King James may protect Christmas for now, but he could change his mind about it tomorrow. Or our next king or queen could agree with the Puritans."

"They might take everything else, but nobody could ever take Christmas," I said suddenly, finishing my last bite of cheese and pushing my plate away. "The Puritans can try, but there aren't enough of them."

Arthur looked thoughtful. "Actually, their numbers are growing. People still remember their terror when Queen Mary sent Protestants to the stake. So many in England are frustrated with their lives, which are controlled by the beliefs or even whims of those in power. Ordinary folk want power over someone or something, too. The Puritans tell them they can raise their voices against anything that remotely seems Catholic, and for the first time many of these people feel their opinions might make a difference. They're told by the Puritans that if they join the cause, they'll instantly be better than anyone who believes differently, even if it's a king or queen. How tempting that must be to anyone who has never before been shown respect! But I'll agree with you that the Puritans can't touch Christmas so long as two things don't happen. There cannot be a weak English king, someone who says and does foolish things that give the Puritans excuses to encourage outright rebellion. And the Puritans can't have a charismatic leader, someone intelligent enough to harness their energy, to organize and lead them. If ever we have that terrible combination in England, watch out!"

Less than three years later, Charles I succeeded his father, James, as king of England. Three years after that, an obscure country squire named Oliver Cromwell became a member of Parliament, the elected body that was supposed to advise the king. As Arthur predicted, catastrophe resulted.

In a pleasant sort of way I was telling a vendor he was asking too much for a few pieces of cod when someone bumped violently against my arm. The basket I was holding overturned and beets rolled everywhere. I turned and found myself staring into the thin, mournful face of Charles I, recently crowned king of England, Scotland, Wales, and Ireland after the death of his father, James.

Seven

 met England's new king in a London marketplace soon after his coronation. I was there at Leonardo's request, shopping for beets, a reddish-colored vegetable that was quite popular with poor people in 1625 Britain. Leonardo didn't want beets to eat, however. He planned to extract the juice of the vegetable and see if it could be used to dye peppermint candy.

"The appearance of a sweet is almost as important as its taste," he explained to me in his laboratory at the toy factory. "The peppermint treats we make here are pleasing to the tongue, but insulting to the eye." He brandished a handful. "Here, look! Round and white—how boring! But if we could only add some color, some flair, how delightful it would be. Bright red, I think, would be the most attractive. But this candy should not be completely red, either. I am picturing it as white with red stripes. Don't you think this would be just right?"

I agreed that combination would be attractive. In those days, no one yet decorated hard-boiled candy with vivid colors. Remember, there were no modern machines to shape and color products. Everything had to be done by hand, and, besides, people were still in the primitive stages of learning how to dye clothes, let alone confectionary. But Leonardo da Vinci never had the same limits of imagination as anyone else. He asked if I would go to the market for him and buy beets, since he had noticed recently at dinner that when beet juice was accidentally splashed on clothing, the resulting stain was hard to get out.

"Perhaps this juice can be altered in a way that would allow it to retain the red color without the nasty beet taste," Leonardo said. "Then I can discover a way to make the color stick to the candy, but not to fingers or clothing. Please, Layla, go to the market and buy some beets for me. I'm anxious to begin my experiments."

Leonardo did not want to go to the market himself because he didn't want to attract attention. Arthur rarely ventured out in daylight hours for the same reason. They had lived in London now for more than two hundred years, and didn't look a day older than when they had arrived. If too many people saw them often enough to remember them, at some point there would be gossip about why these two fellows apparently never aged. That attention, in turn, might lead to discovery of the toy factory. So it couldn't be risked. Having no real friends besides the other longtime companions was a sacrifice we all had to make. In London, Arthur and Leonardo mostly stayed inside.

I had no such restriction because I didn't always live there. Even after Nicholas and Felix left for the New World, I never moved permanently into the cottage near the London toy factory. I spent much of my time there, to be sure, but I also traveled back to Nuremberg to help out Attila and Dorothea, and, as always, I visited countries in Europe to study their changing Christmas customs and to seek out all the deserving children we would want to reward with gifts. And, unlike Arthur with his forceful personality and Leonardo with his distracted, scholarly airs, I looked and acted perfectly normal. There was nothing remarkable about me. So long as I was careful to keep conversations short and avoid meeting the same people too often, there was little chance they'd even remember me, let alone notice that I never seemed to get older.

It was a sunny summer day, and despite the dusty streets I quite enjoyed my walk from the cottage to the market. Today when people shop in air-conditioned, well-lighted, sterile grocery stores, I think they are missing something. The old outdoor marketplaces of Europe exploded in colors and smells, as people milled about bargaining for squawking chickens and dangling bunches of onions and flapping sets of pantaloons. Vendors set their prices as starting-points for friendly negotiation. If you wanted, let's say, a bushel of apples, you never bought the first ones you saw. Instead, you visited several stands selling the crunchy fruit, and made your final purchase based on which merchant combined the lowest prices with the freshest produce.

I spent many enjoyable minutes shopping for Leonardo's beets, which I placed in a wide basket I held by the handle, and then decided I might buy some fish for our supper, since this marketplace was close by the Thames. It was usually easy to get good prices on freshly caught fish, because they would have just been pulled out of the river and needed to be sold before they spoiled in the heat. In a pleasant sort of way I was telling a vendor he was asking far too much for a few pieces of cod when someone bumped violently against my arm. The basket I was holding overturned, and beets rolled everywhere. I turned and found myself staring into the thin, mournful face of Charles I, recently crowned king of England, Scotland, Wales, and Ireland after the death of his father, James.

"I do beg your pardon, madam," Charles said, stammering a little over the *b* and the *p*. He had a slight speech impediment, though it wasn't severe enough to make understanding him difficult. "Here, let my guards pick up those vegetables for you." He had trouble with the *v*, too.

"Please don't bother, Your Majesty," I replied, bowing as protocol required but not feeling in any way intimidated by the presence of royalty. After all, in my more than twelve hundred years of life I had met many legendary figures. Charles I might currently rule England, but in a few hours I would be sharing supper with "King" Arthur, not to mention Leonardo da Vinci.

Besides, seeing the king and even speaking to him was not unimaginable in that time and place. Though Charles had several country estates, he often had to be in his capital city to meet with counselors and converse with members of Parliament, the elected body whose permission he required to raise money through taxation. It was a testy relationship. Parliament wanted the king to consult them about all important policy decisions, including if and when to fight wars and how religion should be regulated. Like his father, James, Charles very much believed in the divine right of kings. Parliament, he insisted, should be told what their ruler wanted and then always support his decisions. As we stood face-to-face while some of his soldiers scrambled about retrieving beets, I guessed Charles must be in London because Parliament was in the process of considering his request for money to attack the Spanish port of Cadiz. Of course, he had no reason to come to the marketplace to buy his own food; the king had plenty of servants to do that. But since he was in London anyway, a royal visit to one of its busiest marketplaces made political sense. Common people would have a chance to see their new ruler, and be both pleased by the opportunity and awed by his appearance. Charles was dressed in the finest coat and trousers, and his long brown hair—what you could see of it under a wide, broad-brimmed hat—glowed in the sunshine. His mustache and beard were freshly barbered. The colors the king wore—gold and green and spotless white—were in absolute contrast to the grim blacks and grays of the Puritans. I noticed that even his hands were spotlessly clean, with the nails of his fingers neatly trimmed. A half-dozen guards stood around in close proximity, and I expected Charles, now that he had acknowledged me and seen to it that my vegetables were picked up and put back in my basket, to move on and greet some of his other subjects. Instead, he smiled and continued speaking to me.

"I see you have purchased beets, and now perhaps some fish," Charles remarked. Having heard his mild stutter, it no longer really distracted me. "Will these be the things you prepare for your family's delicious supper?"

"Yes, Your Majesty," I said, pleased by his courtesy and not wanting to explain the beets were for one of Leonardo's experiments, not dinner. "That is, we'll eat fish if I can convince this merchant to sell me some for a fair price."

Charles laughed. "I, too, have problems receiving fair prices, and even in getting money to make purchases at all. Parliament is very miserly—often, I fear, to the detriment of our nation. But they will see reason, as this fishmonger will. Now, madam, what is your name?"

"Layla, Your Highness."

"Layla," Charles said. "An odd name, certainly. French, perhaps? Italian? Well, no matter. Tell me, what profession does your husband pursue?"

It was not an unusual question. Women of middle age, as I appeared to be, were simply assumed to be married. If I answered the king's inquiry honestly, though, he would believe I was insane, so I simply responded, "Nicholas is across the ocean in the New World colonies, Your Majesty." I didn't add he'd moved to a Dutch settlement because of his disgust with anti-Christmas rules in the British settlement of Plymouth.

"Well, how wonderful!" Charles said. "My father, of course, was responsible for our first New World colony. They called it Jamestown in his honor. I assume your good spouse will soon send for you. And how do you earn your living while he is so far away?"

I thought of the beets, and Leonardo. "I make candy, Your Majesty," I told the king. "It's of the new variety flavored with peppermint."

Charles beamed. "Your new queen is very fond of sweets, and of peppermint candy in particular. It is much more common in her native France than it is here in England. She will be pleased to learn supplies of it may be more convenient than she believed."

As the king and I talked, a crowd had naturally gathered around us listening to all that was said. When Charles mentioned the queen, there was some angry muttering. Just months after her marriage to Charles, Henrietta Maria was already a very controversial figure. In those times, marriages in royal families were arranged more for political advantage than love. In this case, Charles married Henrietta because she was a princess of France. For the moment, England's chief foreign enemy was Spain, so the British king took a woman of French royal blood as his wife in hopes her country might become an ally against the Spanish if England needed military help. There were two immediate problems with this marriage. One involved the royal couple themselves. Charles was twenty-four, in those times considered a very mature age, since few people lived past fifty. (King James died when he was fifty-nine.) But Henrietta was only fifteen, a grown woman by some standards but still, really, a young girl who did not fall in love with her stuttering, shy husband right away.

Meanwhile, many of the British people, especially the working class, did not like what they knew of Queen Henrietta. Mostly this involved her religion. She was a very devout Catholic. King Henry VIII had rejected the Catholic Church a century earlier, so most current English subjects thought of themselves as Protestants. Part of the formal contract of marriage between Charles and Henrietta stipulated that the new queen must be allowed to continue practicing her

Catholic faith. Charles went to a Protestant church, but that wasn't enough to silence the queen's many critics. Puritans especially argued that husbands could be influenced by their wives, and because all Catholics were treacherous, Queen Henrietta must privately be trying to convince the king to return England to the Catholic faith. This was highly unlikely since, in these early days of their marriage, they hardly spoke to each other at all. Yet, as is often the way with hateful, unfair gossip, some people kept repeating that Henrietta was treacherous, and almost everyone else eventually assumed that she was.

"Do you have any of your peppermint treats with you, madam?" Charles inquired. "The queen is in our coach just over there"—he gestured to the edge of the market, where a magnificent carriage drawn by four coal-black horses was guarded by a dozen soldiers— "and she would surely enjoy a tasty surprise."

I couldn't see the queen inside the carriage. The window curtains were drawn tight, which wasn't surprising, since if the crowd had seen her they might very well have called out insults. I wondered why the king would have brought her along, and decided he was trying, honestly though probably uselessly, to show his subjects that their queen was a normal woman rather than the scheming monster her critics proclaimed her to be.

Henrietta

"I have none with me, Your Majesty," I answered.

Charles looked disappointed. "Well, then, perhaps you will at some future date. Please, madam, prepare some of your finest confectionary and bring it to the palace some time when Her Majesty and I are in residence. Identify yourself as Layla the Peppermint Woman, and if it is a convenient time you will be admitted. And don't fear—I will pay a fair price for your product."

"It would be my pleasure to offer the candy as a gift, Your Highness," I replied, and bowed again. I could see that the king's guards clearly wanted him to move on, and Charles, too, looked ready to leave. Just as he turned away, though, I thought of something else.

"May I ask a question, Your Majesty?" I called out.

Now, this bordered on rudeness, and even on being dangerous. It was one thing for me to speak after the king had spoken first, but quite another to address him when the conversation he had begun was concluded. Several of the guards glared, and one stepped toward me, but Charles gestured for him to stop.

"Your king is always pleased to respond to his subjects, madam," Charles said. "The queen waits in the carriage, and I have business with Parliament, but as all here can see, I pause to take this question from you. What might it be?"

"It concerns Christmas, Your Majesty," I said boldly. "There are some now in positions of influence and power who say it is sinful and should be abolished. Though their voices are loud, many, many more of us love this special day. I wonder, will you protect it for us, so that we may keep Christmas as a time of joyful celebration?"

The king smiled. "I too love Christmas," he said. "It is the day to give thanks to God for sending his most holy son, and I realize the feasting and singing brings great happiness to my people. Do not fear, Madam Layla. While I rule this land, your beloved holiday is safe. I only hope Father Christmas will leave some peppermint candy for the queen this year."

"He very well might, Your Majesty," I replied. "Thank you for your courtesy, and for your protection of Christmas."

That night, after we'd finished our dinner of fish and Leonardo had retired to his laboratory with the beets, I told Arthur about my meeting with Charles.

"He loves Christmas too," I said. "If only he can be strong enough to withstand the Puritans' demands to ban the holiday."

"I'm afraid the Puritans squabbling about Christmas may prove the least of his worries," Arthur replied. "The king is truly at odds with

Parliament. He believes they must obey all his commands, and they believe he must be guided by their collective wisdom. At some point they will either compromise or fight. Another civil war in England is a very real possibility, Layla."

Charles's disagreements with his Parliament continued. Parliament met at the king's command, and three times in the next three years Charles summoned it to meet, then angrily dismissed it when its members refused to give him the tax money he wanted and tried to keep him from appointing the royal ministers he preferred. There was much grumbling about this, not only in the London streets but throughout England. Though its members were all country lords, prominent ministers, or well-off merchants rather than real representatives of the poor working class, Parliament was still considered the one opportunity for the king's subjects to have some influence on his decisions.

Meanwhile, in my own small way, I tried to encourage Charles's support of Christmas. Occasionally, I took some ordinary white peppermints to the palace. I never actually asked to see the king or queen, but just left the package with a servant there. And, though it was not easy making my stealthy way into the royal palace on the night of every December 24 for almost the next two decades, each year England's Queen Henrietta awoke on Christmas Day to find a small package of special peppermints beside her pillow. It was especially lovely candy, from the batches Leonardo was able to successfully decorate with bright red stripes. I was careful, in delivering my occasional packages during non-holiday times, to leave only plain white treats so no one would guess the identity of the Christmas gift-giver. As it turned out, the queen, who had little belief in the

Charles

Pere Noel of her native France or England's Father Christmas, decided the striped candy was a thoughtful present from her husband. She began to feel happier with Charles, and soon their marriage blossomed into a real love affair.

But the king's relationship with Parliament remained anything but loving, and several events during the next few years moved England ever closer to civil war. In the process, Christmas was in even greater danger.

"Do you celebrate Christmas, Missus Nicholas?" Elizabeth Cromwell
gently laid her hand on her husband's arm. "Our guest is here to talk
about America, not to debate the merits of Christmas with you."

Eight

 met Oliver Cromwell nine years after encountering King Charles in the marketplace. Unlike my accidental meeting with the king, my first contact with Cromwell came by appointment—actually, by request.

In 1634, religious and political problems in England remained unresolved. The Puritans were more outspoken than ever against all forms of worship other than their own. Charles infuriated them in 1633 by appointing William Laud to be archbishop of Canterbury. Laud supported what Puritans considered "liberal" church services with music and altar decorations. One of the Puritans, William Prynne, responded by writing a book titled *Histromastrix, or the Player's Scourge*, which attacked as sinful all forms of public entertainment from plays to sports, and particularly argued that Christmas encouraged bad behavior, not worship of Jesus. Few people could read at the time, and if the king had been sensible he would simply have ignored the book. But instead Prynne was arrested, and as a punishment for writing what he truly believed, he had part of his ears cut off. This unfortunately proved that Charles could be as harsh as his critics. "Half-Eared" Prynne became a symbol to the Puritans that they were in terrible danger for openly advocating their religious beliefs, and, frankly, it was hard to blame them, even though I disagreed with them completely about Christmas.

Puritans comprised only part of the king's political opposition. Almost everyone in Parliament was against him. Three times in three years Charles called Parliament to meet, and each time demanded money to fight wars. All three times, Parliament refused to immediately do what he wanted, and all three times Charles told its members to go home, instead of thoughtfully discussing with them how both sides could work together instead of remaining angry and adversarial. Then the king got his money by forcing rich people to make loans to him and by imposing new taxes on some businesses. This was clearly against English law; Parliament had to agree with any form of taxation. Charles said the law was wrong; kings had the God-given right to do as they pleased. Parliament was supposed to help him, not tell him what he could or couldn't do.

The members of Parliament responded by writing what became known as the Petition of Right, which stated that whoever held the English throne could not tax anyone or anything without Parliament's approval—and, further, that no one could be arrested and punished without proof of a crime and that the king could not impose martial law on the country in peacetime, something Charles was always threatening to do. The Petition of Right was delivered to Charles in June 1628, when he either had to get the money to keep fighting his wars in Spain and France or else bring all his troops back to England. So Charles signed it, and in return Parliament gave him some of the money he wanted, but neither side was really happy. Charles believed Parliament had assumed too much power. After signing the petition the king just ignored it, levying taxes and arresting people as he pleased. Then, in March 1629, Charles went further. He announced that, for the time being, Parliament would no longer exist. He would govern without it. And, for the next eleven years, he did, despite continued criticism. If members of Parliament hoped English working people would rise up and demand that their representatives again be involved in government, they were disappointed. People in the so-called "lower classes" had enough to do keeping their families clothed and fed.

So in 1634, the king's political and religious opponents were feeling especially frustrated. There was no swelling of popular support for their causes. This is why some of them, including a rather obscure man named Oliver Cromwell, were ready to give up. Now, in a few more years everyone in England would know Cromwell's name, but at that time he was just another outspoken Puritan.

I certainly had never heard of him until one afternoon in the spring of 1634, when one of the women who worked in Arthur's toy factory hesitantly approached me. Arthur employed several dozen people, who would come to the factory in the morning, work during the day, and then go home to their families. He paid a wage that was more generous than most salaries of the day, but not so high as to attract undue attention. None of these people acquired our special powers of not aging and the ability to work and travel much faster than normal folk. We were careful that they wouldn't work at our toy factories for so long that it would become obvious we weren't growing older. Anyone employed for ten years or so was given a generous pension and, if he or she still wanted to work, help finding a new job. Of course, Leonardo's inventions included some remarkable machines that helped us make toys at a more rapid rate than was possible anywhere else, but this was the result of science, not magic. We asked our employees not to talk much about the toys they helped craft and, mostly, everyone obeyed this rule, especially since their pay was so good and they were treated with such respect by Arthur.

Whenever I was in London, I enjoyed visiting with these employees, chatting with them about their families. So in 1634 when Pamela Forrest asked if I could spare a moment, I was glad to do so. Pamela was in her late twenties and we often spoke about her two sons and her husband, Clive, a London barber. Poor people trimmed their own hair with knives, but wealthier men and women enjoyed having this task done for them. Pamela, who had then worked at the toy factory for about three years, often shared funny little stories about her husband's customers, but I noticed on this occasion that she seemed very concerned about something.

"You appear upset, Pamela," I said. "I hope nothing is wrong. Are your husband and children all right?"

Pamela Forrest

"They're fine, Layla, praise God, but I hope I haven't done something wrong," she replied. "Now, I know none of us are to discuss what we do here, and I promise you I haven't. I'm very grateful to Mr. Arthur for the kindness and generosity he shows to all of us who work for him. But I did have a word with someone about you and your husband, Nicholas, who I've heard of but never met because he's over in the New World colonies."

I was immediately concerned. "Who did you talk to, Pamela, and what did you tell them?"

"Only about your husband in America, ma'am, and precious little about that, because, if for no other reason, I don't know much," Pamela answered, wringing her hands nervously. "It was all quite innocent, and quite natural. My husband, Clive, the barber, was trimming a gentleman's hair the other day, and the man told him he was thinking of going to America as a colonist because he found living here so distasteful."

"I know some people do, Pamela," I said. "Please continue."

"Well, this gentleman is a good customer of Clive's, and as it happens I also know his wife, who I meet now and then in the market. Her name is Elizabeth and she's a lovely lady. Well, her man told mine about maybe going to the colonies, and then I met Elizabeth yesterday and she said she was frightened by the thought, that to her mind all there was across the ocean was starvation and attacks by the natives. Well, you get letters from your husband who's there, and I thought perhaps you could talk to Elizabeth and her husband about what it's really like. I hope I haven't made you angry. I'm just trying to help my friend."

I felt quite relieved. After fourteen years in the New World, Nicholas's letters were increasingly positive. He still disdained the Puritan settlers and their refusal to celebrate Christmas, but both he and Felix felt quite at home with the Dutch and their continued enjoyment of visits from St. Nicholas. In fact, Nicholas had begun urging me to cross the Atlantic and join him, but I was worried about Christmas in England and didn't want to leave Arthur alone to face an uncertain future.

"So long as you didn't mention our toy factory, Pamela, there's no problem at all," I told her. "Am I to call on your friend Elizabeth and her husband? I can only tell them what Nicholas has told me, of course, but I'd be glad to be helpful if I can."

Pamela smiled, happy that I wasn't displeased with her. "That would be ever so nice," she exclaimed. "Though they live most of the time on a farm in St. Ives about seventy miles north of here, they're often in London and have a small cottage near the Thames. Elizabeth suggested, if you were agreeable, that you meet them there for conversation and refreshments this Saturday about four o'clock. I'll see her in the market tomorrow. May I tell her you'll come?"

I had no particular plans for Saturday afternoon. "Please do, Pamela. Now, your friend's name is Elizabeth. Who is her husband?"

"His name is Oliver Cromwell," Pamela told me, and went on to explain that he had been a member of Parliament, who, having suffered some business misfortunes, was currently farming in St. Ives. "He and Elizabeth are Puritans, by the way," she added. "Will that bother you?"

"No, it will only make our conversation more interesting," I replied, and on Saturday afternoon I walked to the Cromwell's London cottage, which was quite small and undistinguished. When I knocked on the door, it was opened by a fresh-faced woman in her early thirties dressed in the usual Puritan colors of black and gray.

"You must be Pamela's friend Layla," she said cheerfully. "It's so good of you to come. My husband is in the kitchen. We're just enjoying some fruit—apples and pears, nothing fancy. But I hope you'll have a bite or two."

The afternoon sun cast shadows through the kitchen windows. Seated there at a table was an average-sized man with close-cut hair and a small mustache. When he stood to greet me, he smiled pleasantly and said, "I'm Oliver Cromwell, missus." This was a common way for Puritans to address adult married women; they preferred the simpler term to the more formal *madam*, which they believed copied the social style of the French, who, in turn, they found to be influenced by Catholicism. "Please remind me of your given name."

"I'm Layla, Mr. Cromwell," I replied, being friendly but formal in my turn. "Thank you for inviting me to your home."

"Layla?" he answered, gesturing for me to sit down at the table with him and Elizabeth. "An unusual name, which I hope isn't French. And what is your last name?"

Now, here was a problem. In my youth, people just went by their first names. Further identification involved where you were from, like "Layla of Niobrara" or "Bishop Nicholas of Myra." By the time cultural custom got around to requiring last names, too, people like me and my husband and Arthur and Felix simply kept the shorter names we were used to. No one, over the centuries, had ever asked me my last name before. I would learn, though, this sort of question was typical of Oliver Cromwell. He was always every bit as interested in other people as he was in himself, a rare quality in someone with the ambition to become a national leader.

"Your last name, again?" Cromwell repeated, sounding pleasant but determined to keep asking the same thing until he got an answer. This, too, I would learn was typical of him. Once he started something, he never stopped until it was accomplished.

"Nicholas, Mr. Cromwell," I finally replied. It was, after all, my husband's name, and could be a last name as well as a first one.

"Layla Nicholas," he said, cutting a bit of pear and using the tip of his knife to raise it to his mouth. "And your husband's name?"

"Nicholas," I answered.

"You've said that already. I mean, what's his first name?"

"Nicholas."

"That's his last name. What's his first?"

Oliver Cromwell

There was something about Oliver Cromwell that made me feel not nervous, but perhaps unsettled. Over the centuries I had met many famous people, and a few who were great, which is an altogether different thing than being famous. Cromwell had an air about him that was only common to great men and women, individuals who had rare qualities of leadership. My husband had this quality, too. Something about them made everyone else feel compelled to be honest. In times of crisis, you would look to them for guidance. Now, in his kitchen, I could have made up some name or other for my husband, but I simply could not lie to Oliver Cromwell.

"Nicholas is his first name, too," I answered, because this was, after all, the truth.

Cromwell looked amused. "Nicholas Nicholas, is it?" he asked. "Well, that's quite a name. How long has Nicholas Nicholas been in the New World, and what took him there?"

This was not much safer a topic. As a Puritan, Cromwell would not be pleased by the prospect of the real St. Nicholas bringing Christmas to the New World. What I told him, though, was accurate enough in itself—that my husband and his friend Felix (I was glad Cromwell didn't ask what *his* last name was) had longed to see this place known as America, and they'd now been there for several years. They wrote that they were happy enough, and at some point I expected to sail across the ocean myself and rejoin my husband. The Cromwells didn't seem surprised when I mentioned they were living in a Dutch settlement rather than an English one. Traders and craftsmen went wherever they could make their fortunes, and most New World colonies founded by one country would soon include settlers and merchants from other lands.

"I am considering taking my family to this place called America," Cromwell told me. "Though Elizabeth here fears that those natives they call Indians will slay us as we step off the boat onto the shore, I've heard America is a place where a man can make his living based on his own ability. Here in England I'm only a person of very modest means—I have a small farm, and must make my living from my own sweat. Though I've been elected to Parliament, the king won't allow Parliament to meet. And you know, of course, how we who call ourselves Puritans are persecuted. In America, at least, you can worship as you like without fear of reprisal."

I thought about Plymouth, and how the Puritan leaders there refused to allow anyone to worship differently than they did. "This seems to be a time when few people are willing to tolerate different faith in others," I said carefully. "That may be the case in the New World as well as in England. I, myself, find it sad when anyone attacks the religious beliefs and activities of anyone else. Take, for example, the matter of Christmas."

"Ah, Christmas!" Cromwell exclaimed, putting down his knife and pear. If he had been Richard Harris in the *Cromwell* film he would have stamped his feet and pounded the table, but he was Oliver Cromwell in real life, and not so theatrical. "A day that has become an occasion for bad behavior rather than worship. Do you celebrate Christmas, Missus Nicholas?"

Elizabeth Cromwell gently laid her hand on her husband's arm. "Our guest is here to talk about America, not to debate the merits of Christmas with you."

"No, she is the one who raised the subject," Cromwell replied. "I can guess the holiday is dear to you, Missus Nicholas, but do you deny that it encourages drunkenness and other sinful activities?"

"Nothing in this world is perfect, and certainly there are isolated instances of bad judgment," I said. "But will you, Mr. Cromwell, deny that the poor working people of England look forward all year to Christmas, and that it is the one time they can set aside their problems and give thanks for Jesus in the happiest of ways?"

Cromwell shook his head. "If the purpose of the holiday is to give thanks, why must anything else be involved, like singing loudly in the streets or marching as a mob to rich men's houses and demanding strong drink from them? Giving thanks to God ought to be a constant thing, and something done solemnly. December 25 is nothing more than a date based on old pagan beliefs, which in themselves are insulting to God."

"You would ban Christmas, then?" I asked carefully, trying to keep the anger out of my voice. "You would take that joy away from the English people?"

Cromwell looked thoughtful. "I have nothing against joy, so long as it is tempered with respect for God. Given the opportunity, I would try to persuade people that there are better ways than Christmas to express pleasure in all God has given us, including his son. Unless the situation was dire, though, I do not believe anything involving religion should be forced on anyone, or taken away, for that matter. Surely you do not deny me my right to believe Christmas is wrong?"

I was always ready to defend Christmas with all my heart and spirit, but I saw Elizabeth Cromwell looked very uncomfortable. I was a guest in her home, I reminded myself, invited to discuss America rather than the holiday, so I tried to bring my debate with her husband to quick conclusion.

"Certainly, so long as you do not deny me my right to believe Christmas is precious and must be preserved," I replied.

"So be it," Cromwell said, smiling, and then he cut me some pieces of pear. The Cromwells and I sat at their table for another hour, talking about the New World and the possibilities in it. A few weeks later Pamela Forrest met Elizabeth Cromwell in the marketplace, and learned that the Cromwells had decided to stay in England because they could not find a buyer for their farm. Two years after that, Oliver Cromwell inherited a considerable fortune from an uncle and didn't have to plow his own fields anymore. This enabled him to focus more on politics, so in 1640 when King Charles finally recalled Parliament after eleven years, Cromwell was among its many members who were determined that this time, the king was going to learn that "divine right" was a thing of the past. As Parliament reconvened, Oliver Cromwell was still not considered one of its leaders. But that would come, and soon.

"Perhaps you and I can debate the issue here in the park. But that must come later." He gestured toward a half-dozen men gathered nearby. Their hair was cut in the Roundhead style. All but one wore somber black garments. The other man wore black trousers, too, but his cloak was blue.

Nine

ivil war is inevitable in England, I'm afraid," Arthur said in November 1640. "We know from experience that, in times of war, our powers become limited. Layla, this might be the right time for you to go join Nicholas and Felix in the New World. Leonardo and I must stay here, to keep the toy factory operating if we can. But there's no reason for you to take the risk of remaining, too."

"Perhaps there won't be war," I said hopefully. "The king has just recalled Parliament again. This time things may go better than in the spring." In April, Charles had summoned Parliament for the first time since 1629, mostly because he needed money to put down an uprising in Scotland. Instead, members of the House of Commons—the largest branch of Parliament, designed to be the voice of ordinary people—wanted to talk about unfair taxes, and about Charles's continuing habit of doing whatever he wanted without consulting Parliament first. So, once again, the king told Parliament to go home, but later in the year there was a rebellion in Scotland, and he needed money to raise an army to put down that threat. So now in November, he had asked Parliament to re-form, but its members, including Oliver Cromwell, were in no mood to cooperate.

"There are more Puritans than ever in Parliament," Arthur noted. "They have no intention of compromising with the king about anything, particularly since they learned the two oldest princes have gone to Catholic church services with their mother. They're now convinced the king might return England to the Catholics at any time. Wait and see—something is going to happen that will make war inevitable." Sadly, he was right.

Instead of giving the king the money he wanted, Parliament voted that William Laud, Charles's archbishop of Canterbury, and the Earl of Stafford, the king's military advisor, were guilty of treason and had to be removed from office. Stafford was executed. Then, before finally giving Charles some of the money he requested, certain new laws were made, taking away many of the king's powers and requiring him to allow Parliament to meet at least once every three years. Charles hated these laws. As he had in the past, he agreed to them and then ignored them. He still believed in divine right—God had made him king, and so anything he wanted to do was what God wanted, too.

While Charles was away fighting the Scottish rebels in 1641, Parliament went even further. It wrote prospective laws that required the king to get Parliament's approval for any ministers he wanted to appoint, and created the Assembly of Divines, a committee that would make new rules for religion in England—rules that would reflect the beliefs of the Puritans.

"They're going to ban Christmas right away," Arthur predicted when the news reached us at the toy factory.

I thought of Oliver Cromwell, and how he had told me he would try to persuade people to give up Christmas rather than order them to do it. Though he was still not the most prominent member of Parliament, people were starting to mention Cromwell's name more often. Many poor people in particular admired him. Whenever he made speeches, he always emphasized that the best government was one that let ordinary people have some influence—"democracy" was what he called it.

"If the Puritans truly want to respect the wishes of the working class, they'll soon learn that Christmas is too important to too many people for it to be outlawed in England," I said. "I've told you about Oliver Cromwell. Surely if reasonable people like him are involved, Christmas can still be preserved, and peace in England, too."

"Don't be too certain that this Cromwell is going to be around much longer," Arthur said. "There are rumors that the king intends to charge his main opponents in Parliament with treason, and have them arrested and perhaps even executed. Cromwell could be one of them."

On December 25, 1641, Christmas in England was celebrated as usual. Waits strolled through cities and villages singing their joyful holiday songs. Poor people scraped together their few pennies to buy a goose, and on the wonderful day itself groups of working-class people marched to the homes of their wealthy neighbors and shared fine food and drink with them there. Some churches held special holiday services, though Puritan congregations ignored the holiday completely. Arthur, Leonardo, and I had a wonderful time making our quiet way into many, many English homes to leave small gifts of toys and peppermint candy for the children living there. We regretted very much that we could not leave something for Puritan children, but our tradition had always been to avoid homes where, for one reason or another, parents did not want us to go. Still, the overwhelming number of families in England very much wanted visits from Father Christmas, and it was our pleasure to oblige.

As soon as our special night of gift-giving in England was over, I left for Italy, since the children there hoped to discover gifts from Befana when they woke up on Epiphany, or January 6. There were no Puritans in Italy complaining about this wonderful way of helping celebrate the birth of Jesus. I dressed up as the old woman who had given directions to the Wise Men and loved every moment of it.

From Italy, I returned to Nuremberg, intending to spend some time there with Attila, Dorothea, and Willie Skokan. In Germany, as in Italy, holiday celebrations were universally enjoyed. For the past hundred years, Germans had started the fine new custom of bringing small evergreen trees into their homes around Christmas, and decorating these trees with candles and bits of bright paper. These Christmas trees were lovely to look at, and their clean scent would perfume the room. Willie Skokan had an idea about these trees, and shared it with me when I briefly stopped in Nuremberg before Epiphany to collect the toys and candy Befana would leave in Italy a few days later.

"Candles are dangerous, and these trees, once they dry out, might easily catch on fire," Willie told me. "I'm certain there are already many people who would like decorations that involve less risk. Someday, Leonardo and I will invent some safer kind of lights, but this will take awhile. Meanwhile, I think we ought to find other colorful things to hang from these trees—peppermint candy, for instance."

"You're experimenting with peppermint candy, too, Willie?" I asked. "You know that back in London, Leonardo has found a way to decorate peppermints with bright red stripes."

Willie looked reproachful. "Of course I do. Leonardo and I write to each other constantly. He was interested in improving the appearance of the candy. I propose to change its shape. If, instead of round little lumps, we could stretch them longer and thinner, then perhaps we could wedge these bright red-and-white sticks between the fir tree boughs. Even better, what if this candy took on some sort of curved shape, so it could then dangle from the Christmas tree branches?"

"You mean, something like the kind of cane old people sometimes lean on, Willie?" I replied.

His eyes lit up with excitement. "Perfect, Layla! Peppermint candy *canes*! I'll get to work right away!" I knew Willie would soon have samples to show me, but I wasn't able to remain in Nuremberg long enough to see them. A letter arrived from Arthur telling us that a final, terrible

mistake had been made by the king and that war would erupt in England at any moment.

"Under no circumstances should you return to England, Layla," Arthur wrote at the end of his letter. "Any war is bad enough, and this one may cost everyone here their beloved Christmas holiday. Leonardo and I will do our best to carry on, but things in this country are so dangerous that you must go over to the New World and help your husband spread Christmas joy there."

Three days later I walked back into the London toy factory and informed Arthur in friendly but firm fashion that I would decide when and where I went, not him. "I married Nicholas to be a full partner in his mission," I told my old friend. "You wouldn't tell my husband it wasn't safe enough to stay and help you. I know you're trying to protect me, Arthur, but I really don't need protection. Now, tell me what has happened."

The king, Arthur said, had finally had enough of Parliament telling him what he could and could not do. Acting on their own authority, its members had already tried and convicted his archbishop and his most trusted general, and right after Christmas rumors began to circulate that Parliament next intended to accuse the queen of treason, too, because the Puritans believed she was telling the king to make the country Catholic again. Now, Charles dearly loved Queen Henrietta, and he immediately decided he would eliminate her enemies. He had his staff draw up warrants for five members of Parliament, all of them outspoken critics of the king. Then, leading one hundred musket-bearing soldiers, Charles actually marched to Parliament, interrupted its meeting, and announced he was there to arrest the men.

"But they had learned he was coming and left the building before he arrived," Arthur told me. "The king demanded to know where they had gone, and no one would answer. He then dismissed Parliament and told everyone to go back home, but no one left. He stormed out and Parliament carried on with its daily business." Now, Arthur added, the king had left London for the north of England, where he was beginning to gather an army. Not enough Englishmen were willing to fight for him, so he was trying to hire what were called "mercenary" troops from Europe. Some of the European royal families had also promised to send soldiers to Charles—the last thing they wanted was for their own subjects to see a king deposed in favor of democracy. Queen Henrietta supposedly was ready to cross the English Channel and meet with foreign rulers to make sure they supported her husband.

In London, Parliament recruited its own army, one consisting mostly of landowners and their workers. Leaders of this rebel army were working very hard to convince working-class people that their lives would be better without a king. For once, the Puritans among them were careful not to threaten Christmas. Instead, they talked about taxes based on what was best for the majority instead of what a single ruler wanted, and how law should be based on the common good rather than a king's whim. What reasonable poor person could disagree? Other than Charles and Parliament, though, it soon became clear that nobody else wanted this inevitable war. In the end, Charles and the rebels would collectively have about fifteen thousand troops, even though almost a million British men could have enlisted to fight.

When I heard that Oliver Cromwell was going to make a speech in a public park about the war, I decided to go. He stood on a tree stump so everyone in the crowd of about two hundred could hear him, and he spoke very well.

"We did not choose to quarrel with the king, and still don't wish him any harm," Cromwell insisted. "If he will simply abide by the law and honestly consult Parliament before he imposes taxes or makes new laws, then Charles may come back to London and we will welcome him."

"You Puritans just want to take over so you can force your religion on us," someone called from the back of the crowd.

"Not at all!" Cromwell replied. "This war, sir, is not about religion. It is about whether the king will listen to the voices of the people. I hope that someday all of you might understand God's will as we Puritans do. I pray for this constantly. But all we would impose on anyone is a nation where every voice has importance."

"So you would not take away Christmas?" I called out.

Cromwell's eyes locked on mine, and I knew he recognized me, though it had been eight years since we met in his kitchen.

"No one is mentioning Christmas just now, missus," he replied. "The fate of our nation is at stake. Let us discuss Christmas after the larger matters are settled."

Cromwell talked a little longer, about how he was raising a company of soldiers in Cambridge and why the able-bodied men listening to him should sign up to fight against the king. One or two asked directions to his estate and set off to enlist. Everyone else drifted away, but not before several muttered to me that they were also worried that the Puritans would ban Christmas if they won the war against Charles.

I was leaving, too, when Cromwell came up behind me and tapped my shoulder.

"So, Missus Layla Nicholas, wife of Nicholas Nicholas the colonist, I perceive you still love your sinful holiday right well," he said, a slight smile on his face. "I had hoped, because you seem to be an intelligent woman, that you might have changed your mind by now."

"I'll never change my mind about Christmas," I replied.

"Then you entirely support the king and his Catholic ways," Cromwell said. "I would not have suspected you for a royalist sympathizer."

"My sympathy is for the poor people of England, and I understand, as you apparently still do not, how much Christmas means to them," I said. "Can you not look all around you, Mr. Cromwell? Most of the people you see are wearing rags. They work hard all day and have very little to eat at night. But they still love God and their special day on December 25 to give thanks for his son while having some brief joy for themselves. Why would an apparently decent man like you want to take this away from them?"

Cromwell sighed. "Why cannot *you* understand? I see the same poverty you do. I see the backbreaking labor, the empty stomachs, the desperation. But I also see the everlasting glory ahead for all who renounce this pagan celebration. God will give eternal reward to those who worship respectfully, not obscenely. Christmas represents all the sin in our modern age. It is no surprise that the king and his evil queen love the holiday. One day soon we will remove its temptations from this land, and when we do God will be pleased and bless Britain accordingly."

It would have been easier for me to think Cromwell was just using Christmas as one more excuse to go to war with the king, but that wasn't true. He hated Christmas just as passionately as I loved it, and we both felt we knew what was best for the people of England.

"You told me you would never simply take Christmas away," I reminded him. "You said you would try to persuade the people to give it up instead."

"And so I will, missus, once the king is brought to his senses," Cromwell replied. "With God's grace we will avoid war, the king will listen to Parliament instead of his Catholic queen, and once political peace is restored we Puritans will convince everyone about Christmas and its evils. Perhaps you and I can debate the issue here in the park. But that must come later. As you can see, my friends are ready to leave." He gestured toward a half-dozen men gathered nearby. Their hair was cut short in the Roundhead style. All but one wore somber black garments. The other man wore black trousers, too, but his cloak was blue.

"I thought Puritans found bright colors to be sinful," I said to Cromwell.

He grinned. "Ah, missus, Richard Culmer wears blue as a sign to the common people that he holds their interests close to his heart. A godly man, Richard, but beware. He is less inclined than I to respect the opinions of others. If he believes you are set on preserving Christmas, he is likely to mark you down for future reference."

"Is that some sort of threat, Mr. Cromwell?" I asked.

"I hope you know that I personally wish you no harm," Cromwell said, looking directly into my eyes. "But understand there are those who feel the best way to ensure God-fearing, Christian democracy is to eliminate all dissenting voices. It was not wise, Missus Nicholas, for you to raise your question about Christmas in such a public place with men like Mr. Culmer present. If you make that mistake again, it may have painful, even fatal consequences."

I looked at the man in the blue cloak. Richard Culmer was tall and thin, and his smile bothered me. It was an odd smile because his lips were stretched in a wide grin, but there was no matching pleasure in his eyes. These remained dark, hard, and cold. I was reminded less of another human being than a shark baring its teeth just before biting.

"How can you associate with such people?" I demanded.

Cromwell shrugged. "We must use the tools God sends, missus, and in Mr. Culmer he has given us a hammer. Don't let yourself become a nail."

All during the spring and early summer, both sides prepared for war. It was a leisurely process. This was the way, in those days, that

Blue Richard Culmer

war was often conducted. The two armies gave each other time to get ready, and when they finally did fight it was often in an agreed-upon place at an agreed-upon hour. The king had the support of most of the wealthiest lords, many of whom lived in northern England. The parliamentary, or Roundhead, troops came primarily from the small landowners and other members of the middle class. London was solidly Roundhead, probably because Parliament continued to meet there.

As the summer days of 1642 grew long and warm, a preacher in London calling himself Praise-God Barebone began delivering fiery street sermons about the sinfulness of non-Puritan worship in general and Christmas in particular. To my dismay, large crowds began to gather and, often, cheer his words. Many of them were the same people who, I was sure, still intended to go out on Christmas day to sing and feast. But to hear Praise-God Barebone tell it, Christmas was a trick devised by Catholics and pagans to lure innocent Protestants into terrible sin.

"They're cheering the entertainment as much or more than the message," Arthur reassured me. "If you listen carefully, his real theme for the common folk is that rich people have too long taken advantage of them and that support for the Puritans is the best way to become powerful and important themselves."

"He shouldn't tell such terrible lies about Christmas without someone standing up and disputing him," I said. "Perhaps, whenever he is speaking, I should be there, too, and present the other, truthful side."

"You can't do that, Layla, and for two very good reasons," Arthur cautioned. "First, you know it is our rule to never personally interfere in major historical events. Yes, Nicholas spoke with Charlemagne, and several of you supported Columbus with Isabella the Queen, but never did you tell anyone what to do in matters of public policy. We are gift-givers, not history-changers. Second, Oliver Cromwell warned you about coming to the attention of Puritan thugs like Mr. Culmer, who is becoming known as 'Blue Richard' because of his oddly colorful cloak. If you attract Culmer's wrathful attention, you do more than place yourself in danger. He might then discover the toy factory, and, from there, begin to guess all our gift-giving secrets. I realize it is hard, but you must remain quiet."

I knew Arthur was right, and because of his advice I refrained from engaging Praise-God Barebone in any sort of public debate. But I couldn't resist joining the crowds listening to Barebone and other fanatics like him. This was a mistake. Over the many centuries of my life, I have made my share, but this was one of the most foolish. True, I never raised my voice to disagree with Barebone, but his Puritan allies, keeping careful watch on those who came to listen, must have noted my obvious disgust. I discovered this in October 1642, when Pamela Forrest again said she had to speak with me, this time because she had dreadful news.

I swung my small pack onto my shoulder, pulled the hood of my cloak tight around my face, and went out into the London night.

Ten

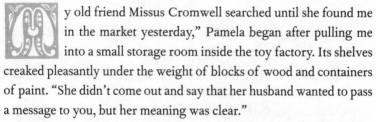 y old friend Missus Cromwell searched until she found me in the market yesterday," Pamela began after pulling me into a small storage room inside the toy factory. Its shelves creaked pleasantly under the weight of blocks of wood and containers of paint. "She didn't come out and say that her husband wanted to pass a message to you, but her meaning was clear."

"What would Oliver Cromwell want to tell me?" I asked. "Perhaps once again that he's right and I'm wrong about Christmas?"

Pamela looked stricken. "No, Layla, it's more serious than that. It seems that Blue Richard Culmer has your name on a list of possible spies for the king. All the people on this list are to be arrested on sight tomorrow, because the Roundheads are about to go into battle against His Majesty, and they fear a few royalist sympathizers might pass him information about their troops and war plans."

"That's ridiculous," I replied. "I know absolutely nothing about any war plans, and, if I did, I would not take sides in this war by telling the king about them."

"I know that, Layla, but Richard Culmer doesn't," Pamela said. "Missus Cromwell says he has your name right at the top of the list."

"How can he do that?" I replied. "To my knowledge, I've only seen Culmer once, and that was when I spoke to Oliver Cromwell after a speech he made. I asked a question there about Christmas, but how, based on that, am I considered a king's spy?"

"It's far worse, I'm afraid," Pamela said. "According to what Mr. Culmer has told Mr. Cromwell and other Roundhead leaders, you have taken to stalking Praise-God Barebone. Mr. Culmer, it seems, has his people watching everywhere for such acts of dissent. And then there's what seems to be the worst evidence of all, though I'm sure it can't be true."

Everything I'd heard so far seemed nothing less than ridiculous. "What could that possibly be?" I asked.

"According to what Mr. Culmer told Mr. Cromwell, for several years you have been seen making visits to the royal residence in London, obviously to inform on Puritan activities to the king and queen."

I couldn't help laughing. "Pamela, that is so silly. I would go there occasionally to leave peppermint candy for the queen, since she is so fond of it. I never even see her or her husband. If Blue Richard Culmer bothers to get the full story from his own spies, surely he'll learn that I was never in the palace for more than a few moments, certainly not long enough to pass any sort of information to his royal enemies."

Pamela Forrest shook her head. "All Mr. Culmer needs is the *appearance* of guilt to accuse you, Layla. He has decided he dislikes you, and that's all the reason he needs to have you arrested."

The foolishness of the whole situation astonished me. "But Pamela," I protested, "one of the reasons Parliament is going to war against the king is because they didn't want Charles arresting his opponents without solid evidence of wrongdoing. If Blue Richard arrests me on such flimsy charges, the Puritans are doing exactly the same thing!"

"But the Puritans are in control now, at least here in London, and so they no longer have to justify their actions," Pamela said gently. "That is the way of power, I suppose, to feel no real need to explain yourself beyond the general principle of, 'I am completely right, so anyone who disagrees must be wrong.'"

Well, there was no doubt I was in danger, and I honestly didn't know what I should do. In all our centuries of gift-giving, none of the companions had ever before found himself or herself being hunted by the authorities. I had to discuss this with Arthur, of course, and asked Pamela if she would go into the factory to get him. I sat down at the small table in the storeroom and rested my chin on my hand, thinking hard.

When Pamela brought Arthur, we told him about Blue Richard and his warrant for my arrest. For a few moments Arthur was furious on my behalf, and then, with great effort, he tried to calm down.

"No problem is ever solved with impulsive decisions based on anger," he said, more to remind himself as anyone else. "Certain facts are obvious. First, we can't reason with Blue Richard Culmer because he doesn't care about the basic truth, which is that you never collaborated with the king and queen. Second, you cannot allow yourself to be arrested. Torture and even execution is not uncommon for political prisoners. Third, whatever we do now must not in any way reveal the existence of this toy factory. Pamela Forrest, I hope you understand this. And now, so that you are not placed in further danger yourself, please return to work, with our thanks for this warning."

"I'd prefer to stay, Mr. Arthur," Pamela said firmly. "My loyalty is to you and Layla, not Blue Richard Culmer and his nasty accomplices. Let me help you, if I can."

Arthur was about to refuse, but I caught his eye and nodded. Pamela Forrest was placing herself at considerable risk by passing on the message from Oliver Cromwell. Though she shouldn't—couldn't—be made aware of all our secrets, she had at least earned the right to involve herself in my escape, if we could think of a way to accomplish that.

"All right," Arthur said. "Culmer and his henchmen are to arrest you on sight tomorrow, which must mean they do not know where you live. Maybe you can just stay inside the toy factory for however long it takes them to forget about you."

"We can't take the chance that they will, at some point, begin a door-to-door search," I replied. "If they found me here at the factory, and if they saw the toys, they might make the connection to Christmas and gift-giving and then you and Leonardo and everyone working here might be arrested, too. No, I can't stay here."

"But you can't go out on the London streets, either," Pamela noted. "They'll have posters of you up on every wall. Mr. Culmer and his helpers are fearfully efficient, Layla."

"Then I have to leave London," I said. "I'll pack a few things and leave as soon as it's dark tonight. I'll quickly make my way to the channel and take the short voyage across to France, and from there I'll go on to our friends in—" I remembered Pamela must not know much about our other operations. "Well, I'll go to our other friends and their factory. Blue Richard's reach doesn't extend outside of England, surely."

Now it was Arthur's turn to point out something obvious. "If the war is about to finally begin, and if Culmer is preparing to make his first arrests, then Parliament has set guards on all the ports. They expect Queen Henrietta to try and flee across the channel to France, you know, and it's very likely Culmer has warned the soldiers placed at the ports to watch out for you and the other so-called spies he intends to arrest. As Pamela has pointed out, Culmer is fearfully efficient. I'm afraid, Layla, that you're stranded here in England."

"But if I can't stay here in London, then where in England can I go?" I asked. "Truly, we don't know anyone who might offer shelter." This was no exaggeration. To protect our privacy, to keep our secrets of being ageless and able to travel much faster than ordinary people, we had not made friends outside our small circle of longtime companions. This now caused a terrible problem. I was going to be a fugitive on the run, but I had no particular place where I *could* run, no trusted friends somewhere in England away from London who would hide me without asking too many questions. For the first time since Pamela had told me the news, I felt some fear. Perhaps I *would* be arrested and thrown into prison. I hope my confessing this doesn't disappoint you too much. But anyone in that dangerous situation would have been afraid.

"If only Nicholas were here," Arthur mused. "He might see a way out of this."

"I wish he were, too, but there's no sense wasting time on forlorn hopes," I said. "There seems to be no other choice than for me to pack a little food, wait for nightfall, and be on my way. I'll have to trust to God to somehow protect me until this terrible time is over. I'll try to get word to you, Arthur, when I find a place to take shelter. Meanwhile, don't write to my husband about this and alarm him. He has plenty to do in America, and in the time it would take him to return here, who knows what the situation might be. In your letters, tell him I'm just too busy to write."

"Think this through carefully," Arthur warned. "You'll be a wanted criminal on the run. You won't know who to trust, who might betray you to the Puritans. And, if there's truly war, you know how that will affect your ability to travel fast." He suddenly remembered Pamela, and added, "I mean, with battles all around you, you won't be able to make your way directly to many places."

"I'll just have to do my best," I said. "Well, Pamela, I really think you should go back to work now. I'm grateful to you for helping me avoid immediate arrest, and I pray you won't find yourself in trouble for doing it. I'll go pack now and be gone as soon as it's dark."

"Wait, Layla," Pamela said haltingly. "I think I may know somewhere you can go, someone who would take you in. Do you know about the town of Canterbury?"

Of course, I did.

Canterbury, about sixty miles southeast of London, grew from a camp scratched out of swamps by primitive tribesmen. The Romans established a town there, and later St. Augustine arrived, sent about the same time we met Arthur, to strengthen Christianity in what was a pagan land. In 597, construction began on a great cathedral, which, almost five hundred years later, had expanded into one of the most towering, impressive places of worship in all the world. In 1170, King Henry II had his archbishop Thomas à Becket murdered in the cathedral, which brought Canterbury a great deal of national attention and shame. Pilgrims began to come to Canterbury for special worship after the Catholic church declared Becket to be a saint. As in Myra at the supposed tomb of my husband Nicholas, many people thought if they came to Canterbury and prayed to St. Thomas à Becket they would be cured of all sorts of diseases.

In the late 1300s, an official of the English government wrote a book called *The Canterbury Tales,* all about some very odd pilgrims who were on their way there to worship. This book, which poked fun at its characters, became one of the most popular ever written. You can still find copies quite easily today. It only added to the town's reputation. Except for the income generated by visiting pilgrims, who would buy food and rent places to stay, Canterbury was mostly a farming community. When King Henry VIII broke away from the Catholic church, Canterbury particularly felt his wrath. He ordered the shrine of St. Thomas à Becket completely destroyed—Henry did not want any of his subjects worshipping at the grave of a Catholic saint. As soon as the shrine was gone, so were most of the pilgrims, so with their tourist trade evaporating it was lucky people in Canterbury had farming to fall back on. In particular, they raised sheep. Wool from Canterbury was prized in foreign markets.

But Canterbury's religious reputation continued to work against the town. In the 1550s, when Henry VIII's Catholic daughter, Mary, was queen, she ordered some Protestants burned at the stake in Canterbury. All the English monarchs since—Elizabeth I, James I, and Charles I—had supported Protestants over Catholics, and Canterbury became a haven for Protestants fleeing persecution by Catholics in Europe. Now the town was considered by the Puritans to be one of their strongholds, and I wondered why Pamela Forrest would mention Canterbury to me as I tried to pick a place to hide.

"Who would shelter me in Canterbury, Pamela?" I asked. "I don't know anyone there, and, to hear the Puritans tell it, no one there would want to know me."

"That isn't so, Layla," she replied. "Most of the people in and around Canterbury are just good, hardworking folk who want all war to go away and with it any people who try to tell others how to worship and what to believe. It's true that Avery Sabine, the town's mayor, happily serves the Puritans in any way he can, but the vast majority of Canterbury citizens still love Christmas. I know all this because I have a younger sister who lives there. Elizabeth is a wonderful, warm person who I know would become your good friend. She and her husband, Alan Hayes, live in a pretty little cottage about a mile outside the town walls. Alan is often away, because he is a fine sailor and much in demand on voyages to and from the New World, so Elizabeth and her eight-year-old daughter, Sara, are left to carry on as best they can. Elizabeth, in fact, works in the manor of Mayor Sabine and his wife, Margaret. I know she and Alan would give you shelter if I asked."

"I couldn't impose on strangers like that," I said. "Your sister hardly needs to be placed in danger by hiding a fugitive."

"She would want to help, I promise," Pamela said firmly. "Elizabeth has a warm heart and a keen sense of justice. Let me write a note for you to take to her. I'll tell her something about your circumstances, asking that she let you stay with her, at least for a little while so you have time to make further plans. Canterbury is far enough from London for you to be safe there, I'm sure."

"I can't do it," I repeated, but Arthur agreed with Pamela.

"It's already getting dark, and you're to be arrested in the morning, Layla," he pointed out. "There is very little time left. And I like the idea of Canterbury, since the Puritans believe they are so popular there. They would never expect you to hide in *their* city. Also, to be honest, it doesn't seem that you have any better option."

"Let me write the note to Elizabeth," Pamela urged.

It seemed I had no real choice. I privately decided that if this Elizabeth Hayes in any way seemed reluctant to take me in, I would not stay at her home at all. Even if she was willing, I would still leave as soon as I came up with another idea. The thought of running, of hiding, was so disturbing to me. I was branded a spy because I loved Christmas. How foolish! How very, very sad!

While Pamela wrote her note I packed a few items of clothing, along with some bread, fruit, and cheese.

"I really don't need to take along food," I reminded Arthur. "Sixty miles is nothing to you or me. Even walking, I'll probably be in Canterbury in less than a day."

"It never hurts to be prepared," Arthur said. "You might have to leave the road to avoid patrols and hide along the way for a while. If you do, the food will come in handy. And if you don't need to eat it, you can contribute it to the larder of your hosts."

He hesitated a moment, then said, "There is one other thing I must ask you, and I didn't want to while Pamela was here. Layla, why on earth would Oliver Cromwell want to warn you about Blue Richard? Could this be some sort of trick on his part?"

I shook my head. "Although we disagree about Christmas, I think

Oliver Cromwell is an honorable man who acts on his beliefs, just as you and I do. He realizes I'm no spy for the king. Cromwell will always be faithful to those causes he believes are just, but never at the expense of truth."

Then I took a few moments to write a hasty letter to my husband, telling him I was off for a while to scout the English countryside for children deserving of gifts from Father Christmas. I hoped he and Felix were well and happy. Then, after a long pause, I added: *"Remember always how much I love you, and how glad I'll be when we're together again. I especially thank you for letting me be your equal partner in this grand gift-giving mission. You are the finest man in the world, and I'm so honored to be your wife."*

After twelve hundred years of marriage, Nicholas and I seldom put into spoken or printed words our feelings for each other. We usually felt we didn't have to. Our mutual devotion was obvious. But this one time I wanted him to have those words to remember me by if my flight from Blue Richard Culmer did not prove successful.

In a while, Pamela finished her note to Elizabeth. She pressed the note into my hand and whispered, "God be with you, Layla."

"And with you," I replied. Farewells should be kept brief under the best of circumstances, and this particular moment was dreadful. I hugged Arthur, patted Leonardo on the arm—he was absentmindedly gazing at a circling moth, wondering, perhaps, how its wings carried it through the air—and then I swung my small pack onto my shoulder, pulled the hood of my cloak tight around my face, and went out into the London night.

Streetlamps were lit at varying intervals, but mostly I walked through the city in shadow. For the first time ever, I felt the need to occasionally look behind me to be certain I wasn't being followed. I didn't see anyone, but the very thought of being pursued made me nervous. Still, I encountered few people, and no one challenged me when I walked through a city gate and out into the country on the road to Canterbury. If Blue Richard was going to put up posters with my likeness on them, he hadn't gotten around to it yet.

At that same moment forty miles to the north, the armies of the king and Parliament were preparing to clash. The Battle of Edge Hill wouldn't officially begin until the next day, but cavalry scouts from both sides were picking their way through the dark to determine the best routes of attack. A few of these scouts accidentally encountered one another and fired some futile shots. Though I had no way of knowing the exact particulars, I had immediate evidence that there was fighting. With my usual powers to travel at great speed, I could have covered the sixty miles between London and Canterbury in a few hours. I had expected to greet Elizabeth Hayes as the morning sun rose. Instead, it took me that night plus three full days to make the trip, walking at the usual human pace. Any sort of fighting had that effect on our special powers. So, to my great dismay, I realized that somewhere in England a dreadful civil war had begun, and Christmas hung in the balance.

Unlike her dark-complexioned mother, Sara was light, almost pale, with white-blonde hair and sparkling blue eyes. It seemed to me that there was something very special about this child, a sort of inner glow.

Eleven

 finally reached Canterbury about eight o'clock on a gloriously sunny Sunday morning. The temperature was cool but not cold, just right for October. Though I had been walking for almost four days, and my legs were tired—an odd sensation for someone used to traveling a hundred miles or more in a night and never becoming weary—I was still overwhelmed by the combination of bright blue sky, fluffy white clouds, rolling green hills, and golden falling leaves. Canterbury itself, nestled in a cozy, shallow valley on the banks of the Stour River, which actually bisected part of the town, added to the overall loveliness. Its ancient origins were evident in the number of old Roman and early medieval structures that made up much of the central district, which was surrounded by a stout wall of flint and other stone. You could enter Canterbury by any one of six different gates, but the main one, the West Gate, was placed on the main road leading to and from London. This gate was comprised of two massive wooden doors, and a drawbridge had to be lowered to allow access. Behind the West Gate were two round towers, each sixty feet high. This is where the town's magistrate and military force were stationed. Because Canterbury was, at least in a military sense, controlled by the Roundheads, the soldiers there had close-cropped hair and dressed in much simpler, drab uniforms than the colorful costumes of the king's forces. The left-hand tower also housed the town jail, which seemed to be a rather fearsome place. Its few windows were crisscrossed by massive bars.

But the forbidding wall and gates and towers and jail still didn't spoil Canterbury's overall impression of country welcome. On this Sunday morning, all the gates stood open and the drawbridge was down. Few people were stirring yet. The calls of the birds and the gentle rushing of the river were easy to hear. Soon, though, everyone would be up, and most, after breakfasting, would make their way to church. There were several churches in the town, but all of them paled in comparison to the limestone Canterbury Cathedral in the eastern corner. This glorious cathedral towered high, dwarfing everything else in both height and breathtaking majesty. Seeing it in daylight for the first time—my few previous visits to Canterbury had been by night to deliver Christmas gifts—I was especially struck by the gorgeous stained-glass windows that adorned all the cathedral's long walls. Even from the outside, they reflected the sun in great rainbows of colors. How wonderful, I thought, that human beings had mastered the skills necessary to craft such beautiful things.

Before Henry VIII's edict changing England from a Catholic to a Protestant country, long lines of pilgrims would have circled the cathedral, each waiting for a turn to pray at the shrine to St. Thomas à Becket in a small side chapel. So many pilgrims went there for so long that grooves were worn into the hard stone chapel floor—often they would fall on their knees when they entered and actually *crawl* to the altar to pray. Now such behavior was frowned upon, especially with

Puritans running the town, and so no pilgrims came and crawled and prayed.

About eight thousand people lived in Canterbury, quite a respectable number for that time, and their homes were much the same as those in London. The few wealthiest residents resided in fine stone structures. From my vantage point of a roadside hilltop a quarter-mile from the West Gate, I could look down over the town wall and see clearly where these well-to-do folk lived. I suspected that one particularly large home must belong to the city's mayor. Then there were the middling homes of merchants, their plaster walls supported by wooden beams. The vast majority of the houses were modest, squarish cottages with thatched roofs. The portion of the town streets I could

see looked much cleaner than those in London. At least, there were fewer pigs on the loose, rooting through trash.

I was tempted to go into the town and find some small, quiet church at which to do Sunday worship, but there was another matter that needed immediate attention. I had Pamela Forrest's letter to her sister Elizabeth, and no real idea of whether or not this Elizabeth Hayes would even consider taking in a stranger, and a fugitive from the Roundheads at that. If she turned me away, I wasn't really sure what I could do next, besides try to hide myself away in the country until I could think of a different plan. Pamela had assured me Elizabeth would make me welcome, but I couldn't be certain this would be the case.

The same number of people lived outside the town walls as inside them. These "outer" families usually owned or worked on farms, and their cottages were within easy walking distance of Canterbury's shops and churches. Elizabeth Hayes, I'd been told, lived a mile to the east of the city with her husband, Alan, and daughter, Sara. Anne's directions to me were to go to the river just past town and follow the path beside it past a grove of poplars. I would soon see a cottage surrounded by flower bushes, with a mighty oak tree towering over it. That, Pamela said, was her sister's home. Of course, Pamela couldn't provide me with a specific address, because these things were not yet in use. People lived where they lived, and you found them by looking around and asking.

Church bells had begun to peal back in the town by the time I saw the Hayes cottage. The cheerful ringing echoed down the road as I

walked, and I thought again how foolish it was for a country to go to war, even in part, because people could not agree to let each other worship as they pleased. Then I paused, because the door of the Hayes home was opening, and I got my first look at my prospective hostess.

Elizabeth Hayes was slender and dark, a lovely looking woman of perhaps thirty. Her brown hair cascaded past her shoulders, and her smile was warm and unforced. I liked her on sight, but didn't have the chance to speak,

Elizabeth Hayes

for she was dressed in a long, clean frock and clearly on her way to church. She paused just outside the door, gesturing for someone to follow, and a moment later was joined by a sturdy-looking child I knew must be her eight-year-old daughter, Sara. If I liked Elizabeth Hayes the first time I saw her, I loved her daughter. Unlike her dark-complexioned mother, Sara was light, almost pale, with white-blonde hair and sparkling blue eyes. It seemed to me that there was something very special about this child, a sort of inner glow. Was it obvious to everyone else, or only to me? Sara had a serious expression as she tugged a kerchief in place over her hair, and took her mother's hand as they walked toward the town. They nodded to me as they passed where I stood perhaps twenty yards from their cottage. Elizabeth said, "Happy Sabbath," in a bright, friendly voice, while Sara quietly murmured, "Good day," and looked quickly away. It was obvious she was a very shy child. It would be a bad thing, I decided, to interrupt their stroll to church by presenting Pamela's letter, and so I decided to sit for a while in the shade of the towering oak and eat the last of my fruit and cheese. Time enough when Elizabeth returned from worship to introduce myself. I did wonder where her husband might be, since only mother and daughter had left the cottage. Either he was sleeping in— not likely in those days and that place—or else he was away on one of his voyages.

I rested my back against the tree and munched an apple. Families made their way down the path, heading into town and church. Many people called out greetings to me. It seemed almost impossible that the same England that was home to such warm, friendly folk was at the same time split by civil war. During the time it had taken me to walk from London to Canterbury, I had heard bits of gossip about the first clash between royalists and Roundheads at Edge Hill. The king's forces, apparently, had barely gotten the better of the fight, and the Roundheads had retreated back toward their strongholds near London. Oliver Cromwell, I guessed, would have taken part in the fighting, and I hoped he had survived.

The breeze was cool, but the sun was warm, and after I'd eaten I suppose I must have dozed, for suddenly I snapped awake with the feeling of being watched. My pleasure in the fine morning had made me forget, for a while, that I was on the run, but now my fear of capture overwhelmed me. I gasped, opened my eyes, and there, perhaps five feet away, was little Sara, who must have been as frightened as I was, for she whirled and scampered back to her mother, Elizabeth, who stood at the cottage door.

"Sara, remember your manners," Elizabeth cried. "Ma'am, I apologize for my daughter. She should not have approached you as you slept. Are you hungry, perhaps? I'm about to prepare our Sabbath meal, and you're most welcome to join us."

For English country folk of the time, inviting a stranger in to eat was not an uncommon thing. Hospitality was cherished, even among the poorest people. Whatever God gave you was to be shared with open arms and a generous heart. Elizabeth's invitation provided me with a perfect opportunity to introduce myself, and I took advantage of it.

"Missus Hayes?" I asked politely. "Please don't be surprised I know your name. Mine is Layla, and I'm a friend of your sister Pamela Forrest in London. We work in the same place."

"Well, now!" Elizabeth exclaimed, her smile growing even wider. "Pamela has told me often about how much she enjoys where she works and the kind people there. Though, you know, I can't ever get her to provide many details, like what, for instance, you *make*."

It was gratifying to know that Pamela was keeping our secrets, even from her beloved sister. "Oh, we make many things," I said vaguely. "I don't know from one day to the next what we'll be putting together." That, certainly, was true.

"Well," Elizabeth said, "by the sun I can see it's getting past noon, and some food will make a pleasant day seem even better. Sara, get out an extra plate, and please see the table is free of dust." The child hurried inside. Elizabeth took my arm and led me through the door.

The cottage was unremarkable. It was, in the 1640s tradition of rural England, one large room with a narrow ladder leading up to a small loft. In one corner of the downstairs room was a fireplace, which provided both warmth and a means to cook. Pots dangled over the fire on hooks, while pans might be placed directly in its embers. A pallet covered by a quilt in another corner was where Elizabeth and her husband slept. I knew little Sara would have her own place up the ladder in the loft. There were a few simple chairs with high, straight backs in front of the fire, and there was a small table where Sara was busily setting out three sets of plates, cups, and knives. She had taken these from a cupboard standing against the plaster wall. I could see these things clearly because the sun was shining through several open windows. The windows had no glass—only the very richest people could afford such luxury—but were protected by heavy wooden shutters that could be closed and latched in case of bad weather or when the people inside wanted privacy. Somewhere behind the house, I knew, would be the "privy," and some yards away from that, a well.

"I'm sorry my husband, Alan, isn't here to greet you, too," Elizabeth said as she poured some water from a bucket into a bowl. "Here, please soak this cloth and wipe the dirt from your face and hands. I can tell you've been traveling for some time. Anyway, Alan has just left as part of a crew sailing over to the Americas and will be gone at least a year, since they are delivering goods in several places and then picking up other goods to bring back to English markets—mostly tobacco, I believe."

"You and Sara must be lonely with him gone," I said.

Elizabeth reached out and affectionately ruffled her daughter's fine blonde hair. "Well, of course we miss Alan, but we're a sailor's family and have learned to accept his lengthy absences. Are you hungry, Layla? What we have to offer isn't fancy, but it's healthy and filling. Bread to start, from local wheat. Fine cabbage and carrots from Sara's garden in the back. I'm sorry we can't offer you beer, but the water from our well is so fresh and clear that it's what we prefer to drink. The cheese is good; all our local dairy is excellent. And, for an after-sweet, we'll have pears from our very own tree. Will that do?"

"It all sounds delicious," I replied, and helped Elizabeth get out the food and set it on the table. Sara helped, too, but I noticed she still avoided looking directly at me, and she didn't say anything at all. When everything was ready, we pulled chairs to the table. Elizabeth offered a short but eloquent blessing, thanking God for both food and a new friend to share it with. As we ate, Elizabeth and I enjoyed pleasant conversation. Sara didn't talk, but I could sense she was listening and remembering every word I said about my husband, Nicholas, being a colonist in the New World, and how someday soon I planned to join him. Elizabeth told some amusing stories about Pamela and their happy childhood together. She'd always thought her older sister would live right beside her in Canterbury, Elizabeth said, but then Pamela met Clive, whose ambitions took him to London—"We country folk don't need barbers, really"—and so now the sisters seldom saw each other.

Sara Hayes

"We send letters back and forth though, whenever someone we know comes to Canterbury from London or vice versa," Elizabeth said as we finished the last of our cheese and prepared to wipe the plates with cloths to clean them.

"That reminds me of something," I said, though I really hadn't needed reminding. I'd just been waiting for the right moment. "Your sister sent you a letter that I hope you'll read." I took it from my pocket and handed it to her.

"Lovely!" said Elizabeth, and she walked over to a window where she would have more light. I watched anxiously as she bent over the note. A moment later, she began to frown.

"Sara," she called out to the little girl, who was putting the cleaned plates back into the cupboard. "Go out, please, and pick us some pears from the tree. Take them over to the river and wash them before you bring them in."

"The well is closer," Sara replied. It was the first time I'd clearly heard her voice, which was soft and sweet.

"I prefer you rinse them in the river," her mother said firmly. "Now, get to it." Sara disappeared out the door. Elizabeth looked at me thoughtfully, then returned to her sister's letter. After several long, silent minutes, she folded the note, placed it in the pocket of her dress, and said to me, "This message is quite interesting."

"I can leave at once," I said carefully, not certain of her mood.

"No," Elizabeth said. "Pamela tells me you are her good, honest friend, but that you've somehow come to the attention of bad people and must stay away from London for a while. I already know Richard Culmer's name. He was minister for a brief time at a church here, but he spent his pulpit hours informing everyone they were doomed unless they embraced God exactly as he did, with no music or altar decorations or even, it seemed, happiness. Archbishop Laud removed him from office. Of course, now the archbishop is in a Roundhead prison, and Blue Richard is free to arrest whoever he will. And that number includes you. Why?"

"He claims I must be a spy for the king," I answered. "It isn't true. I believe my real crime has been to believe in the celebration of Christmas, which, as you know, the Puritans would take away if they could."

Elizabeth nodded. She wasn't smiling now. "Christmas is important in this house, always a welcome time to celebrate Jesus with songs and treats. I too would hate to lose it. But I also realize it can be dangerous to flaunt opposing beliefs around those with the power to arrest anyone who disagrees with them."

"Unfortunately, you're right," I said. "In any event, I certainly don't wish to put you or your child in any danger. Pamela said I might be able to stay with you for a time, but if you feel that isn't possible, don't be embarrassed to say so. I know there's no real reason for you to risk what you have to help a stranger."

Elizabeth smiled again. "There's a very good reason. The Bible tells us that the blessing works both ways when strangers are treated as welcome guests. My husband is away for a long while. I'd be glad to have another grown-up for company. I will ask you not to tell Sara about this arrest warrant. There's no reason for a child to be implicated if, for some reason, they find you here. But otherwise, please be a welcome guest in our home. Though the Puritans rule in Canterbury—our mayor is outspoken in his support of their cause—the rest of us just want to live in peace and have goodwill toward people of all beliefs. So long as you don't draw too much attention to yourself, you should be safe here."

Relief washed over me. I hadn't realized, until that moment, how nervous I had felt as a fugitive on the run with no specific place to find shelter.

"If, at any time, you feel I'm imposing, don't hesitate to tell me," I said. "And, of course, I'll want to do my share of chores and help out in any other way I can. I have a blanket in my pack, so just show me where you'll want me to sleep, and I thank you for your generosity."

"If you don't mind, I'll have you sleep up in the loft with Sara," Elizabeth said. "She has a wide pallet, and you'll find it more comfortable than just a blanket on the floor. And it will do her good to have company, even if she doesn't want any. You may have noticed she's very shy and doesn't talk much. She's always been that way, hesitant to make her opinions heard. But she is a very intelligent child, and I love her dearly."

"Will your neighbors wonder why you suddenly have a guest?" I asked. "I know, in the country, such events can cause gossip."

"We'll just say you're a cousin who's come to stay a while," Elizabeth said. "It makes perfect sense, with my husband away on a voyage and your husband being a colonist across the ocean. Sara," she called out to the child, who was just coming back in with an armful of pears that dripped river water on her arms and dress, "it turns out that Layla is a distant cousin. She's part of our family, and will be staying with us for a bit. Isn't that splendid?"

Sara nodded.

"Can't you welcome our cousin?" Elizabeth urged.

The little girl looked up at me, and I again was struck by her lovely blue eyes and sweet face.

"Welcome," she muttered, and blushed as she spoke that single word.

"Do better than that," her mother suggested. "Say, 'Welcome, Cousin Layla.'"

Now Sara spoke up, though to her mother and not to me. "It's rude to call a grown-up 'cousin,'" she said.

"All right," Elizabeth said, "then call her Missus—" She looked at me, a question unspoken but obvious. I didn't want to repeat my mistake with Cromwell, when he had ended up thinking my husband's name was Nicholas Nicholas. I thought furiously for a moment.

"Please call me Aunt Layla, Sara," I said.

The girl looked at me, and this time she smiled just a little.

"Welcome, Aunt Layla," she said softly, and put the pears down on the table. For a moment I hoped she might hug me, but she didn't. I still felt pleased. This was the first time in my life, I realized, that a child had ever addressed me as anything other than an adult stranger. I liked it very much.

I would lug wooden buckets to the vats, fill them with water,
then bring the heavy, swinging buckets into the washing shed,
where I would empty their contents into the tubs.

Twelve

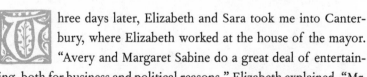hree days later, Elizabeth and Sara took me into Canterbury, where Elizabeth worked at the house of the mayor. "Avery and Margaret Sabine do a great deal of entertaining, both for business and political reasons," Elizabeth explained. "Mr. Sabine has made his fortune as a trader in cloth goods, and also in farm tools like plows and lathes, buying them from factories in big cities and selling them to local people. He and Mrs. Sabine have some hopes of him getting an important place in national government, at least if the Roundheads prevail in this current struggle. So, quite often, they have prominent dignitaries in to dine. Mostly my job is to help keep their home clean, but sometimes at these dinners I also help serve food. It's not a bad job, and we need the money I earn. Sara keeps outgrowing her dresses."

Walking along between her mother and me, Sara made a face, but didn't say anything.

"Oh, my sweetheart, I'm just glad you're a healthy girl," her mother said gently. "And a smart one, too. She can already read, Cousin Layla, and write almost any word in the English language."

"How wonderful, Sara," I exclaimed. "Do you go to school in town?"

Again, Sara grimaced, and let her mother answer for her.

"Canterbury has no school for girls, I'm afraid," Elizabeth said. "There's some basic grammar instruction for the boys when it's not harvest time. But the Sabines have a daughter named Sophia who is the same age as Sara, and the girls are good friends. Sophia has begun private instruction in reading and spelling and sums, and Sara has been allowed to share these classes with her. It's a rare opportunity, and one we appreciate very much."

"Sophia says she will marry a great lord some day, and when she does I will become her lady-in-waiting," Sara said. I waited, hoping she would say more, but she didn't.

"Do you want to be a lady-in-waiting, Sara?" I finally asked.

After a few moments of silence, Sara said, "I want to *see something*," and skipped on ahead. Her mother shook her head and smiled fondly.

"Sara is a quiet little girl with big dreams," Elizabeth confided. "She has heard of wonderful cities around the world, and longs to visit them."

"Do you want her to do this?" I asked.

"I want my daughter to be happy, and it's a hard world we live in," she replied. "If Sophia does marry well and travel with her husband, and if she does make Sara her lady-in-waiting, well, perhaps some of Sara's dreams will come true. But you and I are old enough to know about the danger of dreams, aren't we? If a poor girl wishes for too much, she's likely to be bitterly disappointed. I hope Sara will be realistic as she grows up."

"I believe in dreams," I said. "Well, back to present problems. Do you think Mrs. Sabine will hire me?"

After just three days as Elizabeth and Sara's guest, I was entirely bored with staying inside the cottage all day. I didn't know whether keeping out of sight was really necessary. The civil war had erupted, and surely Blue Richard Culmer's attention was directed at something other than a woman who loved Christmas. Today with modern technology, perhaps my picture would have been circulated everywhere, but this was 1642 England and the sixty miles between Canterbury and London were, probably, as good as six thousand. As long as I didn't call too much attention to myself, I decided, I would probably be safe.

This was another reason why I thought I'd better find employment. In country towns, people took notice of everyone else's business, and while a distant relative staying for a time with her cousin wouldn't be considered worthy of gossip, an able-bodied woman remaining home while her hostess worked certainly would. Elizabeth said Mrs. Sabine often hired women to do menial, time-consuming chores like laundry and cooking. The work certainly wouldn't be very interesting for me—I was used to traveling the world and giving gifts, after all—but it would fill the hours and help me blend into the community.

We came into Canterbury through Riding Gate, one of the town's easternmost entrances. There were two guards at the gate, and Elizabeth had to stop and let them look through the basket she was carrying.

"Sorry to trouble you, missus," one of the guards said. "But we've got orders to be extra careful, what with the battle and all." He was referring to the fight at Edge Hill, where the king's army had gotten the better of the Roundheads. Everyone in Canterbury, and, I assumed, England, was talking about it. Parliament's army had marched in shouting that God was on their side, but their soldiers were mostly untrained farm hands and the king had somehow found enough money to hire a few experienced foreign militia. The result wasn't what the rebels had thought God had guaranteed them. According to the rumors, Oliver Cromwell—who was an officer in the Roundhead army, but not its commander—was angry because his troops hadn't received the training they'd needed before being sent in to fight. Cromwell had retreated with his soldiers—who were mostly the men who normally worked for him in his fields—to his estate near London, promising that he would only return when his troops were properly prepared. The king's victorious army stayed farther north. His commanders wanted to get better organized, too, and finish off the rebels for good when next they fought.

Since Canterbury was a Roundhead town, everyone was afraid of what would happen if the king triumphed. Cer-

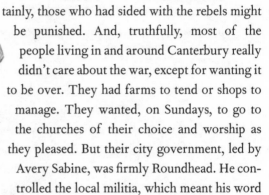

tainly, those who had sided with the rebels might be punished. And, truthfully, most of the people living in and around Canterbury really didn't care about the war, except for wanting it to be over. They had farms to tend or shops to manage. They wanted, on Sundays, to go to the churches of their choice and worship as they pleased. But their city government, led by Avery Sabine, was firmly Roundhead. He controlled the local militia, which meant his word was law. Even if there was popular demand for a new election, Sabine's people would be the ones counting the ballots.

Avery Sabine

"If the king's forces win, won't that mean the end for Avery Sabine?" I asked Elizabeth as we made our way through the town's streets toward the house of the mayor. "If he and his family have to flee, I supposed that's the end of your job, and Sara's chance to be a lady-in-waiting."

"Somehow, I believe Mr. Sabine will do quite well no matter what," Elizabeth said, looking to be certain Sara was too far away to overhear. "When you meet him, you'll understand. He's one of those people who know how to be a good friend to whoever is in power. He's with the Puritans now because he thinks they'll eventually win, but if it turns out that the king retains control, then Mr. Sabine will be His Majesty's most loyal, and most visible, supporter. Meanwhile, here we are at the house. Let's go through the kitchen in back, and I'll see if Mrs. Sabine is available." She called sharply, "Sara, wait with Cousin Layla."

The mayor's home was a sprawling brick structure, obviously very expensive to build. I stood in the kitchen watching people bustling around, carrying loads of food or clothes and talking to one another about the big dinner party the next day, and *would* the venison haunches arrive in time to be properly grilled before serving? But there was order to the bustle; someone ran this great household with efficiency, and soon enough Elizabeth returned with her. Margaret Sabine was a towering woman, almost six feet tall in an era when men seldom surpassed five and a half feet, and she was wide to match. Mrs. Sabine's dress was silk, rare for everyday wear, and her auburn wig was spectacular in both size and color.

"Elizabeth tells me you are her cousin who wants work," she said briskly, her tone matter-of-fact without quite becoming rude. "We may have some for you. Sara, Sophia is upstairs and her lessons are about to begin. Hurry if you want to join her." Sara hurried, and Mrs. Sabine returned her attention to me. "Please look directly at me, missus. Well, you've got an honest face. We have an organized household here. Phyllis, do *not* fold the towels that way. Here. Watch. See? Isn't that better? Well, Missus—Layla, is it? Odd name. I've had one of the washing women leave me at a *very* inconvenient time, since some of Mr. Sabine's suppliers from Portsmouth—very wealthy, influential people, all of them—are coming to dine tomorrow, then staying for another day, and we must impress them and everything from sheets to shirts needs cleaning. I'll take you on to help with the washing for a while. Two pennies a day is the wage. If you please me, we'll talk about a permanent position. Oh, and you get your dinners here in the kitchen. Elizabeth, take your cousin back into the washing shed and get her started, then come back and help me arrange things in the parlor."

We watched as Mrs. Sabine marched from the room, barking out suggestions on how best the kitchen floor might be swept and *don't* let that pitcher of milk spill; Sophia wants two cups of it sent up to her room immediately.

"One cup of milk will be for Sophia and the other for Sara," Elizabeth explained. "I know Mrs. Sabine seems gruff, but in her way she's very kind. Most rich employers wouldn't allow their children to mingle with the children of servants. Sophia treats Sara almost like a sister. Well, you're hired, so let's take you over to where you'll work. Washing is hard business, I know, but with luck you'll please Mrs. Sabine and she'll soon set you to more pleasant tasks."

Like the kitchen, the washing shed was a bustling place. There were two huge wooden tubs, one for soaking and the other for rinsing. My job was the most demanding. There were dozens of sheets and lots of outer garments and underclothes and towels and pillowcases and every other imaginable item to be washed, and to accomplish this water had to be hauled in from huge vats in the backyard. I would lug wooden buckets to the vats, fill them with water, then bring the heavy, swinging buckets into the washing shed, where I would empty their contents into the tubs. A fire burned under the soaking tub, so the water could be heated, and all the clothes in there had to be scrubbed by hand with soap. It was hard work, but not as hard as hauling the water, which I was doing. Then, when the things in the soaking tub were considered finished, they were transferred to the rinsing tub and wrung out by hand again. Finally, they were hung on long lines in the backyard to dry in the sun.

I had wondered, before I began, if I would be able to work at much greater speed than everyone else. But I quickly learned I had no special powers as a washerwoman. Soon enough my arms and back began to ache from hauling the heavy buckets, and the heat from under the soaking tub made me feel sweaty and uncomfortable. By the time someone came in to tell us it was time to break for dinner—that was what the midday meal was called—I was having some difficulty standing up straight. I could not remember ever having worked so hard.

"Tie a little cloth around each palm, dearie, so you won't get no blisters from carrying the buckets," an old woman who worked at the rinsing tub suggested. Her face, though deeply wrinkled, was very kind, and I asked what her name was. "I'm Janie," she said, and remarked that she'd been working for the Sabines, mostly in the washing shed, for twenty years.

"What did you do before that?" I asked, mostly to be polite. My back throbbed horribly.

"Why, I helped my mother in the fields," Janie replied. "Now that I'm thirty-five, I hope I'll stay healthy enough to keep working here a while longer. But it wears you out, it does."

I was thirty-five when I met Nicholas and stopped aging. Janie looked haggard and ancient, old enough to be my mother or perhaps even my grandmother. I'd never really understood before how constant hard, physical work could age people. Though I was an enthusiastic

Janie

gift-giver, I realized that, in my more than twelve hundred years, I'd never really had to do anything so exhausting before.

Elizabeth joined me at the long kitchen table as we ate the bread and cheese provided for our meal. It was good bread and cheese, and there was plenty of it. I asked why Sara wasn't eating with us, and Elizabeth said she usually ate with Sophia in her room. I valued the break from hauling water even more than I did the meal, which seemed to be over in minutes. Then Elizabeth went off to another part of the house and I trudged back to the washing shed. For the next five hours, I took water from the vats to the tubs, slowing considerably as the day wore on, but never completely stopping. Janie's advice about wrapping cloth around my hands helped, but I still wore blisters on my palms. Finally, though, the last sheet and shirt were hung up on the line, and everyone got ready to go home.

"You've tried hard," said a voice behind me, and I turned to see Mrs. Sabine. "You've not done this kind of work before, have you?"

"It was quite tiring," I admitted.

"But you kept at it, and that's commendable," she said. "Because of your attitude, I have something better for you. So you're staying with Elizabeth and Sara? Elizabeth is a good worker, and little Sara gets along so well with my daughter. I like them both. Well, I'll need you here by sunup tomorrow, since the guests will arrive around noon. Lots to do, lots to do. Have you polished much silver before? No? By this time tomorrow you'll be expert at it. Now go home and rest."

The walk back to the Hayes cottage seemed endless. Elizabeth had to slow down so I could keep up. Sara scampered ahead, not tired at all.

"They worked on sums today," Elizabeth told me. "Sara likes to practice them, but I'm hopeless with numbers and can't help her much. Say, should I carry your pack for you? I'm sorry you're so tired."

I could barely keep my eyes open. "Elizabeth, I can't understand how people can work so hard every day of their lives," I moaned. "If I'm suffering so much after just one day, imagine how weary Janie must feel after twenty years! No wonder working folk are desperate to keep the few pleasures they have, like Christmas."

"Eating is a pleasure, too, and we have to work to earn money for food," Elizabeth replied. "People find the strength to do what they must, Layla. I saw you talking to Mrs. Sabine just before we left. She must have been impressed with you to take time for conversation. I'm to be at the house by sunup tomorrow. What about you?"

"She asked me to come then, too," I said. "Something was mentioned about polishing silver before the guests arrive at noon. That sounds easier than hauling water."

"Ah, the silver," Elizabeth said thoughtfully. "Well, I'm sure you'll at least find it different from water hauling."

Working-class people didn't have forks. No one in England did until the early 1630s. But the Sabines had hundreds of them—no exaggeration!—and hundreds of knives and spoons and fine plates and goblets, all of them tarnished and desperate for cleaning. I sat down in the kitchen a good hour before dawn, and didn't stop polishing until, finally, the last silver was shining brightly just as a carriage pulled up outside with the Sabines' guests. My fingers ached, and my eyes stung—the polish had a harsh aroma that burned as well as smelled bad. But the silver did look lovely, and Mrs. Sabine even complimented me on it as she bustled past to greet the men and women who suddenly filled her parlor. They were all Puritans, as evidenced by their sober dress. Mrs. Sabine wore plain black instead of the brighter silks I'd seen her in the day before. Her husband stood by her side, looking stout and prosperous in his formal black coat and trousers. The greetings were long and loud, with God repeatedly thanked for welcome guests and gracious hosts, and Mrs. Sabine said how everyone must be tired and hungry after their journey, and please come into the main dining room, where a little light refreshment had been prepared. The light refreshment would have fed a dozen families for a week. There were all sorts of rare, wonderful treats—things like tomatoes and grapes, and perfectly roasted venison, which had arrived in plenty of time. We servants were kept busy picking up this and moving that. The women guests praised the furnishings and the shining quality of the silverware—I felt proud—while the men huddled over glasses of wine and talked about the war.

"I hear Cromwell swears he won't fight again until his troops are ready," one said. "Imagine that, a glorified farmer telling lords and real gentlemen how they're supposed to fight!"

"Don't underestimate Oliver Cromwell," another responded.

"There's a sense of destiny about the man. Say, Sabine, are your people here getting nervous about the royals' battlefield success? Can you keep your pro-Catholics in line?"

"My people will always obey me," Sabine said confidently. "They're really good and God-fearing, I promise. We'll find a way to get the king whipped, and then we can really get this country straightened out."

"Cromwell's been saying he doesn't want the king deprived of the throne at all," the first man said. "He just wants him to learn a lesson about sharing power with Parliament. Be a shame to win the war and still have Charles and his Catholic queen."

"Mr. Cromwell hasn't thought this through," Sabine said. "It may be he isn't tough enough for leadership. But we have others who are sufficiently stern, and useful for keeping doubters in their places."

"Blue Richard Culmer, perhaps? Is that who you mean, Sabine?"

"Certainly, I mean Mr. Culmer."

The man sipped some wine. "Now, Culmer's one fellow I wouldn't want after *me!*" and the others laughed and agreed. I winced; with all my exhaustion from hauling water and polishing silver, I'd almost forgotten that I was one of the unfortunate ones Richard Culmer was pursuing.

After the guests had eaten and we'd cleared the dishes away, the Sabines brought down their daughter to present to the company. Sophia came

Sophia Sabine

dashing down the stairs, with Sara trailing quietly behind. The two girls were complete physical opposites. Where Sara was sturdy and blonde, Sophia was tall and slender and her hair was almost black. There was also another obvious difference—while Sara hardly ever talked, Sophia never seemed to stop. She ran from one guest to the next, chattering constantly, asking where they were from and what they'd seen on their journey and telling about her latest lessons—"Sara thought eight and three made eleven, but I told her they made twelve."

"Well, eight and three *do* make eleven, dear," one of the women told her, and instead of becoming angry Sophia threw back her head and laughed.

"Sara, you were right after all," she called to the back of the room, where Sara perched quietly on the staircase. "Let's go back up and practice numbers some more." In the manner of well-raised children in company, Sophia curtsied to the grown-ups before she turned to leave the room.

"Is Sara your sister, dear?" the woman asked. Before Sophia could answer, her mother said sharply, "Oh, no, not at all. She's the daughter of one of the servants. We sometimes allow her to play with Sophia, however."

"How *democratic* of you, Margaret," the woman said, and back on the staircase I saw Sara's cheeks flush bright red before she turned and followed her friend Sophia. So, along with intelligence and ambition she also had pride.

So eight-year-old Sara woke up on the morning of December 25, 1642, to
discover a dress and a doll by her pallet, as well as several candy canes
on her pillow. She shrieked with delight, trying to pull the dress on
over her nightgown while cuddling the doll at the same time.

Thirteen

hat night, Elizabeth asked if I would take Sara home. She explained she'd just heard a friend was about to give birth, and needed to go to her and help with the delivery of the baby. While rich women brought their babies into the world surrounded by physicians and midwives, poor women usually had to rely on their friends. I told Elizabeth I'd be glad to, and went upstairs to fetch Sara from Sophia's bedroom. I found the girls sprawled on a wide bed with silk covers and a canopy. Sophia was talking about a dress her father had promised to buy her, and Sara was bent over a slate, studying arithmetic.

"Time to go home, Sara," I interrupted. "Your mother has to go help a friend, so it will be just you and me."

"You're Sara's Aunt Layla, aren't you?" Sophia inquired. "The one who's come to stay at her house while your husband's in the colonies?

Do you like living with Sara and her mother? How long do you expect to stay with them?"

"I really don't know," I replied, trying to sound respectful as befitted a servant speaking to an employer's child. "I'm just glad Sara and her mother have offered me their hospitality."

"Sara says she likes you," Sophia observed, and I felt immensely pleased to hear it, though Sara had never said anything to me that indicated like or dislike, for that matter. "She's glad you're her aunt."

"I'm glad, too," I said, and Sara and I set out for the cottage. Since it was just the two of us, I thought the girl might chat with me along the way, but she didn't. We walked in companionable silence though. I found pleasure simply in her presence. It occurred to me that, although Nicholas and I and the rest of the companions had devoted our lives to children, we never actually spent time with them besides briefly coming into their homes at night to leave holiday gifts.

When we reached the cottage we went inside and lit some candles. Today, with electric lights that shine brightly at the touch of a switch, that Canterbury cottage in 1642 would probably seem like a dark, depressing place. But back then, a few candles and their meager light were what we were used to, and so Sara and I found their glow cheerful. Neither of us had eaten, so she fetched water and I sliced bread and washed a few carrots and pears. As we ate our simple meal I asked, "What cities do you want to visit someday?"

"Paris," Sara said promptly. "Athens, in Greece. Rome, of course, and Alexandria. I suppose I'll start with London, since it's the nearest great capital and I haven't even been there, yet. What is it like?"

I told her about the high towers and palaces, the great hall of Parliament, and the other impressive buildings. Then I described London Bridge over the wide Thames, and the marketplaces where so many things were for sale, and the theaters and gardens and the streets with cobblestones. I did leave out details about trash and smells, because this little girl had plenty of time to temper her dreams with reality, as we all must eventually do. Sara smiled hugely as she listened, and after I'd talked about London I couldn't resist beginning to describe Paris.

"You've been to *Paris?*" she exclaimed. "However did you get there?" I explained that my husband Nicholas was a craftsman and trader, and that his work had brought us all over the world. When Elizabeth finally came home around midnight, reporting that her friend had given birth to a healthy baby boy, Sara and I were still at the table, and I was describing the unique scent of tabouli that permeated the streets of Constantinople.

"Cousin Layla, I'm glad you and Sara have had such fine conversation, but eight-year-olds need their sleep!" Elizabeth said. "Young lady, off to bed with you! We all have to get up early."

Sara obediently rose and walked over to the short ladder that led to her pallet in the loft. "I'm glad the baby is fine, Mother. Good night. And good night, Auntie Layla." Now I was *Auntie* rather than the more formal *Aunt.* That thought warmed me as Elizabeth chatted for a bit about her friend and the baby, and when we blew out the candles and went to bed ourselves I almost hoped Sara was still awake in the loft pallet we shared so I could tell her more about the places she wanted to go, but the child was fast asleep. And soon, so was I.

For a few more weeks, life remained simple and mostly good. All day from Monday through Friday, and then half-days on Saturdays, I worked in the Sabine house, doing all sorts of chores. Saturday afternoons were spent with Elizabeth and Sara shopping in town or enjoying walks through the green hills around Canterbury. On Sunday mornings there was church—I was pleased Elizabeth attended one where the minister did not adhere to the stern tenets of the Puritans—and then, afterward, perhaps a picnic.

After so many centuries of magical gift-giving, it was in some ways pleasing to live what would be considered a "normal" life. I was often reminded, though, that I was still a fugitive. Reports of the war reached us regularly, often in my letters from Arthur and Elizabeth's from Pamela, which they sent whenever they knew someone who was going between London and Canterbury. In those letters, we learned the king was winning most of the battles against the Roundheads, but he was never quite able to end the war by marching all the way into London.

"Even without Cromwell, who is still supposedly training his troops, the rebels fight just well enough to keep the king from complete triumph," Arthur wrote. "The Puritans still go around saying God will not let them lose. They're trying to convince the working people that few, if any, real Englishmen are fighting for Charles at all. Their new rude nickname for the king's troops is *Cavaliers,* which, I think, is based on the French *chevalier* or 'cavalry.' If the rebels don't win a major battle soon, I don't think they can hold out much longer."

But besides the English rebels, Charles had other troubles. The Scots kept raiding up along the northern border, and there was outright rebellion in Ireland, where most people were Catholics who wanted English Protestantism completely gone from their country. It was rumored that the Roundheads were holding talks with the Scots, Arthur said, hoping to form an alliance with them against Charles—who, other rumors had it, was trying to get the Irish Catholics to join him!

It was all very confusing, and ordinary people had trouble keeping track of who was doing exactly what. So long as Avery Sabine was in charge, Canterbury would officially belong to the Roundheads, but as fall 1642 turned into winter, it seemed quite likely Charles was going to beat the rebels of Parliament. In Canterbury's markets and streets, working people began to grumble about Sabine, and how the king might just wreak some awful vengeance on the town in retaliation for its mayor supporting his enemies.

Almost everyone, I think, began looking forward to Christmas that year as an especially welcome time to forget the war. I personally found it quite odd, when October gave way to November, not to be part of annual holiday preparations at either the London or the

Nuremberg toy factory. There, I knew, Arthur and Leonardo and Attila and Dorothea and St. Francis and Willie Skokan would be overseeing toy production and planning who would deliver what and where, while, over in America, Nicholas and Felix were doing much the same. I hadn't heard directly from my husband while I was in Canterbury. Arthur mentioned he'd had one letter from Felix saying everything there was fine, and that he'd replied all was generally well in England, though I was away from London for a while.

I missed Nicholas terribly, and planned to join him in America just as soon as the war in England was over, which promised to be soon. The king would win, the Puritans would be commanded to give up trying to force their beliefs on everyone else, and Christmas would once again be safe. At that time, I would no longer be a fugitive, and it would be possible for me to move on and resume my life as an ageless gift-giver. I longed for that moment and, yet, I knew I would be sorry to leave Elizabeth, who I'd grown to love as a sister, and Sara, who I certainly loved like a daughter. She talked to me all the time now, about her dreams and also her disappointments, such as often being reminded in little ways that although she could be friends with Sophia, she could never be considered her equal.

"I'm actually better than Sophia at spelling and sums, but the teacher only praises her and not me, Auntie Layla," Sara said. "Sophia talks all the time about *her* education and the important man *she* will marry and how I'll be *her* lady-in-waiting. It doesn't matter how smart I am; I'll always be the servant, and, if I marry at all, it will probably have to be to some farmer in Canterbury. I don't think it's fair."

"Much in life isn't fair, Sara," I replied. "It's for us to find and take advantage of its possibilities, though, instead of being controlled by gloomy thoughts. I had a dear aunt who told me often to keep my dreams and make as many of them come true as I could. That's my advice to you, my love."

"Your aunt sounds very special," Sara said. "What was her name?"

"Lodi," I answered.

"That's a pretty name. Is she still living?"

"In my heart, at least, and now in yours," I said, and gave Sara a huge hug.

In early December, a package arrived from Arthur along with the usual letter. Anticipating Christmas morning, I had asked that Leonardo personally craft a fine doll for Sara, one with blonde hair and painted blue eyes. He'd outdone himself, fashioning a marvelous wooden toy with real working joints, and I felt some satisfaction that Sophia Sabine, for all her father's wealth, would never own a finer one. There was something in the package that I hadn't expected, too, wrapped carefully in paper. I had never seen the likes of the candy that spilled into my hands.

"Leonardo and Willie Skokan have been collaborating," Arthur wrote. "These things they call 'candy canes' are the result. Willie says you were the one who suggested them."

The peppermint sweets had been stretched into sticks about four inches long, and then one end had been curved around in the shape of an upside-down *u*, mimicking exactly the sort of canes older people used to walk, and also resulting in a shape that could, as Willie hoped, dangle as a decoration from the branches of Christmas trees in those countries like Germany that had developed this new holiday tradition. Leonardo's striking red stripes remained on the canes, and they were lovely in their color and simplicity. Since neither Elizabeth or Sara was around—I wanted to keep the confectionary as a surprise holiday treat—I sampled a cane, and the sharp peppermint taste was astonishing.

I knew it would be all right for Sara to wake up on Christmas day to discover Father Christmas had left her a doll and some candy, because Elizabeth had assured me he was a welcome visitor in their home.

"Of course, Father Christmas can't be everywhere, so my husband, Alan, and I are careful to help him with Sara's presents," she said. "It's been a hard year with Alan away at sea, but still there will be a new dress for her on Christmas morning." When I told her I would like to give a doll, she hugged me in thanks for adding to her child's holiday joy.

"It's really a gift straight from Father Christmas and his companions," I said truthfully, and Elizabeth stared at me in surprise.

"Father Christmas has companions?" she asked.

"Of course," I replied, smiling.

In my months at Canterbury, I had been accepted into the community, with my plain looks and unremarkable job. Though I'd been careful to make no close friends other than Elizabeth and Sara—I didn't want questions about where I'd come from, because in Avery Sabine's town I assumed there would be Puritan informers—I did have passing acquaintance with a number of people, including the other women who worked for Margaret Sabine. They began talking, during the second week in December, about what the Canterbury mayor might do to discourage the celebration of Christmas.

"I hear he thinks his Puritan masters in London will be angry if people here do the usual things on the holiday," Janie confided one weary day as I lugged water buckets into the washing shed. Occasionally I still had to perform this backbreaking chore. "You know, Layla—the feasting, and the singing in the streets, and all that. He'd like to impress them with his control of the city by making sure that doesn't happen."

"I don't really see how he can prevent it," I replied. "There are no laws against celebrating Christmas—at least, not yet."

"He'll try to find a way," Janie predicted, and she was right. Only a few days later, town criers began walking around Canterbury's streets urging people "at the suggestion of our beloved mayor" to treat Christmas like an ordinary day. Shops should remain open. Everyone should go to work. If the savior's birth must be celebrated at all, it should be with a moment's silent meditation. No gifts, either, because that was only continuing a pagan tradition.

"Are Christmas gifts really bad, Auntie Layla?" Sara wanted to know after listening to the criers.

"Not at all, my darling," I said. "Gifts anytime are simply a token of love and caring, and gifts at Christmas are meant to add joy to a wonderful celebration. Please remember that the kind thoughts of the giver are even more important than the gift, and then you'll have the perfect spirit of Christmas."

Christmas fell on a weekday that year, and on the Saturday before Margaret Sabine called her servants together to tell us we would be expected to report to work as usual on December 25.

"I know some of you may disagree with my husband's—that is to say, my *family's*—position on Christmas, which is more properly called Christ-tide, but that is just too bad," she said. "Those who do not report for work will have to find employment somewhere else, and there are few other jobs to be had in Canterbury right now. And if any of you have any thoughts of the usual caroling at our home with drinks and food provided for all, forget them. We are a godly Puritan household and will no longer honor drunken, pagan traditions."

No one dared argue, most because they knew Margaret Sabine would certainly fire them for disobeying, and me because my husband and his companions had long ago decided to always respect the beliefs of others. If the Sabines did not want Christmas celebrated in their home, it should not be. But the rest of us could certainly do as we wished in *our* homes.

So eight-year-old Sara woke up on the morning of December 25, 1642, to discover a dress and a doll by her pallet, as well as several candy canes on her pillow. She shrieked with delight, trying to pull the dress on over her nightgown while cuddling the doll at the same time. As soon as those contradictory tasks were accomplished, she jammed a candy cane in her mouth, mumbling in wonder over the shape, color, and taste.

"And just last night she was privately asking me to tell her the truth about Father Christmas," Elizabeth confided. "Sophia told her they were too old to believe in some made-up Catholic saint."

"Sophia was wrong," I said, and handed a candy cane to Elizabeth, who liked it very much. Leonardo had sent along dozens, so I had plenty. When Sara was sufficiently calm, we fed her breakfast and walked to town and our jobs at the Sabines. Sara reported later that, despite Sophia's parents telling everyone else not to celebrate the holiday, they had given Sophia dozens of Christmas gifts, though Sara much preferred her own doll and dress and candy to anything her friend had received. When the day's work was over, Sara and Elizabeth and I walked hand-in-hand back to the cottage, softly singing Christmas carols. Later, we ate goose and mince pie, both special, once-a-year treats, and only after I climbed into the loft bed I shared with Sara did I realize with a start that not once during the whole day had I even thought about my usual magical gift-giving.

Though the working people in town reluctantly obeyed the Sabines' edict not to come to their fine home for caroling and treats, most of them openly defied their mayor's wishes and celebrated Christmas as best they could. The shops in town that Sabine didn't own were shuttered in honor of the holiday. His remained open, but had few customers. The town's non-Puritan churches held worship services, and the grandest of these was in the fine Canterbury Cathedral. Because we had to work, Elizabeth and I were unable to attend, though we badly wanted to. Well, we told ourselves, we had kept Christmas as best we could, with joy and gifts to celebrate the birth of Jesus.

"Sophia says her father is afraid his reputation has suffered because so many people here kept to their Christmas traditions when he asked them not to," Sara told us a few days later. "She says he wrote to someone in London asking for help."

"What sort of help?" Elizabeth asked absently. Sophia talked about so many things it was impossible to know what was important and what wasn't.

"Just help, Sophia said."

At dawn on the second Sunday in January 1643, there were loud shouts outside the cottage. "Someone's destroying the cathedral," a man bellowed, and Elizabeth, Sara, and I quickly pulled on our clothes and ran with the rest into town. What we saw there was horrifying. A number of men with heavy clubs, some high on ladders, were smashing the cathedral's lovely stained-glass windows, howling, "Death to Christmas!" Dozens of others, dressed in full Roundhead armor, stood pointing muskets at the dismayed crowd.

"The mayor called in troops!" someone said, and it was true. Avery Sabine stood safely inside the line of soldiers holding everyone at gunpoint, his arms folded as he watched the destruction of the church windows with every appearance of satisfaction.

"It's horrible, Auntie Layla," Sara whispered to me. Elizabeth and I held her tight between us. Then my own blood ran even colder, because one of the stick-wielding men broke away from his terrible work and walked to Avery Sabine's side. In the early morning light, I could see that his cloak was a color other than traditional Puritan black.

Blue Richard Culmer turned to the crowd and shouted, "Your mayor told you not to celebrate Christmas. You should have listened!" As in London, his lips split wide in a happy leer while his eyes remained dark and joyless. "If you do it again next year, we'll break you like we broke these sinful windows!" Then, with an animal-like howl of triumph, he signaled for the club-wielders and musketmen to march back toward London through the West Gate while Avery Sabine preened solemnly and almost everyone else stood numb with despair.

"Don't test me on Christmas again," Sabine said to the stunned crowd, and walked back to his fine house.

Elizabeth, Sara, and I returned one night from work to find there were candles already lit in the cottage. Both mother and daughter knew what this must mean and ran shouting through the door. I followed, and found them wrapped in the arms of a tall, wide-shouldered man who nodded briefly in my direction before burying himself back in this joyful three-person embrace.

Fourteen

he Christmas-loving people of Canterbury were terribly shaken by the assault on their cathedral, just as Avery Sabine and Blue Richard Culmer intended. A few brave souls boarded up the gaping holes in the sandstone walls where the stained-glass windows had sparkled and inspired for centuries, but no one suggested new windows should be installed. In the moment the original windows were shattered, so too was the resolve of some in Canterbury to keep celebrating Christmas no matter what the mayor and his Puritan masters had to say about it.

"I doubt there'll be many around here welcoming Father Christmas from now on," Janie suggested as we wrung out tablecloths in the washing shed. It was the spring of 1643, and I had been employed by the Sabines long enough that I was no longer the newest servant. Much of my time was spent indoors, where the work was easier. Melinda, hired soon after the assault on the cathedral, now had the dubious honor of always being assigned the hardest chores, which included water hauling. But there was a lot of washing to be done on this particular day, and I had been instructed to go out and help.

"No act, no matter how terrible, can destroy Christmas," I replied. "Somehow, the holiday will prevail."

Sometimes, though, I wondered, especially when, over the next months, the Roundheads won a series of victories over King Charles and his army. Oliver Cromwell had returned with properly trained cavalry, and his troops were instrumental in winning several battles. There were rumors the king might now be willing to negotiate a settlement that would allow him to remain on the throne in return for certain concessions, which would give more power to Parliament. In general, I simply hated the whole idea of civil war, and hoped it would end as quickly as possible. But I also knew men like Blue Richard Culmer would never really compromise about anything, although they might pretend to for a time. If Parliament defeated the king, the Puritans would find ways to dominate Parliament, and, eventually, force their beliefs on everyone else in England.

By late summer, the Scots had allied themselves with the Roundheads, and the king's forces gradually lost control of their few ports. Avery Sabine strutted down the streets of Canterbury, and was often called away to London on mysterious business, which Sophia told Sara her father would not even discuss with his family, though he promised his wife and daughter that great things were in store.

"He sometimes mentions Christmas, and laughs when he does," Sara reported. "Sophia says I should throw away that doll Father Christmas left me, but I won't."

In September 1643, just after the king's forces suffered a terrible defeat at Newbury, Alan Hayes came home from his long voyage. Elizabeth, Sara, and I returned one night from work to find there were candles already lit in the cottage. Both mother and daughter knew what this must mean and ran shouting through the door. I followed, and found them wrapped in the arms of a tall, wide-shouldered man who nodded briefly in my direction before burying himself back in this joyful three-person embrace. I went outside for a little while, to give the reunited family some privacy, and wondered what I would do if Alan Hayes did not want a houseguest who had already been living in his home for more than a year.

It turned out I had no cause for concern. After about ten minutes, Sara came to fetch me, saying her father very much wanted to meet his wife's cousin.

"If Elizabeth and Sara love you, then so do I," Alan proclaimed, and by the time we had finished dinner—eggs from a neighbor's chicken made up the main course—Alan was insisting I stay as long as I liked, "up to and including forever." Actually, I had no idea of how long I wanted to remain in Canterbury, or even in England. If the Roundheads won—it now seemed possible they might—then Christmas would soon be abolished. Avery Sabine and Blue Richard Culmer had demonstrated the lengths to which the Puritans would go to frighten people into giving up the holiday. If England had no Christmas, there was no longer any reason for Arthur and Leonardo to operate the toy factory in London, and certainly no reason for me to delay any longer my reunion with my husband, whom I now had not seen in twenty-three years. True, for ageless gift-givers like Nicholas and me, twenty-three years was the merest hiccup of time, but I still missed him so very much, and knew he missed me equally.

Alan Hayes

But somehow I believed I must stay where I was. Arthur, certainly, thought I should get out of England immediately. He said as much when, in November 1643, he came to Canterbury to see me.

"I decided this couldn't be communicated as effectively in a letter, Layla," Arthur said. We were off in the hills outside Canterbury on a late Saturday afternoon, out of sight in a grove of trees so no passing neighbors might start wondering aloud to their friends about the stranger visiting Alan and Elizabeth's longtime guest. "We hear constantly at the toy factory in London that Parliament is determined to eradicate Christmas and everything about it. Blue Richard Culmer grows more powerful each day. I doubt he's forgotten you—such men remember everyone they consider to be their enemies. The Roundheads now control almost every port city, but we can find some way to get you through. Go back to Nuremberg, or, better, across the ocean to join Nicholas and Felix. But leave England—*now.*"

"What about you and Leonardo?" I asked. "You're in danger, too. If Culmer ever discovers the factory, and why we make toys there, you'll end up in the Tower of London."

Arthur sighed. "I've come to the conclusion that, at some point, it will be better to close the toy factory down. I won't until I absolutely have to, and for now there still is no specific law against Christmas, just strong suggestions by the Puritans that it's no longer wise to celebrate it. Everyone in England has heard about what happened here in Canterbury."

"Do you think Parliament will legally outlaw Christmas, Arthur?"

"It's only a matter of time," he said. "If, in another year or two, enough people in England don't voluntarily accept the Puritan view of the holiday as sinful, then the Puritans will stop trying to persuade and start commanding instead."

I reminded Arthur of how Oliver Cromwell once told me no one should force religious beliefs on anyone else. "Cromwell is growing in influence among the Roundheads," I said. "Maybe he will prevent them from passing anti-Christmas laws."

"Cromwell is a devout Puritan who hates Christmas as much as any of them," Arthur replied. "Besides, power changes the way people do things. When he told you he believed in persuasion rather than force, he was an unimportant member of Parliament who had very little power. Of course he believed in persuasion. That was the only way he could get things done. But now he's one of the most important men in England, and as people grow in power they usually grow less concerned about the opinions of others. Don't fool yourself that Oliver Cromwell will protect Christmas if he sees the chance to destroy it." He shrugged. "But we really can't do anything about Cromwell. Let's talk about you."

I wasn't accomplishing anything for our overall gift-giving mission by staying in England, Arthur pointed out. I couldn't be in London, helping at the toy factory, because of the warrant for my arrest issued there by Blue Richard Culmer. In Canterbury, all I did was wash clothes and sweep floors for the wife of a Christmas-hating Puritan. In Europe, children in Italy still waited for Befana on January 6 and French children loved Pere Noel, who'd leave gifts in their shoes while they slept on Christmas Eve. A holiday custom unique to France was that children could open their presents on Christmas morning, but adults had to wait until New Year's. So many countries had their own special traditions, meaning Attila and Dorothea and St. Francis and Willie Skokan had all they could do preparing for the holidays and delivering all the right toys to all the right places. They badly needed my help. And what about the New World, where Nicholas and Felix were working so hard to spread the wonder of Christmas? Didn't I think they needed me, too?

"Isn't it possible, Layla, that you're being selfish by insisting on staying here?" Arthur concluded.

That stung me, because, in a way, he was right. *Selfish* is such an awful word, implying a person cares much more for himself or herself than about others, and for twelve centuries I had devoted my life to gift-giving. I had been granted very special gifts, and while I remained in Canterbury I was not using them.

I was quiet for a few moments, thinking—about my husband, so far away in America; about Oliver Cromwell, and whether he was as special a leader as I had once believed; about all the children in the world who depended on holiday gift-givers for moments of joy; and, yes, about the person in the world who, next to Nicholas, had become dearest to me. Every moment I spent with Sara was a delight. I had to admit that part of the reason I refused to flee England was that I couldn't bear to leave her. She was so hopeful, so anxious to see the world and do special things and not become just one more country farmer's wife. So much, I realized, like I had been back in Niobrara.

But there was something more at work here, and finally I tried to explain it to Arthur and, perhaps, to myself.

"Not long after we married, Nicholas told me he felt there was no coincidence where our gift-giving mission was involved," I said. "He believes, and helped me to believe, that we find ourselves in certain places at certain times because there is some great purpose to our being there. You've heard the story more times than you wanted, I'm sure, of how Nicholas and Felix and I just happened to bring gifts to the same nomad camp outside Constantinople one night in 412, or 1,231 years ago. Constantinople is a sprawling city in a huge world—what brought us together there in that one modest spot? I'm here in Canterbury now as a result of many apparently coincidental things—Nicholas wanting to see the New World, the Puritan 'Saints' making a voyage just as we came to London, Pamela Forrest working at your factory and having a kind, generous sister here when I needed some place of refuge . . . Arthur, I believe if I leave now, I ignore a message from God, who has so generously given us the special gifts to carry out our mission."

"A message to do what, Layla?"

"It's hard to say," I admitted. "Surely it has to do with Christmas, and the danger to the holiday. Canterbury is where Blue Richard Culmer made clear the Puritan determination to eliminate Christmas forever. Canterbury, then, may be the place where it is saved."

Arthur looked doubtful. "Who will save it, Layla?" he asked gently. "You? Remember, you're running from Blue Richard because you're not strong enough to fight him. I understand why you say God is with you, but don't forget the Puritans believe just as strongly that God is with them. Please, be practical."

I took a deep breath. "I'm staying, Arthur," I said. "We have been friends now for more than a thousand years. Support me in this, as we have all supported one another for so many centuries. There is no co-incidence in our lives, and somehow Christmas will be saved."

Arthur embraced me and returned to London. I went back to the Hayes cottage and resumed my life there. Parliament continued to combat both king and Christmas. December 25, 1643, was one of the saddest holidays in memory. Parliament still did not demand that Christmas no longer be celebrated, but it deliberately met on Christmas Day as a sign business should be carried on as usual. Across England, a few brave church leaders put holly on their doors and invited working people in to celebrate. Many of those who conducted services soon afterward received visits from vandals sent by Blue Richard Culmer.

The vast majority of the English people still loved Christmas and kept the holiday quietly in their homes, sharing special dinner treats and summoning up their courage to sing some carols, though not too loudly. Those with Puritan employers reported for work. Arthur wrote me that so many families feared reprisals that they made it clear Father Christmas should not enter their homes and leave gifts for hopeful little ones. Reluctantly, he complied, since we never left gifts where we were not welcome. "For the first time, we had a surplus of toys left over after Christmas," Arthur wrote. "We sent them immediately to Attila, so they could be distributed on Epiphany." He added that he didn't think he could keep the factory open much longer, especially since there was so much less gift-giving to do now in England.

On December 25, 1644, Parliament took another step toward eliminating Christmas completely. Just before King Charles had fled two years earlier, in a last-minute effort to appease his rivals he had agreed that the last Wednesday of each month should be set aside for fasting, since Puritans believed the act of going hungry would remind everyone of how grateful we should be to God for providing us with food. Now, in this year, the twenty-fifth happened to be the last Wednesday of December. In towns like Canterbury where the Puritans had control, town criers offered reminders that, by law, December 25 was a day to fast, not feast. Singing Christmas carols in your home might not be illegal, but eating a Christmas goose or holiday pudding certainly was.

Though there still was not one final, heavy-handed decree that Christmas was unlawful, these acts and edicts gradually wore down the Christmas spirit all across the land. Fewer people grumbled about having to work on December 25 because it seemed like one more permanently sad fact in life, rather than something temporary. Poor villagers were much less likely to band together and march singing to the homes of their richest neighbors because, in too many cases, they would be met with curt reminders that Christmas was a pagan holiday, and then have heavy doors slammed in their faces.

Not everyone rejected Christmas out of either conviction or, more likely, fear. Some wealthy families encouraged their poorer neighbors to make the traditional holiday visit and gave them wonderful things to eat and drink when they arrived. Brave working-class families declared what happened in their homes was their business, not Parliament's, and feasted on Christmas and exchanged small gifts. The very bravest even ventured out to church, knowing spies among their neighbors might report them for doing it. In Canterbury, the Hayes family tried to balance Christmas spirit with common sense. Elizabeth and I were employed by Margaret Sabine, so we had to work. But Alan Hayes was home between voyages, so he had the whole holiday free to celebrate if he wanted—and he did.

"When I was a boy, my family was probably the poorest one in Canterbury," Alan explained. "We counted ourselves lucky, during the year, if we had vegetables more than once a week to go with our bread at mealtimes. Then my father got work with a farmer who loved

Christmas. One of the ways he celebrated it was to give a goose to each of his employees to enjoy for their holiday supper. I cried on that first Christmas when we had goose, Layla, because it was the most wonderful thing I'd ever tasted. When my parents brought me to church that day, I thanked God for sending us his son *and* the tasty goose. When my mother served it to us, that was the one time that year I can remember her smiling. I promise you, while I live we *will* celebrate Christmas in my home, and I feel sorry for all those who deny themselves and their families the joy of the holiday."

So while I went to work with Elizabeth, Sara stayed home with her father, and Elizabeth and I returned home at the end of the day to find the cottage decorated with holly and a fine goose sizzling on a platter.

Sara received another dress that Christmas morning, and Leonardo had sent me more candy canes from London, which I left on her pillow. But she announced as Alan carved the Christmas goose that Father Christmas probably shouldn't bring her gifts in the future.

"I'm ten now, and will be eleven next month," Sara said. "I know this is a hard time for Father Christmas, and so I'm ready to do without presents."

"Is this because of something Sophia has said to you?" her father asked sharply. "I know her father is a powerful Puritan and won't allow Christmas in their home, but in this house your mother and I make the decisions—and Auntie Layla, too. If you want Father Christmas to keep coming, I promise you he will."

"I do want him to, but I know there's danger in it," Sara replied. "I would not want Father Christmas or anyone helping him to get in trouble. Sophia does say her father expects new, stern laws about Christmas to be passed very soon, since the king's troops are losing nearly every battle and the war will be over before next year's holidays."

I was proud of Sara for putting concern for her parents ahead of any desire for Christmas gifts. It was another sign that my beloved girl was indeed growing up fast, in mind as well as body. She was almost as tall as me, and the instruction she still shared with Sophia Sabine now included drawing and dancing in addition to reading, writing, and sums, since privileged young ladies were expected to master such social graces. Of course, the purpose of the instruction was to prepare Sophia, not Sara, for society life, but Sara admitted to me she enjoyed dancing very much, though, being so shy, she would never dance anywhere but in a small room with only her best friend and the dancing instructor there to see. Then she wanted to know if I had ever done much dancing. I replied that I hadn't—but didn't add that twelve centuries of making and giving gifts all over the world had left little time for such things.

The year 1645 in England started with very bad news. Meeting on January 4 in London, Parliament began considering a rule that would allow only Sundays to be considered holy days. Confident now of complete victory, not long afterward its members put former Archbishop Laud, who'd been appointed by King Charles and then appalled the Puritans by not restricting religious worship, on trial. He'd been held for a long time in the Tower of London, but now he was brought out, sentenced to die, and promptly executed.

Oliver Cromwell caused a stir by temporarily leaving the battlefield to make a speech. In it, he accused Parliament of still promoting rich men to be military leaders rather than more talented working-class men. Hearing this, I felt hopeful about him. Clearly, power had not altered Cromwell's commitment to the common people.

Then members of Parliament turned their attention back to King Charles, and soon they convincingly defeated him at Naseby, with Cromwell leading what was known as his New Model Army to victory there. Now the king's soldiers were in full retreat, and the holiday haters were about to have the power they had craved for so long.

But they hadn't destroyed Christmas quite yet. As December 25 drew near, I found myself wondering if it was right for me to remain safe in hiding in Canterbury, while Arthur and Leonardo and their employees risked so much operating the toy factory back in London. Dusting in the parlor while some visitors from London chatted over tea there with the Sabines about the war and its most prominent figures, I overheard that, on Christmas Day, Blue Richard Culmer intended to prowl some northern English cities, punishing those who celebrated the holiday there. Meanwhile, Oliver Cromwell was going to be visiting his wife back in London.

I told Alan, Elizabeth, and Sara that I would be spending Christmas 1645 in London. They were dismayed, Sara in particular.

"But if you're on a trip, how will Father Christmas find you, Auntie Layla?" she asked.

"Oh, I never have to worry about that, my love!" I said, and I knew Sara wondered why her innocent question had caused me to laugh. Her parents, of course, had another concern, and asked me quietly if I really wanted to risk being seen by Blue Richard Culmer. I replied that, to the best of my knowledge, he would be away to the north, and I should be safe if I only stayed in London for a day or two.

Just before I left, I informed Margaret Sabine that I would not be able to come to work on December 25. "There are some people in London who might only be there on that day, and I must see them," I told her.

"You've worked for me for three years, honestly and well," she replied. "With someone else, I might suspect this was an act of defiance over that pagan Christmas holiday. But if you say you must see someone in London, I believe you. I would not want you to have to walk all the way there. My husband is sending some goods to London by wagon on the twenty-third. You may ride along, though you must find your own way back."

Margaret Sabine

So the Christmas-hating Sabines helpfully gave a ride to someone who intended to save Christmas from people like them.

These brave young men were making it clear that no law
could prevent them from thanking God for his son as they saw fit.
They kicked footballs around the streets and market stalls, cheering
and laughing and enjoying the lives that God had given them.

Fifteen

was dismayed by what I saw at the toy factory in London. I arrived early in the afternoon on December 24, since the wagon ride from Canterbury took a day and a half. I'd anticipated a merry reunion with Arthur and Leonardo and their employees, but instead I found most of the Christmas toys being packed for shipment to the factory in Nuremberg. There was another package, too—Leonardo was sending a box of several hundred left-over candy canes on to me in care of the Hayes cottage in Canterbury.

"This is the last Christmas we'll have this London operation, at least for a while," Arthur informed me. "Blue Richard Culmer has his spies everywhere in London, so it is only a matter of time before we are discovered. Tonight we're going to distribute gifts to those few remaining children in England whose parents defy the Puritans by allowing Christmas presents. With the very limited number of boys and girls who are still allowed to accept our gifts, it won't take very long.

Then Leonardo and I will be off to Germany. The fine people who work for us will have to find other jobs, I'm afraid. Within a year or two, I'm sadly certain, Christmas will no longer be celebrated in England. For a while, at least, its enemies have won, Layla."

"Perhaps they haven't, Arthur," I argued. "I suppose you're right to close the factory for a while, though it breaks my heart to see you do it. But this new government may very well find it is harder than they imagine to make the holiday simply go away. It won't. Those who cherish it so much won't allow that to happen."

That night, I helped Arthur and Leonardo distribute gifts—dolls and puppets and hoops for spinning and balls for bouncing, tokens to remind children throughout the coming year that they were loved. Even in such a sad time for Christmas itself, there was still so much joy in giving presents as one way to celebrate the wonderful gift God gave the world so many, many centuries before. Then, on Christmas morning, I hugged my dear friends good-bye as they prepared to leave for the toy factory in Germany. By government order, all the British ports were open despite the holiday, and so Arthur and Leonardo could leave immediately.

"Give my love to Attila and Dorothea and St. Francis and Willie Skokan," I reminded them. "Arthur, when you write my husband to inform him you've closed the London factory, please tell him as well that I send my love and hope to see him very, very soon."

"You really should come with us," Arthur said. "I'm worried that you have some dangerous plan in mind. If you like, I can send Leonardo on ahead and stay to help you."

I smiled and said gently, "I really don't have a specific plan, Arthur. But I'm not going to give up on England and Christmas quite yet."

I had two visits to make on that holiday morning. Many of the shops in London were open, signifying December 25 was just another ordinary working day. Most of the people who were at work wore sad expressions, for they truly believed it was wrong not to celebrate Jesus' birth with songs and small gifts and feasting. When I arrived at my first destination, Pamela Forrest told me her husband, Clive, had been summoned to cut the hair of some Roundhead generals and asked if I had brought any messages from her beloved sister Elizabeth. I had, of course, and spent some happy minutes sitting with her in her small, pleasant home while describing to Pamela how much her niece Sara had grown. Pamela had a few small tokens she wanted me to take to Elizabeth, Alan, and Sara, and they, of course, had sent some modest gifts for Pamela, Clive, and their two sons.

"With the factory closed, Pamela, how will you make your living?" I asked.

"I'm not certain," she replied. "There are some businesses that hire seamstresses, and I'm very talented with needle and thread. But no matter where I go to work, I'll keep hoping that Mr. Arthur and Mr. Leonardo return someday, so I can go back to helping them make toys. I'm not going to ask you any awkward questions, Layla, but I think I have a rather good idea of what the three of you really do. I'll just say that Father Christmas is *very* real to me, and we'll leave it at that."

When I stood up to go, Pamela hugged me. I thanked her again for sending me to her sister Elizabeth in Canterbury and promised I would keep in touch. Then I went on to my second stop, a fine brick house near Parliament. Oliver Cromwell's dwelling reflected his rise in rank; though he was not officially the commanding general of the Roundhead army, everyone knew he made all the important decisions. Years ago, I had just knocked on the front door of his middle-class cottage, then joined him in the kitchen. Now he had guards outside his home, and it took several minutes before they would even agree to tell their commander that a Mrs. Nicholas wanted to see him.

After another quarter-hour, a young Roundhead soldier came out to fetch me.

"Colonel Cromwell is fearsomely busy, missus," he said. "I'm surprised he'll see you at all. Please state your business and then be on your way."

Cromwell received me in a large, well-lit room. He stood by a table that was strewn with maps. Looking up as I entered, he said, "So it's Layla Nicholas, wife of colonist Nicholas Nicholas. Missus, I would have hoped by now you'd be safely across the ocean with your husband, and instead you come knocking on my door in London. Aren't you afraid Blue Richard Culmer may run in and catch you?"

"I'm sure Mr. Culmer has more important things to do," I replied.

"Don't be so certain," Cromwell said. "Blue Richard is never pleased when someone escapes his clutches, and he surely hasn't forgotten how you avoided arrest—what, three years ago?"

"Three years," I agreed. "I assume you know I was never a spy for the king, and thank you for your warning so that I could escape. I don't deny I am a great friend of Christmas, but I don't believe that is, at least as yet, a crime. Will you make it one, now that you've beaten the king and England is yours to do with as you wish?"

Cromwell rubbed his face. He looked very tired. "We began to debate this Christmas issue once before in my home and again in a public park. We obviously will never agree. But I wish you would at least try to understand what I am really attempting to do, what we true Puritans have intended from the moment this terrible civil war began. Yes, the king is defeated, and I believe that, within a few months, he will finally negotiate the peace that we have sought for so long. Charles will be welcome to return to London and reclaim his throne—don't look so amazed! We never said we didn't want a king at all. We just want one who will consult with Parliament, which is elected to give voice to the people, before the king makes his decisions. When Charles agrees to this, why, I'll dust off his crown for him myself."

"And if the king refuses?"

Cromwell rubbed his face again. "He won't. He doesn't have much of an army left. So Charles will come back to London, Parliament will have its rightful influence, England will be at peace, and I can return to my farm. See if it doesn't happen just that way."

"It won't be as simple as you make it sound," I argued. "People like Blue Richard Culmer will shut down any churches that don't worship God the way they want. Christmas, the happiest, most joyful day in the lives of almost every working family in England, will be banned. You say you want a government that listens to its people. But you don't seem eager to hear what they say, only to impose your will on them. How is that an improvement?"

Cromwell walked over to me and looked hard into my eyes. "Yes, there will be some new rules. Only godly men, those who truly understand the will of the Lord, shall control this government. We will allow worship for any faith—Catholics or Jews or whoever. But non-Puritans will never hold any positions of power, as, indeed, they should not. Though we will protect them, we will not allow them to taint our laws or godly nation with their false beliefs. As for Christmas, all right. I will state it for you one more time. Christmas is not a true Christian holiday. December 25 is not the actual birthday of Christ, but instead a pagan date appropriated by sinful people who want to practice bad behavior. Singing and gift-giving and feasting are not proper ways to give thanks to God. In short, missus, Christmas is not holy."

I stared right back at him. Years before, I had held my tongue in deference to Elizabeth Cromwell, but now there was no reason not to reply in detail. I had come to London hoping to meet with this man and offer a complete defense for the celebration of Christmas. I would take advantage of the opportunity.

"Very well, Mr. Cromwell," I began. "You have told me what Christmas is not. Now allow me, sir, to tell you what Christmas *is*.

"Christmas *is* a day when we can reflect in our words and deeds the same generosity of spirit that moved our Lord to send us his son. It *is* a day when, for a few fleeting hours, every man, woman, and child can remember all the joyful things in their lives instead of being worn down by problems and hardship. It *is* a day when, for a little while, there are no masters and servants, no rich and poor, just human beings equal in their love of Jesus and in their respect for one another. In short, Mr. Cromwell, Christmas *is* holy."

Cromwell looked frustrated. "Surely, missus, you cannot see these Christmas drunks and troublemakers and tell me their actions are appropriate in the eyes of God?"

"I suggest, Mr. Cromwell, that you consider the actions of Blue Richard Culmer smashing windows in churches and arresting people on trumped-up charges. Are these things holy? Just as you, I know, would tell me Mr. Culmer does not really represent the Puritans, so I promise you that those who abuse the holiday for their own purposes do not represent Christmas. Let us be honest with each other, Mr. Cromwell. We both know very well that even if King Charles regains his throne, you personally will be the real power in England. When you have that power, will you use it to represent the people or to force your own beliefs upon them?"

Oliver Cromwell started to say something, stopped, thought a while, and then sighed. "I will always do what I know is best for England. I've learned a hard lesson during this war, that sometimes right-thinking leaders must impose their will if the common people prove incapable of understanding. At first, some new rules may seem harsh, but everyone will accept them after they see how much more improved their lives are, living as God wants. When Christmas is gone, it will only be missed until a pleased Lord bestows new blessings on England, a country that turned away from pagan celebration. I am acting as I think right for the land I love, Layla Nicholas, and I hope you accept that."

I did. It is very hard, when you believe in something as completely as I believed in Christmas, not to decide anyone who disagrees must be evil. Oliver Cromwell and many, perhaps most, of his Puritans thought they were doing the right things for England, including making everyone give up Christmas. I wanted everyone to celebrate it. The difference between us was that I would never force my beliefs on others, and Cromwell and his supporters would. This did not make them evil, but it did make them wrong.

I held out my hand, and Cromwell shook it. "We understand each other, even if we cannot agree," I said. "You can defeat a king, Mr. Cromwell, but Christmas will prove too powerful."

"Please leave London immediately, missus," he replied. "This is not a safe place for you. Neither is England, for that matter. Go to your husband in the New World, and I will pray that God helps you understand the sinfulness of this holiday you mistakenly love so much."

"Good-bye, Oliver Cromwell," I said.

"I sense that you might be very dangerous, Missus Nicholas," he replied, and turned his attention back to the maps on the table.

I had wanted to make a final appeal to Cromwell, and I had done it. The London factory was shut up tight. I had visited with Pamela Forrest. I had no other friends in the whole city. There was nothing to prevent me from beginning the long walk back to Canterbury, where I would do—what? The Roundheads controlled England. I had no doubt, now, that Parliament would order Christmas ended forever. It seemed there was nothing I could do to stop them. I walked along the London streets, avoiding pigs and piles of garbage and thinking my gloomy thoughts until, quite suddenly, I became aware of a great commotion.

Even though it was officially a workday, many people were bustling about in the central marketplace on the banks of the Thames. They were mostly young men of what was called the apprentice class, hired out to work for pennies for carpenters and cobblers and other tradesmen, serving until they had learned the craft for themselves. Christmas was a special holiday for apprentices, who were otherwise required to work from dawn until dark every day but Sunday. Christmas was their one day a year to sing and feast and do silly, enjoyable things like playing football in the streets. But Parliament's order to keep December 25 as an ordinary working day took that single holiday away from the apprentices, whose masters were glad to have them putting in extra work. Now, in the marketplace, some of these young men were congregating, defying the law that required them to work on Christmas Day. Many of them were quite young—a boy could be apprenticed out at eleven or twelve—and none seemed much over twenty. Quite a few looked fearful as they defiantly walked away from the shops where they worked. They were taking a considerable risk. Their masters, of course, could tell them never to come back and the years they'd served to begin learning a useful trade would be wasted. They could also be arrested by the Roundheads, if not officially for celebrating Christmas then for some made-up charge like disturbing the peace.

And yet hundreds of them were gathered together in the marketplace, apparently without any prior planning, and they were running about chanting in unison, "God bless Christmas! God bless Christmas!" until even more others like them heard the shouting and couldn't resist leaving their jobs to join in. Later, there would be reports that a thousand apprentices joined in courageous protest that day, and it might be true. I was there to see it, and though I didn't count the participants, I know there were many of them.

Despite what the Puritans subsequently claimed, the Christmas protestors did not overturn marketplace displays and threaten shop owners who refused to close in honor of the holiday. No one was beaten, or even spoken to harshly. Instead, these brave young men were making it clear that no law could prevent them from thanking God for his son as they saw fit. They kicked footballs around the streets and market stalls, cheering and laughing and enjoying the lives that God had given them. By high noon, they were singing "We Wish You a Merry Christmas" over and over, somehow louder every time, and Roundhead soldiers stood by watching helplessly, not certain what they should do. There were too many of the apprentices to arrest, and even the Roundheads didn't want to fire their muskets into the crowd. Then, older men began to join in the singing, and women and children, too. I really believe almost everyone in London would have been swept up in the excitement, had not, at that moment, several carriages rolled up in the marketplace. The Lord Mayor of London got out of one, and Oliver Cromwell was at his side, whispering in his ear.

The Lord Mayor waved his arms for silence; the singing stopped. "What is this gathering?" he cried. "Everyone, back to work at once, do you hear me? In this godly nation, December 25 is a working day!"

"We want Christmas!" several apprentices shouted back.

Cromwell whispered again in the Lord Mayor's ear. Nodding at Cromwell, he shouted, "If you disperse at once, there will be no arrests. I will forgive this terrible behavior. Tell your masters I said you were not to be punished. All will be as it was."

There was a great deal of murmuring. Cromwell nodded to the Roundhead soldiers, who brandished their muskets. The apprentices had no leader to rally them, to assure them that the soldiers most certainly would *not* fire in fear that the peaceful protest would then become a riot. So, first one by one and then in pairs and finally in dozens, the apprentices dispersed, walking unhappily back to their jobs, but warmed, I hoped, by the knowledge they had made their love for Christmas known.

Cromwell and the Lord Mayor remained in the marketplace. Cromwell talked; the Lord Mayor listened and nodded. Finally, the apprentices were all gone, and the marketplace activity went back to normal. The Lord Mayor got back into his gilded carriage. Just as he, too, was about to climb inside, Oliver Cromwell took one last long look around and saw me standing there. He thought about ordering some of the soldiers to arrest me, I'm sure, but didn't. Instead, he gazed at me thoughtfully before getting into the carriage and closing the door behind him. The horses pulled the carriage down the street and past me; Cromwell watched me from the window, his face wrinkled with concern. I knew he was wondering how it happened I was in the very place where the apprentices' Christmas protest took place. I did not believe in coincidence, and neither, I guessed, did Oliver Cromwell. He would think I had somehow organized that protest, even though I had not.

On the long walk back to Canterbury I had much to consider. One surprise was that the walk took a single day rather than three or four. I was regaining some of my power to travel faster than normal men and women; that was because the English civil war was finally winding down. Soon, once a peace treaty was signed, I would be able to go from one border of England to another in hours rather than weeks.

But there was something else to occupy my thoughts. The apprentice protest in London had been a spontaneous event, yet one that made a powerfully effective statement. The Lord Mayor and the Roundhead soldiers had been confounded by the sight of so many citizens insisting boldly, yet peacefully, that Christmas not be taken from them. Had Cromwell not been on hand to offer guidance, I believed, the Lord Mayor would not have acted decisively, and all of London might eventually have joined in sending the holiday message. What if there was another such protest, one that was better organized, one that had strong leadership? I had seen Oliver Cromwell in the marketplace afterward; I had looked into his face. He had been worried. If the people spoke in defense of Christmas again—even more of them, and louder—then perhaps Cromwell would not be able to ignore what they were telling him.

Some churches, usually only one or two in each community, bravely
sported holly and evergreen boughs on their doors, windowsills, and altars,
and there were services in them giving thanks to God for sending his son.
In almost every case, black-robed Puritans made a point of gathering
outside the churches and staring hard at the worshippers as they left.

CHAPTER

Sixteen

he power of the protest came from so many voices uniting in their demand to be heard," I told Elizabeth and Alan Hayes as we sat at the table in their cottage. "One person shouting out support for Christmas would certainly have been arrested. The same is true for five or ten or two dozen. But hundreds of men, women, and children standing shoulder to shoulder, peacefully but forcefully demanding the right to enjoy their beloved holiday, was too much for the Puritans. If the crowd had been better organized, I think they might be singing 'We Wish You a Merry Christmas' yet!"

It was mid-January in 1646. Sara, who had just celebrated her twelfth birthday a few days before, was up in her loft bed. Almost everyone in and around Canterbury was surely asleep at this late hour of perhaps ten o'clock, but my two friends and I had much to discuss. Ever since I had returned from London, I'd burned with excitement whenever I thought of the apprentices' Christmas protest. Rumors about it had swept through England, gladdening the hearts of everyone who still loved their special holiday and wanted to keep it as an important, joyous part of their lives. Elizabeth and Alan sat transfixed as I offered them my eyewitness account.

"It must have been amazing, Layla," Alan said, lighting his pipe and puffing happily. In those times, of course, no one realized how bad smoking was for your health. "I wish I could have seen it. Very soon I'll need to go to London myself and sign on with some company for a new voyage. But I doubt there will be more Christmas protests there until the holiday draws close again."

Elizabeth looked sad, and I certainly couldn't blame her. Families of sailors had to accept long, frequent absences of their loved ones, but that didn't make the separation any easier. I knew how it felt to miss your husband. I hadn't seen Nicholas now for more than twenty-five years. When I wasn't thinking about how to save Christmas in England, I often found myself remembering his warm smile or the softness of his wide white beard.

"Perhaps the next protests won't happen in London," Elizabeth mused. "Country folk don't want Christmas taken from them, either. Sometimes I believe the members of Parliament only think about what happens in London, because that is where they spend most of their time. If they really want to know what people want in England, they ought to get out into the rural villages for a change."

"Some sort of big demonstration out in the country supporting Christmas could be very effective," I agreed. "Why couldn't it happen, for instance, here in Canterbury?" I began imagining some grand gathering on High Street near the cathedral, with hundreds of participants, even a thousand, so many people singing songs and shouting out their love for the holiday that their example would inspire similar pro-Christmas demonstrations in every corner of England.

Alan, though, said he doubted it could happen.

"The livelihoods of so many people here depend on the goodwill of

Mayor Avery Sabine," he reminded me. "Sabine, for instance, owns all the mills that grind local farmers' corn. They can't sell the crop as it comes directly from their fields. If the farmers join a pro-Christmas protest and Sabine sees them, he can simply refuse to grind their corn, they'll have nothing to sell, and their families might starve."

"Think about those of us who work for Mrs. Sabine, Layla," Elizabeth added. "If she saw any of us, or any members of our families, involved in some Christmas protest that might embarrass her husband and hurt his prospects in politics, she would certainly dismiss us immediately."

"I think the Sabines couldn't retaliate if there were enough protestors," I argued. "The mayor's mills, for instance, can't make profits for him if they have no grain to grind up. If enough of the farmers were part of the protest, Sabine couldn't deny them the use of his mill because, at the same time, he'd be shutting down his own business. And Mrs. Sabine has no intention of ever doing her own laundry or sweeping her own floors."

Alan shook his head. "You make it sound easier than it would really be, I'm afraid. Just persuading enough people to participate in that sort of demonstration would take months, perhaps even years. As much as all of us love Christmas, we have to consider our responsibilities to our families, too. The risks for anyone involved would be great."

That night, up in the loft bed beside the sleeping Sara, I thought about what Alan had said. He was right, of course. I reminded myself that the risk for any of the working-class folk in and around Canterbury would be much greater than the danger to me. They would have to stay and face the consequences of their actions. I, on the other hand, would be leaving soon to rejoin my husband in America. I had to, and not only because I missed Nicholas so much.

All of us involved in the gift-giving mission had to be careful not to stay in one place for too long or if we did, like Arthur and Leonardo in London, to keep out of sight. Normal people aged quite rapidly. In

Europe and in England, living to sixty was rare. The passage of three or four years resulted in obvious signs of aging. Peoples' faces creased with wrinkles. Their hair rapidly turned gray. I had been in Canterbury since 1642, arriving as a thirty-five-year-old woman, about the same age then as Elizabeth Hayes was now. She was still lovely, but there were new lines around her eyes and streaks of white in her lustrous brown hair. Sometimes, now, she teased me a little, saying things like I must have a guardian angel who kept my hair from turning gray, and wasn't it wonderful how a few lucky women like me never seemed to get wrinkles around their eyes and mouths? In another year, perhaps, certainly in two or three, it would be obvious that I was not growing any older. Though I knew there was nothing sinister in this or my other special powers, that view would not be shared by the Puritan clergy or a superstitious public. Arrest and burning at the stake for being a witch would not be out of the question. So I would have to leave soon, whether Christmas in England was saved or not.

In the spring of 1646, Alan Hayes made several short trips to London, talking to various captains about their upcoming voyages and trying to choose which ship's crew to join. He didn't want to be away from his family for two or three years on some around-the-world adventure; instead, Alan hoped to find a berth on a ship making a direct voyage from some British port across the ocean to America, taking on tobacco or some other cargo, and then coming straight back to England.

"Six months is as long as I want to be gone from now on," he told us. "My little girl is growing up, and I've missed too much of her life already. You're going to be thirteen, Sara, and for all I know I'll come back from my next voyage to find you've married a young man and started a family of your own."

Sara squirmed and made an awful face. "I don't want to marry anyone," she insisted. "All Sophia ever talks about now is what rich man might become her husband. It's boring!" I sympathized with Sara, but I also knew what Alan meant. Being with Sara had helped me understand how precious every parent should find each day of a child's life. Already, my darling girl no longer played with dolls. She was becoming a beauty. At church on Sunday, some of the boys couldn't stop staring at her. As yet, she didn't notice, but someday soon she might. At least up in the loft at night she still whispered to me about her wish to travel and see all the great cities in the world. I would tell her to keep her dreams and make them come true, just as my Aunt Lodi had once encouraged me.

When he returned from London, Alan also brought us up to date on the latest news. For anyone who loved Christmas, it wasn't good. By June, the civil war was officially over. Commanders of the royal army had signed peace treaties, and King Charles had surrendered—to the Scots, not the Roundheads. While in their custody, he was rumored to spend his days secretly communicating with leaders in Ireland and France, trying to convince them to send armies and restore him to his throne. Queen Henrietta was in Europe trying to do the same thing; the two oldest princes, Charles and James, were with their mother.

In London, Alan reported, Parliament seemed divided on what to do next. Some wanted to settle with the king on almost any terms, as soon as the Scots could be persuaded to hand him over. These members were mostly businessmen who had made great profits during the war and now hoped to have a royal blessing to do the same in times of peace. Oliver Cromwell led a faction that wanted the king to remain on his throne, but only if he would agree to accept Parliament as a full partner. Then there was another group called the levelers—they wanted to abolish the crown and, indeed, every form of social class. All who lived in England must be equals, they insisted.

Many leaders in Parliament wanted the Roundhead army to be disbanded. Now that the king was defeated and the English government no longer planned to meddle in Europe, there was no need for a standing army, they argued. Cromwell loudly disagreed; the army, he insisted, was necessary because the king's supporters might, at any time, attack with new troops. It was also true, although Cromwell didn't say it, that so long as the Roundhead army remained intact, he, as its chosen leader, was the most powerful man in England. Though he never threatened it, no one could doubt that if Parliament didn't do what Cromwell wanted, he could muster the army and take over the country. Some people even believed Cromwell eventually intended to make himself the new king.

So the last months of 1646 were nervous times, because no one could be quite sure what was going to happen next. Would Charles again be England's king? Would Queen Henrietta be successful recruiting invaders from Europe to sweep Parliament out of power? And, of course, everyone wondered about Christmas. Charles had always supported the holiday—I knew this from our single conversation—but the Puritans would never let him remain on the throne without extracting certain concessions, one of which would surely be his support in abolishing Christmas celebrations. It may seem to some of you now that one holiday would count very little in the minds of working people, compared to who would rule their country. But you must remember how hard these times were for the poor, and how December 25 was really the only day when they could forget their troubles and deprivations by celebrating the birth of Jesus. The more it seemed obvious they would lose their single real holiday, the more precious it became to them.

Alan Hayes left on a voyage to America in September 1646, promising his wife and daughter he would return to them no later than spring. At the same time, I began mentioning to Elizabeth and Sara that I might soon be leaving, too, and my departure would be permanent. I couldn't tell them I had to go before they discovered I wasn't aging, of course. I told them that it was soon going to be time for me to join my own husband, though I loved my Canterbury "family" dearly.

"We can't be selfish about Auntie Layla," Elizabeth reminded her daughter; Sara had burst into tears at the thought of my going away.

"She wants to be with her husband just as you and I want to be with your father. Do you know for certain when you will leave, Layla?"

"Probably within another year," I replied. "It will take some time to book passage on a ship, and, of course, I don't want to cross the ocean during the cold storms of winter."

"You are welcome in our home for as long as you want to stay," Elizabeth reminded me. "At least we'll have you with us for one more Christmas."

That was another reason I didn't plan to leave right away. With the Puritans and Roundheads in full control, Blue Richard Culmer wasn't constantly on the track of those he accused of being royalist spies. He spent most of his time now in London, waiting, perhaps, for orders to persuade reluctant members of Parliament to do whatever it was Cromwell and the Puritans wanted. I wasn't in quite as much danger of discovery and arrest if I tried to organize one last, great Christmas protest in Canterbury. But I had to be certain that the time was just right.

In 1645, Parliament had essentially banned Christmas, but many celebrated it that year anyway, usually quietly in their homes, and they had not been arrested or otherwise persecuted. People had begun to hope that Parliament, having passed its Puritan-inspired law against the holiday, might now be content after making that gesture to let each English citizen decide whether or not to completely comply. As long as there wasn't any *public* celebration, some believed, perhaps the Puritans really didn't care who enjoyed a goose dinner or some family carol-singing on December 25. I knew that wasn't the case—the Puritans were just distracted with setting up a whole new system of English government. When they had completed that task, they'd turn their attention to Christmas again, because Oliver Cromwell was their leader, and Cromwell never left anything uncompleted. Because people were so uncertain how to celebrate it, and what might happen to them if they did, I realized it would do no good yet to organize a protest supporting the full enjoyment of the holiday. In a few more months, when the unsettled state of English government was resolved, then we would all know for certain what the fate of Christmas would be. Until then, no one would be willing to do too much.

So Christmas 1646 was a very curious day throughout England. Some churches, usually only one or two in each community, bravely sported holly and evergreen boughs on their doors, windowsills, and altars, and there were services in them giving thanks to God for sending his son. In almost every case, black-robed Puritans made a point of gathering outside the churches and staring hard at the worshippers as they left. This was rather unpleasant, but there were no physical attacks, just shouted threats of God's stern judgment if they didn't renounce the celebration of a "pagan" holiday. Most people couldn't go to church, anyway, because all the shops were open and lots of men and women had to work. A few shopkeepers did ostentatiously keep their doors bolted and their windows shuttered, and, afterward they received no further trade from Puritan customers. Because most of the major landowners now were either Puritans or defeated royalists who wanted to get back in the government's good graces, no wealthy families encouraged or accepted Christmas Day visits by groups of townspeople to their homes. No waits strolled singing through the streets, but there weren't any protest marches, either, even in London. Out in public, the day was subdued.

In private homes, of course, it was often different. With the toy factory in London shut down, I wondered if Arthur, Leonardo, or any of the other companions were making Christmas visits to children in England. I had not heard from them since they left for Germany the year before. This did not particularly worry me. There was no official mail service, so getting a letter to me in Canterbury from Nuremberg would have been difficult. If there was something they thought I needed to know, they would find a way to bring me word.

On the morning of December 25, Elizabeth and Sara found candy canes on their pillows. Leonardo had sent along a whole boxful, and it

was only right to share the bright, tasty treats with my friends, though
there were many dozens left over. We went to the Sabine house, Elizabeth and I to work, Sara to visit upstairs with Sophia. She told us later
that Sophia's gossip once again concerned her father: Avery Sabine had
hopes that if he could exhibit one last year of firm control over Canterbury he might be appointed to some important government office.

"Then, Sophia says, she and her parents will move to London,"
Sara reported as we walked slowly home afterward. "She told me not
to worry, though, because she will surely marry some nobleman soon
after that, and then I will be called to London as her lady-in-waiting."
Elizabeth and I sighed. Sophia was a very pretty girl, and a rich one,
too. If she did move to London, she wouldn't lack for suitors, and her
ambitious parents would be eager to make a good social match as
quickly as possible.

"And will you go to London if Sophia asks you?" Elizabeth asked
carefully, trying and failing to keep concern out of her voice.

"I want to see London, but I don't want to be anyone's servant,"
Sara replied. "When I tell Sophia that, she just laughs."

That Christmas night, Elizabeth and Sara and I dined on vegetables
and fruit, but not goose. Alan was still away on his voyage, and his
wages for the trip would be paid after his ship returned to England.
Elizabeth and I had our earnings from Margaret Sabine, but lately
prices had increased on every kind of food, and we simply could not
afford goose that year. It made little difference, though. The three of
us heartily enjoyed the food we did have, and after dinner we sat in
front of the fire and sang carols. If Oliver Cromwell doubted that the
spirit of Christmas mattered less to those celebrating it than fine food
and gifts, he could have learned better by watching us that night. After
we had sung every carol we knew, some of them twice or three times,
Sara asked me about the wonderful candy canes, and I explained to her
that a special friend of mine had made them. When she tried to learn
more about this mysterious friend, I changed the subject, telling her

about the waits who used to walk the streets of London and about the great churches I had seen where thousands gathered to praise God and his son on Christmas Day.

I meant, very soon afterward, to make my plans to go, only waiting until Alan Hayes arrived home in the spring so Elizabeth and Sara would not be left on their own. I thought about how wonderful it would feel to be with Nicholas again and tried very hard not to imagine the empty place that would be left in my heart without Sara. So long as the Puritans allowed people to at least quietly celebrate Christmas in their own homes, I believed, I might as well leave. Even the smallest spark of Christmas spirit and joy was better than none. Somewhere, someday, enough people in England would demand their full, wonderful holiday again, and it would be restored. Until then, I reasoned, my place was with my husband, fulfilling our gift-giving mission in lands where Christmas was still completely welcome.

Alan's return home was delayed until late May, which still left me plenty of time to book passage to the New World and be with my husband before the onset of winter. But the news Alan brought with him from London convinced me I could not leave England after all.

Alan and I were the first to arrive, but soon afterward
we saw flickers of small lanterns being carried by people
making their way up the hill toward the barn.

Seventeen

he first months of 1647 were difficult for the Puritan-controlled Parliament. The war was over, and the king was defeated. But victory did not guarantee the love and loyalty of the common people. Many working-class English men and women, perhaps even a majority, had liked it better when the king was on his throne. They were very suspicious of the Puritans and of Parliament. Even though its members were supposedly voted into office at regular intervals by the taxpayers, this Parliament had been in session since 1640 without benefit of reelection. They kept extending their own current terms without requesting public approval. Many called it the Long Parliament, and they didn't intend the nickname as a compliment.

Parliament made an agreement with the Scots for the return of King Charles. In exchange for several large payments, the Scottish leaders handed the king over to England, where he remained a prisoner while rebel leaders negotiated with him. If Charles agreed to Parliament's terms, there was still the chance he would regain his throne. If not, he faced a life in prison and perhaps even execution. But as soon as Charles was in Parliament's custody, a stunning thing happened. As the defeated king's carriage proceeded south to the estate where he would be kept captive, the common folk of England lined the road and cheered him as he passed. This made the leaders of Parliament *very* nervous—what if there was a popular uprising to restore the king? Parliament had just voted to stop raising money to pay the army, so the Roundhead soldiers might very well refuse to fight anymore.

"Parliament feels it must do something to prove it is in complete control of England," Alan reported after his arrival home in Canterbury. "I believe one of its members, Lord Manchester, called it 'Bringing the rabble to heel.' Rumor has it there will be a new, harsher law against Christmas, because, so far, so many people have ignored the ruling of two years ago that it should no longer be celebrated."

"What can Parliament really do if people want to sing carols or feast in honor of Jesus' birth, so long as we do this in our own homes?" Elizabeth wanted to know. "They can't punish everyone who does. Under the laws of this country, no one is supposed to tell us what we may or may not do within the walls of our own homes, so long as we are not plotting treason."

"No," Alan said thoughtfully, "but they can try—and they might. I'm sorry to say, my love, that those presently in power seem to define 'treason' as any beliefs that do not exactly match their own. Those they cannot persuade, they are quite willing to intimidate. Blue Richard Culmer is stalking through the streets of London once more, followed by his gang of nasty-looking thugs. Parliament meets again during the first week in June. That, I expect, is when we'll have more laws about Christmas. It is on that issue—whether or not it is sinful to celebrate the birth of Christ on December 25—that the Puritans intend to make their stand and to prove once and for all that they can force their beliefs on the rest of us."

Sadly, Alan was right. In early June, Parliament announced again that celebrating Christmas—or Easter, for that matter—was against the law. Violators would be punished. There was no explanation of *how* they would be punished. That was left to the public's imagination. But there was no flexibility in this edict. Christmas could not be celebrated publicly *or* privately. No church services, no carol singing, no gifts, no feasts. Any of these activities would be cause for arrest. Though Parliament still couldn't find money to pay its army, it did set aside funds to pay for a militia, or Trained Band, in each county. These men would enforce the new no-Christmas law.

As a gesture to the poor working class who were losing their beloved holiday, Parliament added that, from now on, one Tuesday of each month would be made into a nonreligious holiday when no one would be required to go to their jobs. This only proved Parliament had no real understanding of what Christmas truly meant; the wonderful, traditional celebration of December 25 had nothing to do with not having to go to work, and everything to do with giving joyful thanks to God for the gift of his son.

After the new, stern law was announced, Parliament was concerned by the negative public reaction. I, on the other hand, was thrilled. The time had finally come. With the right planning, it might just be possible to rouse the public spirit and save Christmas in England after all.

I began cautiously in mid-June, right after news of Parliament's edict reached Canterbury. I asked Alan and Elizabeth to quietly talk with their friends and sound out whether any of them might be willing to risk reprisal by joining in a public protest on behalf of Christmas. I realized, of course, that for the greatest impact the demonstration should take place on December 25 itself, but six months would be barely enough time to recruit sufficient participants.

"You must be aware, Layla, that every town in England is riddled with spies for the Puritans," Alan warned. "Here in Canterbury, that is especially true. Mayor Sabine must have informers all over. If the wrong person learns that you are attempting to organize a Christmas protest, something terrible might happen to you."

I was willing to accept the risk. I had now been living in Canterbury for five years. I knew that most of its people were good-hearted, hardworking men and women who loved Christmas and resented being told they could no longer have it. Avery Sabine's spies might be numerous, but they were mostly obvious, too, in their Puritan black and with their disdainful, superior expressions.

It would be enough, at first, to suggest to people that there might be some way to make it clear to Mayor Sabine and to Parliament that Canterbury and its surrounding towns would have Christmas whether the law allowed it or not. There need be no immediate mention of a demonstration on Christmas Day. Otherwise, people might decide to march before we had recruited a large enough number to defy reprisals—a group of fifty might all be arrested, but there was no jail in Canterbury or anywhere else in England that could hold a thousand. Public indignation was already widespread, but it would grow even more intense when the holiday was imminent.

And so Alan and Elizabeth began making discreet inquiries, and I did the same. At work in the Sabine house, I was particularly careful since I knew at least some of the employees there had to be informers. Only to Janie and Melinda did I carefully mention the possibility of public action on behalf of Christmas, and they both told me they would be willing, even eager, to participate. Shopping for Sunday dinner in the Canterbury marketplace, I made the same suggestion to several people I saw there on a regular basis. A few replied that they had no desire to incur Puritan wrath, and I could not blame them for that. But most liked the idea, and one or two even mentioned the Apprentice Protest of 1645 in London, which pleased me. If that event was still in public memory, think how effective a larger, better organized demonstration might be!

Not surprisingly, I found strong, if secret, support among non-

Puritan church leaders, who were being allowed to conduct services so long as they did not violate the new Parliamentary strictures. In particular there was Father Joel, a staunch Catholic who had been reduced to holding Sunday services in a barn. Because his responsibility was to protect his small congregation's beliefs in general, he told me, he would not personally be part of any Christmas protest I planned. But he could, at least, offer me the use of the barn. Large, clean, and well away from view several miles outside the walls of Canterbury, it stood atop a sprawling hill. No one could approach closer than two hundred yards in any direction, Father Joel said, without being visible, so if I held meetings there I could post lookouts and not have to worry about the area's Puritan-funded Trained Band sneaking up to arrest us.

By late September, I felt we had enough supporters to call a meeting at the barn, where we could discuss more specific plans for a demonstration. Parliament's attention, for the moment, was on issues other than Christmas—the king was being stubborn during negotiations, refusing to give up most of his divine right powers—but December 25 was now just three months away, and more people were beginning to realize that this year Christmas really *was* being taken away from them for good, unless they did something to prevent it. We now had to begin our work in earnest.

"How many people do you expect to come to this meeting?" Elizabeth asked, keeping her voice very soft. It was late at night and Sara had long been in bed, but we still didn't want her to overhear if she happened to be awake. "Six? A dozen? More?"

"I would think twenty or even thirty," I said. "All of them are known and trusted by you, Alan, or me. There won't be any strangers there."

"Well, there will be a few you haven't met, Layla," Alan corrected. "I've made the rounds of the surrounding farms and found a few good fellows who ought to be great additions to our group. We've done what we can to emphasize to everyone that we must keep our effort completely secret. I believe they understand. We all certainly remember Blue Richard Culmer's smashing of the stained-glass windows of the cathedral. No one doubts how severely we'll be treated by the Puritans if they find us out, but we all are willing to take that chance."

"You've made it clear to them that there will be no violence on our part?" I asked. "Everyone understands that whatever we do, it will be peaceful?"

"Christmas is dedicated to the glory of the Prince of Peace," Alan said solemnly. "It would dishonor him if we raised a hand against anyone, even those who might raise their hands against us."

The night of September 30 was unseasonably chilly. A brisk wind blew in from the north and recent rainstorms had left the ground damp. Leaving Elizabeth home with Sara—who indignantly demanded to know why her father and auntie were off somewhere after dark and was told that some friends needed help planning a party—Alan and I walked about two miles to the barn, which was to the north of Canterbury, past the river and across rolling fields of recently harvested wheat. The scent of freshly cut grain carried quite pleasantly on the cold air. We pulled our cloaks about us and didn't need to light our lantern for a while, since the moon was full and the road was wide. A few riders passed us, including members of the Trained Band, but no one stopped us to ask where we were going. The war was over, and, though Alan thought we were walking at a very good pace, I could have made it all the way from Canterbury to London in the thirty minutes it took us to get from the cottage to the barn. But I made certain to match his much slower, normal pace.

The barn was on the property of a farmer named Stone, a devout Catholic who'd had to stop practicing his faith openly, but who allowed Father Joel to hold Sunday services there for the Stone family and other Catholics. Accordingly, it was quite clean inside, with fresh straw strewn across the dirt floor and a thick bale of hay off to one side. I guessed that, on Sundays, Father Joel used that hay bale for an altar.

Alan and I were the first to arrive, but soon afterward we saw flickers of small lanterns being carried by people making their way up the hill toward the barn. Father Joel had been right—it was easy to see anyone coming from any direction. Many of the new arrivals were farmers, but to my surprise I also recognized some town craftsmen and a few shop owners. While I had expected twenty people, perhaps thirty at the most, almost sixty eventually arrived.

"I hope you don't mind, Layla," my friend Melinda from the Sabine house whispered to me. "It's just that my two chums Katie and Kenneth love Christmas so much, and I knew they would want to come."

"Do you trust them to keep our secret?" I asked, and when Melinda nodded, I greeted both her companions, who assured me they wanted to be part of any effort to save Christmas in England. And, like Melinda, it was obvious some of the other people Alan and Elizabeth and I invited had decided to recruit some of their Christmas-loving friends, too. Alan was worried because there were so many arrivals he didn't know personally, but I took it as a good sign. People cared enough about Christmas to come out to a secret meeting on a cold fall night!

Alan called the meeting to order, first suggesting that only a few lanterns remain lit: "We don't want the Trained Band to receive a report that a local barn is on fire!" he joked. "Let me welcome you all, and thank you for coming. I'll begin by emphasizing things I hope you already know. First, we must keep our activities secret. None of us want a visit from Blue Richard Culmer. Second, our purpose is to help save our beloved Christmas holiday by planning some activity, a protest, if you will, that will be so impressive in style and message that all the way back in London Parliament will realize it cannot take Christmas from us. Third, there is to be no violence of any sort. No matter what might be done to us, we will not raise our hands against anyone else. Are all here agreed?"

There were murmurs of assent. Then Alan introduced me as "Layla, aunt of my beloved daughter and someone who has lived here among us for five years now. Though we may not have any official leader, I would suggest that she is the beating heart of this body. No one I have ever met loves Christmas more than Layla or understands better how the holiday can reflect the best in human spirit."

Then I talked for a little while, mostly about the Apprentice Protest in London, how brave it was, and how effective. I was not used to speaking to an audience and found it somewhat uncomfortable. My voice shook a little as I told about the look on Oliver Cromwell's face as he realized there was stronger opposition to the abolition of Christmas than he and his Puritan supporters had ever imagined. I pointed out that the demonstrators had been easily dispersed because they had no real plan. If they had remained organized, no one could have made them stop protesting until they themselves decided they'd done enough.

"If we do something similar here, it will only be effective if we act as one," I pointed out. "Everyone must be agreed beforehand that we will stand together and not waver in any way. Mayor Sabine will certainly order us to go home, and he will threaten us with prison or even the possibility of direct musket-fire from the Trained Band. But if there are enough of us, nonviolent but defiant, all he can use against us are words. The mayor is not a stupid man. If a peaceful Christmas demonstration is marred by bloodshed caused by the Puritans, the whole country might well rise up against them, and Sabine can't risk that."

"You say we need a thousand people involved, maybe more," a gap-toothed farmer said. "How are we supposed to find them?"

"In the same quiet way the first few invited here tonight took it upon themselves to invite others," I replied. "All of you have friends you trust, and those friends will have friends, and so on. An abiding love of Christmas, and a determination not to lose that wonderful holiday, are the only qualifications necessary. Of course, the more people who know, the greater the danger that someone will be a spy for the mayor. Well, that's a risk we must take." As I spoke, I worried I wasn't effectively communicating the urgency of our task, and what I was asked next proved me right.

"Do we really need to do this?" an elderly woman wanted to know. "I miss singing carols in the streets, but last Christmas my family still enjoyed roast goose. We gave each other little gifts, and no one came to arrest us."

"The laws are stricter this year," Alan pointed out. "Blue Richard and his gang are promising that, on December 25, they'll break into homes where Christmas is being celebrated and drag everyone there off to jail. They might miss your home this time, but sooner or later it will be your turn. We're not trying to save Christmas just in 1647. We're trying to preserve it for the future. If we don't act now, people will gradually decide that the Puritans really can take Christmas away, and if enough of them eventually accept this awful new law, then Christmas *will* be gone forever."

"And there's even more danger to Christmas than that," said another man, and my eyes widened and my heart leaped, because his face and voice were so familiar. Arthur, my friend of more than one thousand years, had come back to England!

"Christmas has been gone from Scotland for sixty-four years, taken from the people by Scottish Parliament then and never restored since," Arthur said, grinning as he looked toward me and saw I'd recognized him. "At first, the people there thought it would only be a matter of a year or two before their Puritan leaders came to their senses and let everyone choose whether or not to celebrate the holiday, but it never happened. Across the ocean in their American colonies, the Puritans have banned Christmas for more than twenty-five years. Now, if they succeed in banning Christmas in England, why, they may try the same thing in other countries until, finally, a December 25 will come where no one in the world will dare sing a carol or give a small gift in honor of the birth of Jesus. But we're gathered here tonight. Let this be the moment when we decide this cannot, will not, happen. Let this be the moment when we agree that, no matter what the risk, we join together and take the first step to save Christmas forever."

I understood something then, listening to Arthur. Because we know them so well, we often take our family or friends for granted. We don't appreciate them as much as they deserve. Now, after spending over a thousand years in Arthur's company, I finally realized the extent of his ability to persuade people to act. Perhaps he had only been a war chief and never a magical king, but he was a great leader. He could put words together in a speech to inspire followers in a way I never could. When I talked about the Apprentice Protest, I made the people in the barn think about the possibility of a single demonstration in local streets. Arthur talked about saving Christmas for the whole world, and suddenly everyone understood all that was really at stake. It wasn't just the holiday. It was the right of people to believe as they chose, rather than being told what they could and could not believe. By protecting Christmas, we would even be protecting the rights of those who *didn't* want to celebrate it.

Everyone cheered, and some began chanting, "This is the moment!" until Arthur finally raised his hands and asked them to stop "because we don't need the sound of our voices reaching the mayor's ears just yet!" But now there was a sense of excitement, of exhilaration, that hadn't been there before. Arthur suggested that everyone think about how to recruit more supporters and that we meet back at the barn in two weeks. There was a roar of approval, and people slapped one another on the back and chattered happily as they began making their way home through the chilly, dark night.

Arthur came over and hugged me. I introduced him to Alan as "a dear old friend of mine and my husband's. I thought, though, he was living in Germany."

The two men shook hands, and Arthur said, "I'd heard such fine things about the countryside around Canterbury that I just had to come see for myself. I'm staying with a farm family, helping out with the chores, and when one of them told me about this meeting tonight I just thought I'd come with him, since I love Christmas so much. Layla, perhaps we can meet tomorrow evening and catch up with each other. I just had a letter from your husband Nicholas in America, and I'm sure you'll want to read it."

Alan invited Arthur to join us tomorrow for dinner and gave him directions to the cottage. I hugged Arthur a second time, and then walked home with Alan feeling completely elated. *This is going to happen,* I thought to myself. *Christmas is really going to be saved.*

Arthur distributed candy canes and explained how they were to
be used. When one of us needed to meet with everyone else,
he or she would leave a small drawing of a candy cane stuffed
in a crevice of the big tree outside the Hayes cottage.

Eighteen

 ara didn't like strangers coming into her home. When Arthur arrived for dinner, she nodded stiffly in his direction, then resisted all his efforts to coax her into conversation. But Alan and Elizabeth warmed to my old friend quickly, so despite Sara's shyness—which, I informed her afterward, bordered on rudeness—we shared a happy meal and pleasant talk. Arthur told about himself—that he was a native of England who'd been living in London, then moved abroad for a bit "because of political and religious discomfort" before returning to his homeland, since he missed it so much. By apparently telling everything, he was able to conceal his deepest secrets, specifically how he was about eleven hundred years old and an important member of Father Christmas's gift-giving companions. Once again, I marveled at his amazing ability to draw people to him. After an hour of his company, I could tell Elizabeth and Alan would have followed Arthur anywhere. Only Sara didn't seem capti-

vated by him. As soon as dinner was over, she excused herself and
climbed up to the loft.

"I don't think your young friend likes me," Arthur commented
when the dishes were cleared away and he and I had gone outside to
walk a bit and talk. "Did I say or do something to offend her?"

"That's just Sara's way," I replied. "She is bashful around those she
doesn't know very well, but she must learn to be friendly and gracious
even when she feels uncomfortable. I'll speak to her about it. Now,
last night you mentioned a letter from my husband. Did you bring it
with you?"

"Of course," Arthur said, reaching into a pocket and handing me
several pages of creased, well-worn paper. "After Leonardo and I arrived in Nuremberg I wrote to Nicholas right away, telling him we'd
closed the London toy factory, at least for a while. I *didn't* tell him
you'd remained behind in Canterbury. Perhaps you wrote him about
that yourself? You didn't, did you? Well, that, of course, is your decision. Anyway, it must have taken him a long time to receive my letter,
and it certainly took months for his reply to reach me. Here it is; I'll
just wander around a bit while you read."

Arthur disappeared over a small knoll, and I settled down in the
fading fall grass with Nicholas's letter. Even his handwriting, so grand
and flowing, made me miss him. It had been so many years since we
had been together! Well, we wouldn't be apart much longer.

The first part of the letter described his life with Felix in the New
World. They were now living in the Dutch colony of New Amster-
dam, and very much enjoying the holiday customs there. Dutch children expected visits from St. Nicholas on December 6, and there were
enough of them to keep Nicholas and Felix quite busy making and
delivering toys on time. But the British colonies were still Puritan-
dominated, and Father Christmas was not welcome in them—an ex-
tension, Nicholas noted, of the Christmas troubles in England.

"Though I'm sorry you felt the London toy factory must be closed, I cer-

tainly understand and agree with that decision," he wrote. *"What a terrible thing it is when a few close-minded people force their own prejudices on everyone else. But I hope that, like me, all of you continue to believe in the overall goodness of human nature. Bad times do not last forever. Because the vast majority of the English people want Christmas, I know that they will, somehow, get it back again."*

Then, to my amazement, my husband addressed me directly. He had not done this in his previous letters. After more than twelve centuries of marriage, we did not need to constantly reassure each other of our love. But, separated from his wife by a vast ocean, Nicholas still instinctively understood that just now I did need some extra words from him.

"Layla, none of Arthur's recent letters have made much specific mention of you," Nicholas wrote. *"I don't know for certain, but I suspect that you are planning, in some way, to challenge the English Parliament's outlawing of Christmas. I won't insult you by pointing out the dangers of such action. You will have considered them for yourself. I will only remind you that whatever you do, you have my complete support. We are now, as we have always been, equal partners. Though I can't share these difficult times with you in person, I am always with you in your heart. Do whatever you believe is right, and then board a ship and come across the ocean to me, so I can put my arms around you again after so many years."*

I suppose I sat there for a half hour or more, tears dripping down my cheeks onto the grass, before Arthur returned. He sat down beside me and patted my shoulder.

"I miss my husband so much," I murmured. My throat felt thick, and my eyes burned from the salty tears.

"Of course you do," Arthur said. "You know, Layla, we have received these wonderful gifts—apparently endless life, the ability to travel at amazing speeds, the opportunity to spread joy and comfort to children through our holiday mission. But they come with a price, as all worthwhile things do. You can no more let the Puritans' banning of

Christmas go unchallenged than you can resist breathing. That's why I came back to England. I knew you would be planning something, and now the moment draws close. I'll help in any way I can and, afterward, I'll take you to the dock and smile as you board a boat that will take you across the ocean to your husband."

"Thank you," I gulped. Then I resolutely wiped my eyes, cleared my throat, put Nicholas's letter in the pocket of my cloak, and got to my feet. "All right, Arthur," I said. "I've had my weepy moment, and that is the end of that. Now, we have a Christmas Day protest to plan."

And we did. Back in the Hayes cottage, gathered with Alan and Elizabeth around the table while Sara sulked up in her loft, Arthur and I discussed what might happen, and where. His experience as a war chief came in handy, because he could guess how the Canterbury authorities and Trained Band would react.

"If we have two thousand protestors, and I believe we will, we can't have them all trying to enter the city through the same gate," Arthur warned. "The guards will see them coming—the town is in a valley, after all—and simply shut the gate tight. The protest won't be as effective if Mayor Sabine and his holiday-hating cronies stroll the streets while the demonstrators are held outside the city walls. There are six gates in all. We'll need to have the protestors divided into six groups, each entering the city at the same time through a different gate. That way, even if one or two of the gates are closed to prevent some of us from entering, the others will still get inside the walls."

"What about once we all are inside?" Elizabeth wanted to know. "If we're in six different parts of the city, won't that lessen the impact of having thousands of people involved?"

"We should all meet in one central place," Alan said. "And, by the way, I still haven't said you can march, my darling. It will be quite dangerous. The Trained Band might attack. It would be better for you to stay home with Sara."

Elizabeth looked at her husband, and then said, in tones made all the more frigid by their apparent blandness, "I'm afraid I don't require your permission. Do you intend to insult me by implying I don't love Christmas as much as you do, or that only men have the right to take risks for the sake of a good cause?"

"You know it's not that," Alan sputtered. "But if things turn ugly, Sara must have a parent left to raise her."

"Then *you* stay home," Elizabeth said briskly. "Now, Layla, what time of day do you think would be right for the protestors to enter the city?"

For more than a month, we continued to plan. There were so many little things to consider, and a few big ones, too. As our numbers gradually swelled, it was no longer possible for everyone to gather at the barn for nighttime meetings. Arthur suggested that we appoint captains, who would come to the meetings and then, in their turn, inform everyone else of what had been discussed and decided.

"These captains should be the people we know best and trust most," he added. "They will understand the need for secrecy. We need to establish some sort of password for them, or some secret sign, so we can identify ourselves to one another without anyone else knowing."

I had an idea for that. The box of Leonardo's lovely striped candy canes was still beside the bed Sara and I shared in the loft. I brought it down. There were several dozen canes left.

"No one else would have these," I suggested. "They will provide perfect identification, and Mayor Sabine and his men surely won't consider candy to be something suspicious."

"They're festive, too," Elizabeth agreed. "I think they're just perfect."

That night, about thirty of us met back at the barn. It was much colder now, and everyone wore heavy cloaks. Arthur distributed the candy canes—no one had ever seen anything quite like them before—and explained how they were to be used. When one of us needed to meet with everyone else, he or she would leave a small drawing of a candy cane stuffed in a crevice of the big tree outside the Hayes cottage. Arthur or I would check for such messages every day, and, if we found one, we would come to the barn after dark.

"Don't ask for a meeting unless you really need one," Arthur added. "The more often we gather, no matter how careful we are, the greater the chance we'll be noticed by the Puritans. Also, whenever we meet, hold out your candy cane as a sign everything is safe. If, for some reason, you think you've been followed or there is some other sort of danger, hold out your empty hands, and that will be a sign to the rest of us."

Everyone remarked at the candy canes, about their color and unique shape. A few wanted to taste the candy, but I reminded them that if they ate their secret symbols, they would no longer have them to use.

"After we've marched on Christmas Day, we can have the pleasure of eating this candy," I said. "It will taste very good, I promise." Though Arthur still was much better than me when it came to addressing the group, I was gradually becoming more comfortable in speaking to them.

Arthur and I checked the tree for messages each day, and a few days later we did find a candy cane sketch. That night, up in the barn and after showing us his candy cane, as we showed him ours, a Canterbury bootmaker named Peter told us he thought he'd mentioned the protest to the wrong person.

"He's been coming to my shop for years and has always been very friendly, and sometime we talked a little about how sad it was that Christmas can no longer be celebrated," Peter said. "So this past week I told him there might be some sort of demonstration in favor of the holiday on Christmas Day and would he be interested in participating? He said he might, but then he asked so many other questions, like who exactly was *organizing* everything, that I suddenly had the feeling he was going to run to Mayor Sabine with whatever he could find out."

"You were right to tell us," Arthur said. "I know it is inevitable that some rumors about what we're doing will reach the wrong people. But we can't let any outsiders learn too much. Now, you didn't tell this man anything else? Very good. I expect he'll be back in your shop tomorrow asking more questions. Just tell him that you had misunderstood; there's no demonstration planned at all, and sorry for the confusion. Then be very careful that you're not followed by any of the mayor's spies. They ought to be easy to spot, with their black cloaks."

I still could not really understand why anyone would be against Christmas. This can happen sometimes, when we believe in something so completely that we lose the ability to appreciate someone else's right to a different opinion. Many Puritans sincerely believed God and Jesus were being dishonored by holiday celebrations. Their arguments—that the date of December 25 was based on pagan rituals, that too many people used Christmas as an excuse to get drunk or otherwise act badly—weren't entirely wrong. In choosing to fight for Christmas, I could not, or at least should not, disregard inconvenient facts. But to me and, I believed, to almost everyone else in England, the positive things about Christmas—thanksgiving for Jesus, gifts and food to remind men, women, and children that even hard lives could include moments of joy—far outweighed the problems. How could Puritan-controlled Parliament even consider taking the holiday away from people who drew from it almost the only joy they experienced throughout the whole year?

My own resolve to save Christmas was reinforced one day in early December, when several of Margaret Sabine's servants missed work because of illness and I had to help Janie back in the washing shed. The work there, filling and lugging buckets of water, or wringing heavy sheets and curtains by hand, was still hot and exhausting. I couldn't help but notice Janie's already-exhausted face had gained many more lines and creases in the five years since I'd met her. She was a tired, aging woman who told me repeatedly that she looked forward to Christmas all year long. How thrilled she had been when I invited her to the first barn meeting to discuss the Christmas Day protest, and then I had delighted her further by presenting her with a candy cane and making her one of our group's captains. I really didn't do this because I felt Janie had a shrewd mind and could help us plan. Rather, I just wanted to let her feel important for once in her life, which had mostly been spent doing menial work for Margaret Sabine. It was, in a sense, self-indulgence on my part, but I didn't regret it for a moment.

Now, as I carried buckets of water over to the rinsing tub where Janie was twisting pillowcases to wring water out of them, I saw she was smiling.

"Why, are you enjoying your work today, Janie?" I asked as I poured water into the tub.

"You know why I'm smiling, Layla," she replied, lowering her voice so no one could overhear. "Our big day is coming, and I'm quite looking forward to it!"

I dropped down beside her as she squatted by the side of the tub. "I'm glad you are, Janie, but please promise me that, on Christmas Day, you'll be very careful. Even though I doubt it will happen, Mayor Sabine or his wife might see you taking part in the demonstration, and then you could lose this job. There will be no disgrace if you decide to hang back behind most of the marchers, so there will be less chance you'll be identified."

"But I won't mind being seen!" Janie said proudly. "All my life, I've taken orders, and I've tried to do good work in return for my wages. But this will be a moment when I can speak up for something I believe in, and if it costs me my job I'll just have to find another one, won't I? Christmas is so wonderful, Layla, and don't make any mistake about it. I know that even though Mr. Arthur is getting most of the attention, you're the one who must have really thought of this, because you're so smart and so brave, like."

All of us enjoy compliments, and I am no exception. Janie's words warmed me more than a little. I was never jealous of Arthur being considered the leader. He had so much more of what would one day be called *charisma* than I did. But it was still nice to know that someone recognized and appreciated some of my qualities, too. I gave Janie a brief hug and told her not to work too hard, because she was going to need all her strength very soon. Janie hugged me back and furtively reached into an apron pocket.

"See, I've got my candy cane with me," she whispered. "Just in case I have to use it for a signal, you know."

"Well, be certain not to let it melt around all this steam and hot water," I laughed, and spent the rest of the day feeling happy despite the aching in my arms from hauling heavy water buckets. Janie had reminded me why saving Christmas in England was so important. I wanted to do it for people like her, who really had nothing else.

When there were only two weeks left before Christmas, Mayor Sabine instructed the town criers to begin announcing that any form of Christmas celebration was forbidden by law. Shopkeepers were required to tack up posters announcing all stores, including their own, would be open on Christmas Day. This was mostly a symbolic gesture, since so few people could read.

Arthur and I called another meeting of group captains. As each arrived at the barn, he or she brandished a candy cane. That meant no one was following them, but also represented a certain holiday spirit as well. We'd talked about the Christmas Day protest for so long, and in just fourteen more days it would happen!

"It will soon be time to decide which groups enter the city through which gates," Arthur said. "You all know that we have selected the noon hour to begin. Everyone else in the city, including the mayor, will be up by then."

More strategy was discussed, and all of it involved things Arthur and I had talked about earlier with Elizabeth and Alan at their kitchen table, while Sara, as usual, stayed out of sight up in the loft. We told everyone now that we would only meet once more, on the night of December 24. As always, messages for emergency meetings should be left in the crevice of the big tree.

"Be of good cheer," Arthur called out to everyone as the meeting concluded. "It won't be long now."

I walked back to the cottage with Elizabeth; it had been Alan's turn to stay behind with Sara. We talked about what might happen after the protest. Would Margaret Sabine dismiss all of us who had participated? Would the Trained Band have the nerve to arrest anyone at all? How would Parliament react when it learned two thousand men and women gathered to defy their laws against Christmas?

"I'm a little nervous, but even more excited," Elizabeth confessed. "This may be the only time in my life that I make my voice heard. That's a special thing, isn't it?"

"It certainly is," I agreed, and silently prayed that Elizabeth and all the others would not suffer too much for their moment of honest protest.

I gently turned her face toward me. "You may not care now, Sara, but someday you will. No, don't argue. I know you as well as I know myself. Any time a great wrong is being done—and taking away Christmas is completely wrong—those who know better must not allow it to happen."

Nineteen

en days before Christmas, Sara and I took an evening stroll after dinner. It was a beautiful night. There had been some snow the day before, so the hills were covered with pure white. But the clouds had cleared, so the black night sky was decorated with hundreds of stars and a crisp quarter-moon. We pulled our cloaks tightly about us and wore mittens. It was chilly enough to make our cheeks and noses tingle, but not so cold that we were uncomfortable.

"Don't you cherish this time of year?" I asked cheerfully. "The snow is so beautiful, and in winter I think the stars seem to shine just a little bit brighter. From my husband's letters, I know there are stars and snow in America, but I can't imagine them being as lovely as they are in England."

"When you leave for America, Auntie Layla, will I ever see you again?" Sara suddenly asked. Now I knew why she had asked me to take a walk with her. I had made it clear in the past weeks that right after the winter snows melted I would be leaving Canterbury to join Nicholas in the New World. Of course, I'd already stayed much longer with the Hayes family than I'd ever expected, but five years was the absolute limit before it was obvious I was not aging as they were. Whether the Christmas protest was effective or not, I would still have to go almost immediately afterward. Following this final effort to save Christmas in England, I would help Nicholas and Felix spread holiday joy in America.

But Sara's question tore at my heart. "No one can know the future, my love," I answered gently. "The ocean is quite wide, but people can cross any distance if they want to badly enough. Who knows? Instead of me returning to Canterbury, you might come to the New World instead. Then we could have a wonderful reunion there!"

Sara sniffled, probably as much from holding in tears as from the winter wind. "I think that after you leave, we'll never see each other again. I hate it. Why can't you stay? If you and your husband miss each other so much, he can just come back to England."

I thought of my own frustration with Parliament's banning of Christmas, and how Nicholas would despise it, too. At least in the New World, he had Dutch and French colonists who welcomed his gift-giving. "Right now, England isn't a place where my husband would feel welcome," I replied. "Sara, you know I'm going to miss you, too. I love you as though you were my own daughter. It has been one of the great joys of my life to share these past five years with you."

And this was true. I realized Sara was not a perfect child. There has never been one. Sometimes she was a little too proud of her own intelligence, since her ability to read and write and do sums was so far superior to her friend Sophia's, and Sophia was herself a very clever girl. Often, Sara indulged her natural shyness, giving in to the urge to hide from almost everyone and refuse to talk when it would have shown great maturity on her part to overcome her bashfulness and behave more appropriately. And there had been, lately, some testy flare-ups between her and her parents. At thirteen, Sara was beginning to consider herself a full-fledged adult, and it was certainly true that some girls her age were already married, and a few had children of their own. Alan and Elizabeth, naturally, still thought of Sara as their little girl, and sometimes she responded too sharply when she felt they were treating her like a helpless child rather than a responsible grown-up.

But those bad habits paled beside all her good qualities, which included offering her unqualified love to those she knew best and trusted—her mother, her father, and me. Sara had a generous heart, too. It hurt her deeply to see people in need. If her parents had permitted it, she would have given away all her clothes and food to the beggars who lined Canterbury's streets (the poor, in fact, lined the streets of every English town). And Sara had great spirit. She refused to limit herself to those basic things society allowed young working-class women of her time. It had been her great good fortune to be allowed to study with Sophia, but Sara had also worked hard and taken full advantage of that opportunity. She did not intend to marry some local farmer and spend her days doing chores and raising children, the life working-class girls like her were supposed to accept, whether they wanted to or not. Nor did she intend to become her best friend's lady-in-waiting, accepting that servant's role because Sophia had been born rich and she had not. Instead, Sara planned to somehow find a way to travel the world and do good deeds. She believed in this fine future as deeply now at thirteen as she had when I first met her five years earlier. What a precious, special girl, and how hard it was going to be for me to go on without her.

So we walked in silence for a few minutes, each thinking our own thoughts, until Sara suddenly blurted, "But you can't go to America if Sophia's father puts you in jail."

I whirled toward her. "What are you talking about?"

Sara sighed, the sort of sigh traditionally heaved by teenagers when adults fail to understand the obvious. "I know all about your plans for

Christmas Day, Auntie Layla. You and my parents and that man Arthur are going to lead a parade or something through the city streets to protest Christmas being taken away."

My heart was pounding. "Sara, where did you ever get that idea?"

"Oh, Auntie Layla," she said disdainfully. "All those nights when I've gone up to my bed and the four of you have sat downstairs talking around the table, don't you think I could hear every word being said? Just because you couldn't see me, that didn't mean I couldn't hear you."

"It isn't nice to eavesdrop on other people's conversations, young lady," I said sternly. "But why would you say that Sophia's father might arrest me?"

"Well, not *you* in particular," Sara replied. "But Sophia says her father has heard there will be some sort of demonstration, and he's getting ready to put it down and impress everyone in London with his firmness. She thinks he'll arrest some of the demonstrators and keep them locked up for a while, to teach everyone else that it's futile to try to save Christmas."

We had guessed all along that Avery Sabine would hear some rumors about the protest, of course, but now I wanted to be sure he didn't know everything about our plans.

"Has Sophia said how many protestors her father is expecting?" I asked. "I don't want you to betray your friend's confidence, of course, but anything you feel you could tell me would be helpful."

"Sophia never has secrets because she talks too much to keep any," Sara said. "I don't think her father is expecting much trouble. But that's one reason I asked you to come on this walk. I don't want you to go to jail, or my mother or father, either. I think the three of you should stay home on Christmas Day, and let whoever else wants to march get arrested instead."

"I thought you loved Christmas, Sara," I said.

In the silver light from the stars and moon, I saw her give me a sharp look. "Of course I love Christmas, Auntie Layla. I'm going to miss it very much now that it's against the law."

"And why will you miss Christmas, my love?" I asked. "Is it the presents you will no longer receive, or perhaps the goose we had for Christmas dinner on those years when we could afford it?"

Sara snorted. "I haven't expected presents from Father Christmas since I was eleven! Last year we didn't have goose, and it was still a wonderful holiday because we sang carols and thanked God for sending Jesus. I love Christmas because it's happy. You can forget all the sad things in life for a little while. I'm going to miss there being one special day when everyone is friends with everyone else, and we are reminded of all the good things we have."

"Then if Christmas is such a precious day, don't you think it is worth trying to keep?" I asked.

"Yes," Sara replied, "but I still don't want you being arrested. They'd put you in that big ugly jail by the West Gate. I don't want you or my parents there. It would be horrible for you."

I put my arm around her. "My darling, you're right that it would be horrible. I certainly don't want to go to jail, and I know your parents don't either. But we will, if it comes to that."

Sara jerked away from me, and, in the faint silvery light, I could see tears finally streaking her cheeks. *"Why?"* she whimpered. "Why would you take the chance of going to jail?"

I reached out for her hand. At first she tried to pull her hand loose from mine, but then she relented. "Sara, I'm going to tell you something very important, and I hope you'll remember it. In life, no great achievement is possible without equally great risk. Anything worth having comes with a price, my love. A few moments ago, you described perfectly why Christmas is so important, as a time to thank God for sending us his son and a time when even the poorest, saddest people can have moments of hope and joy. The men who control England now don't understand this, either because they are genuinely mistaken or because they simply don't want to. They say they have taken Christmas away because it is sinful, but there is more involved than that. Taking Christmas, even though most of the English people want to keep it, is a way of demonstrating that they have complete power over everyone else. And if we let them take Christmas, who knows what they might decide to take next?"

"I don't care about that," Sara said stubbornly. "I just care about my mother and my father and you."

I gently turned her face toward me. "You may not care now, Sara, but someday you will. No, don't argue. I know you as well as I know myself. Any time a great wrong is being done—and taking away Christmas is completely wrong—those who know better must not allow it to happen. If we do, then we are as much at fault as the people who are doing the bad thing. Here in Canterbury on Christmas Day, a thousand or more men and women are going to bravely stand in front of the mayor and tell him they will have their Christmas whether he agrees or not. There will be too many for him to arrest, I believe, and so he will have to stand and watch. Then the story of what happened will begin to spread—not just back to London and Parliament, but all over England. In other counties, other towns and cities, all the people who cherish the holiday will be inspired to do the same thing, until finally the men in power realize that, despite all the laws they might pass and the threats they might make, they cannot take Christmas away. It may take another year, or ten, or twenty, but there will be waits singing carols in our streets again and we will all enjoy the grateful fellowship that only Christmas can really bring."

"Do you really believe that's going to happen?" Sara said doubtfully.

"I have always believed in Christmas because I have always believed in the best of human spirit," I told her.

We walked a little more, both of us silent and thoughtful. Then, just as I was about to suggest that we'd been out in the winter cold long enough and should turn back toward the cottage, Sara said something that surprised me.

"Will you let me march with you on Christmas, Auntie Layla?" she wanted to know.

"I thought you found the possibility of prison quite horrifying," I said. "What if you marched, and the Trained Band was called out, and you were the one they arrested?"

Sara shrugged. "I would take that chance. You're right—we must all stand up for what we believe in, and I believe in Christmas."

I was proud of Sara, but wanted her to think it all through. "If you marched, my darling, you would have to be among strangers, and they would look at you and talk to you. You're the girl who runs to the loft whenever anyone but your parents or I are in the cottage. Are you certain you could overcome feeling so shy?"

"I'm not sure," Sara said honestly. "But at least I would try."

"That's all any of us can do," I said. "Well, angel, this isn't my decision to make. You must discuss it with your father and mother. If they agree, you may certainly come with us, provided that you understand the risks and are willing to accept them. If the mayor or Mrs. Sabine happen to see you, at the very least you would never again be allowed to play or study with Sophia, and she is your best friend. How would you feel about that?"

"Mrs. Sabine doesn't think I'm as good as her daughter," Sara replied, and she sounded resentful, which I could certainly understand. "She reminds me in many little ways that she could keep me away from Sophia any time she chooses. I wouldn't care if I never saw Mrs. Sabine again."

"But I asked you about Sophia," I reminded her.

Sara was silent for several moments. "Sophia and her parents will move to London soon," she finally said. "Since I don't want to be her lady-in-waiting after she gets married, I suppose I won't see her anymore. I'll be sad about that. She isn't like her mother. She mostly treats me like we're equal. Sometimes she even says we're like sisters. But deep down we both know we're not. We'd be separated soon anyway. But—" and here her voice broke a little—"I'm going to miss her."

I pulled Sara close, and we walked that way a while, moving back toward the cottage where a warm blaze roared in the fireplace. We had almost arrived when Sara tugged free, ran ahead a few paces, and called back to me, "I'm going to lose Sophia, and I'm going to lose you, but I'm not going to lose Christmas!" By the time I came through the door, she was already huddled with Alan and Elizabeth at the table, making a case for marching with us on Christmas Day. I could have joined them, but I decided this was something for parents and child to work out among themselves. I lay up in the loft bed for more than an hour, and Sara was correct—I could hear every word being said. She insisted she had the right to stand up for what she believed in, and they talked about the possibilities of the Trained Band using violence to disperse the marchers. Elizabeth flatly informed Sara that she would not be allowed to come, but Alan was wavering, and then they finally sent Sara up to bed so they could discuss it further themselves. An hour later, when Sara was finally asleep, her mother and father were still talking about it, but now I could tell Elizabeth was beginning to change her mind. In the morning, Sara was informed she could march, but only at the back of one of the groups, and that at the first sign of possible violence she was to turn and run back to the cottage.

"Will you promise you'll do this?" Elizabeth asked, looking her daughter straight in the eye.

"Will *you* run away, too, if it gets scary?" Sara shot back. "Will my father? Will Auntie Layla?"

"We'll certainly try not to be hurt," Elizabeth replied, which really didn't answer Sara's question. They both knew it. But Sara was pleased that she would at least be allowed to march, and so she didn't press her mother further.

When Arthur and I spoke later, he assured me there should be no real danger to Sara. "I know of several other parents who will be bringing their children on the march," he told me. "Their presence should make it even more certain that Mayor Sabine's constables and the Trained Band won't resort to violence. Think of the massive public reaction if children were injured as they demonstrated on behalf of Christmas Day! I think Sara will be fine, Layla."

In fact, Arthur's main concern was that the march wouldn't have its desired effect on Parliament no matter how many men, women, and children participated. Back in London, he said, it was possible government leaders were more concerned about the king than Christmas.

"You know Charles escaped Parliament's custody for several weeks in November," he reminded me. "Cromwell and his Puritans are starting to realize that the king won't do the convenient thing and cooperate completely with them. There is so much royalist support throughout England. A second civil war is certainly possible, and within months unless Parliament does something drastic. They could ignore our march altogether."

"They *are* doing something drastic, and it involves Christmas," I replied. "You wait and see. In ten days they're going to unleash Blue Richard Culmer and his minions on anyone who celebrates the holiday, and this will be meant to frighten everyone into complete submission, and not just about Christmas. That's why they won't ignore our march. They'll understand exactly what it means, that the people *will* have their voices heard whether Parliament permits it or not. I just hope nothing goes wrong. We're so close now."

"I think, if something was going to prevent us, it would have happened by now," Arthur said. "You've told me that Mayor Sabine has heard some rumors, which we expected. But the magnitude of our march will catch him by surprise."

For a few more days, I thought so, too.

Directly in front of us, Janie stood beside two cloaked figures, both
very tall, one of them thick-bodied and the other thin as a wraith. The heavy
one threw off his hood, and I saw it was Mayor Avery Sabine, whose
expression was disapproving and solemn. Then the thin one pulled back
his hood, and I looked into the leering face of Blue Richard Culmer.

Twenty

felt particularly tired on the evening of December 18 as Elizabeth, Sara, and I trudged home. Margaret Sabine had been in a snappish mood all day. Nothing any of the servants did pleased her. Worst of all, Janie had not come to work—I supposed she was ill—so I had to spend the whole day in the washing shed with Melinda, who was so nervous about the Christmas Day march that she dithered about and I had to do quite a bit of her work, as well as my own. Even Sara reported that Sophia had been very cross. The two girls hadn't exactly quarreled about anything, but by day's end they were mutually irritated and Sara was glad when it was time to leave.

So we walked slowly home, mostly in silence. I was thinking about the protest. We had told our team captains we would meet once more in the barn, on the night of December 24, and now I was wondering if we shouldn't meet on the twenty-third instead, since Avery Sabine's spies might be especially active on the day before Christmas. I asked Elizabeth what she thought, but she was worn out from her own long working day and made it clear she didn't want to talk.

It was already dark when we reached the cottage. I was surprised to see Arthur there, sitting at the table with Alan. The glow from candles was sufficient for me to see that Arthur had a scrap of paper in his hand.

"There was a message in the tree," he told me. "I came by about an hour ago to check, and there it was." He handed me the bit of paper, which had the outline of a candy cane scrawled on it with charcoal—that is what many poor people of the time used to write or draw. "We'll have to walk over to the barn, Layla. Whoever left this might already be waiting, since night has fallen."

"What could someone need to tell us?" I asked. "Christmas Day and the protest are only a week away. Do you think there's a problem?"

"There could be," Arthur mused, "but it's more likely that one of our captains is feeling nervous and wants some reassurance. You must remember, Layla, that most of the people who joined with us have never done something so bold in their lives. As the moment approaches, they're bound to worry. So why don't you and I go to the barn and see if that isn't what's happening. Probably a few soothing words will do the trick."

"I'll go with you, too," Alan said. "It's a cold, clear night and I'll enjoy the walk. Besides, if there is some sort of problem, perhaps I'll be able to help."

Elizabeth then said that she would go, while Alan stayed with Sara. It had been a frustrating day at work, she said, what with Mrs. Sabine acting so angry, and so she wanted a chance to get out and clear her head and think of something else besides why there had been dust under one of the beds when Mrs. Sabine happened to look there. Several minutes went by while Alan and Elizabeth debated who should be able to go with Arthur and me, until finally Sara shouted crossly from her loft that they should both go, she was fine, and after all she was thirteen years old! Just *go,* for goodness' sake!

"I suppose she's right. She's old enough to be left by herself for a while," Alan muttered, and so all four of us adults took the two-mile walk across hills to the barn. We brought a single lantern, but didn't need to light it. The moon was half-full, the stars twinkled, and by now we knew the way very well, even in the dark. As we walked, we talked quietly about the protest, and how wonderful it would be to see thousands of people joining together on behalf of Christmas, and this discussion put us all in better moods.

"Exactly one week from now, we'll be back in the cottage celebrating Christmas with extra enthusiasm," Alan predicted. "The protest will go well, our message to Parliament will be clear, and the holiday in England will be saved. Just wait and see."

When we reached the bottom of the steep hill with the barn above us, we lit the lantern so that if someone was waiting for us there he or she would see us approaching and not be startled when we arrived. Halfway up the slope we could see the silhouette of the barn against the night sky, and in the doorway there was also a lantern casting a small glow.

"Whoever it is, is waiting," Elizabeth said. "Let's hurry and deal with this problem, whatever it might be. I really don't like Sara being alone back at the cottage. I don't care if she's thirteen."

"Remember to be cautious," Arthur warned. "Pull the hoods of your cloaks around your faces. Wait to see the candy cane before you go all the way into the barn and reveal yourselves." But as we reached the crest of the hill and a small, dark figure also wrapped in a cloak stood in the doorway, I knew who it was even before she pulled her beloved candy cane out of a pocket and waved it at us.

"Janie, you weren't at work today," I whispered. "Is something wrong?"

"Come inside, Layla, so we can talk, and bring your friends with you," she replied, and turned back into the barn, her small lantern barely radiating enough light to see where she was going.

"It's Janie," I said to my three companions. "It's all right." We pulled our cloaks away from our faces and filed inside. It was very dark in the barn. Beside me, I could sense rather than see Arthur taking flint and stone from his pocket to strike a spark and light our lantern, too.

Then there was rustling behind us and to either side, and Janie said, "I have some people here, too." The clicking of stone and flint echoed in several places, as did the louder *clack* of musket hammers being drawn back. Lanterns flared with sudden light, and Arthur, Elizabeth, Alan, and I saw we were surrounded by at least a dozen members of the Trained Band, each of them pointing his gun directly at us. The four of us were not armed. There were too many of them to fight, and they were all around us, so we couldn't run. Directly in front of us, Janie stood beside two cloaked figures, both very tall, one of them thick-bodied and the other thin as a wraith. The heavy one threw off his hood, and I saw it was Mayor Avery Sabine, whose expression was disapproving and solemn. Then the thin one pulled back his hood, and I looked into the leering face of Blue Richard Culmer.

"Ah, Missus Layla Nicholas," he hissed with sarcastic courtesy. "You avoided becoming my guest in London five years ago. I'm so pleased to greet you now, and also your friends. *No*, sir!" he barked as Arthur moved to step between us. "You will stay still, or these men will shoot you down where you stand. I don't know your name, or that of these others."

"The second woman is named Elizabeth Hayes," Avery Sabine told him. "She works for my wife as a maid. The fellow with his arm around her is her husband."

"I'm Alan Hayes," my friend said bravely, his voice trembling a little.

It is very frightening to have guns pointed at you. "What is the meaning of this? Mayor Sabine, why do you threaten peaceable citizens?"

"You're hardly peaceable," Sabine replied. "You and your fellow conspirators, here, planned to incite a terrible riot in my city on Christmas Day. It was your intention to destroy property and set fires and encourage other citizens to join in the violence. Well, you're caught."

"Who told you such lies?" Arthur demanded, but, my heart sinking, I already knew.

"Why, Janie?" I asked.

She stood behind Sabine and Culmer and had a sad smile on her face.

"From now on, I'm to be the upstairs maid instead of toiling in the washing shed," Janie said. "That will make every working day like Christmas for me, Layla. And I never said nothing to this man about any violence. I told him the whole thing was to be peaceable, like." She turned to Sabine. "Your honor, may I go now? Your missus wants me at work quite early tomorrow."

"Yes, yes, go," Sabine muttered. "Wait, here's a coin for you. Now, begone while we finish our business here."

Those words chilled me. There were soldiers with guns, Blue Richard Culmer with his evil smile, and no witnesses. Perhaps Alan, Elizabeth, Arthur, and I were all to be shot. Culmer, watching me intently, guessed what I was thinking.

"There will be no executions here tonight, missus," he said. "I have other plans for you and your friends. How foolish you were, what amateurs! Did you really believe you could confide your plans to so many people and not have one of them, at least, betray you? If you're the best defenders Christmas has, no wonder the holiday is going to be gone forever! You trust people, Missus Nicholas, and that's always a fatal flaw."

"I'm the one who planned this, Culmer," Arthur interjected. "These other three only did what I told them. They're frightened now by you and these guns. They've learned their lesson. Let them go."

Culmer laughed—at least, the cackling sound he made was probably intended as laughter. "Oh, no, Mister—what is your name?"

"Arthur."

"Well, Mr. Arthur, you and Missus Nicholas and these Hayes people are going to be helpful to me, which means helpful to England. Even traitors like you can be of use."

Arthur bristled. "I'm no traitor to England, Culmer, now or ever. You're the traitor, terrorizing anyone who doesn't act exactly as you demand. And I don't care what you might have been told about plans for Christmas Day. Violence was never part of them. That's your way, not ours."

"Oh, sometimes cracking heads or smashing windows is effective, but I have other ways, too," Culmer replied. "You're about to find that out. You meant your Christmas riot to symbolize resistance. Now I will use you to symbolize the futility of resisting. Men, get out rope and tie these people up. Then let them sit down on the floor. There's hay strewn all about, so it shouldn't be too uncomfortable. We need to settle in. The night is still long, and we must wait until daylight."

"I can't stay here all night," Avery Sabine protested. "I have many important things to do tomorrow, and I need my rest."

Culmer waved his hand. "Go back to your home and your bed, then. Mind you don't tell anyone about what happened here tonight. We want everyone to be surprised tomorrow."

"Surprised by what?" Arthur asked.

"You'll see," Culmer said. The mayor hurried out of the barn, and we could hear him stumbling down the steep hill. Avery Sabine was not a graceful man. Then Culmer watched as a few of the Trained Band set down their muskets and tied our hands behind us. We were forced to sit down. Elizabeth was crying a little. The sound of her sobs seemed to soothe Culmer, who lit a pipe and sat with his back to the bale of hay I presumed Father Joel used as an altar.

"I hope you're not uncomfortable," he said sarcastically. "We'll be here until dawn. You'll understand why after that. Meanwhile, you may talk quietly, but if I even suspect you are trying to loosen your bonds and escape, I'll have one of you shot in front of the others. Four would be better for what I have planned, but three will do. Perhaps you might sing some Christmas carols to pass the time."

Alan squirmed over to Elizabeth's side. Because his hands were tied he couldn't put his arm around her, but he leaned so that their shoulders touched.

"Don't be afraid, love," he said softly. "I don't think they'll do anything too terrible to us."

"You don't believe that for a moment, and I'm not crying about our predicament," Elizabeth replied. "I'm afraid for Sara. She's all alone at the cottage, and both her parents are prisoners."

Panic shot through me. I had forgotten about Sara. I wondered how long she would sit up waiting for us to return. Maybe, after hours and hours, she would come to the barn herself to see what was delaying us. Culmer might take her prisoner, too! "Don't mention Sara," I hissed to Elizabeth. "If Culmer overhears, he might send his men to arrest her, too, just to make you and Alan feel even worse. She's Sophia's best friend. I don't think Margaret Sabine will let anything bad happen to her. But don't talk about Sara now!"

The four of us talked quietly a little longer. We thought it odd that Culmer was not questioning us about others involved in the Christmas Day protest plan. It was as though he didn't care. Why? And why were we being kept in the barn until dawn? After a while, Elizabeth and Alan, exhausted by fear and stress, dozed. Arthur and I remained awake. Every so often I would glance over at Blue Richard Culmer, who leaned back against the hay bale smoking his pipe and never taking his eyes off of us. Finally, as the first faint streaks of dawn appeared on the eastern horizon, Culmer stood up, stretched, and nodded to one of the Trained Band. That fellow went to a far corner of the barn and, with some effort, picked up a heavy canvas bag that clanked as he carried it over to where we four prisoners sat. The clanking woke Alan and Elizabeth.

"Chains," Arthur said grimly, and he was correct. "Now, I understand. Culmer means to make examples of us."

"Exactly, Mr. Arthur," Culmer snarled. "Men, secure them properly, and take no chances. Keep those ropes tight around their arms until all the chains are in place."

It was horrible. The chains were very heavy. Manacles were snapped around our wrists, which were still kept behind our backs. Then lengths of chain were placed around all of our waists, with about two feet of additional chain linking us up one to another—me to Arthur, Arthur to Elizabeth, and Elizabeth to Alan. Finally, Culmer stepped up and personally secured a final shackle around my neck, much like a master will place a collar and leash on a dog. "Time to go to town," he crooned, and tugged the length of chain attached to my neck. I was jerked forward and forced to follow him, and my three friends staggered along behind me in a grotesque parade. The Trained Band soldiers took up their muskets and fell in on either side of us. "Slowly, now," Culmer cautioned as he led the way down the hill. "Don't stand too close to the prisoners, lads. We want all their friends and neighbors to get good looks at them!"

Country people around Canterbury rose with the sun, so as we reached the main path toward town there already were many people moving along it. As we made our ghastly walk, I recognized quite a few of them—they were all participants in the planned protest. Now their eyes widened and their mouths fell open in shock to see their leaders in Blue Richard Culmer's clutches.

"See what happens to Christmas plotters?" Culmer bellowed over and over as we made our slow, awful way into Canterbury. "All those who unlawfully celebrate Christmas face swift and certain punishment! Would you want this to be *you*?" People who had greeted me every day for five years turned away, trying not to look me in the eye. Culmer was using us to frighten the rest of the people into submission, just as he had used the smashing of cathedral stained-glass windows a few years earlier. And his plan was obviously working. No one called out comforting words to us; onlookers were too afraid for their own safety to offer any show of support.

Culmer led us into Canterbury through St. George's Gate on the eastern wall, and the guards there snapped to attention and saluted him as we passed. High Street, the main city thoroughfare that was lined with shops, ran straight through the center of Canterbury and ended at the West Gate, with its two hulking towers, one of which housed the city dungeon. Culmer obviously intended to take us there, but along the way he wanted as many people as possible to see us in our chains. We tried to walk with some dignity, but with our hands chained behind us it was hard to do. Every so often Culmer would deftly tug at the chain linked to my neck, and I would stumble a little, and in turn Arthur, Elizabeth, and Alan would be pulled off balance and stagger for a few steps. Right through the central marketplace he led us, calling out for the Trained Band soldiers to make the crowd stand clear. As word of our procession spread, black-cloaked Puritans began to appear all along High Street, calling out insults to the four of us and jeering that Christmas was gone forever, and look at the dreadful fate we'd brought on ourselves by not accepting that! I was terribly afraid, though not for myself. I was thinking about Sara. When she woke and discovered that her parents and auntie hadn't returned to the cottage, what would she do? The girl was so shy that she would probably not run to a neighbor and ask for help. Perhaps she'd make her way into Canterbury and her friend Sophia—what if my darling girl was seeing us in chains right now? I began desperately looking at the people lining both sides of the street, my head swiveling back and forth, and Blue Richard Culmer saw me and misunderstood.

"You're feeling panic, I can tell!" he crowed. "Well, missus, not one of those people is going to help you, so there's no sense searching for a friend. You have no friends left!"

We finally reached the West Gate, where the north tower served as the town prison. I thought Culmer would immediately throw us into cells, but he had other plans. Outside the tower were four sets of "stocks," wooden stands with openings that closed around prisoners' necks and wrists, forcing them into an awkward standing crouch until, finally, the stocks would be unlocked and they could move around again. Culmer ordered us locked into these stocks. Hundreds of people gathered about; criminals were usually put into the stocks for extra embarrassment after some particularly disgusting crime, like stealing from church coin boxes. Then Mayor Sabine appeared—I could only see him out of the corner of my eye, because the stocks were tight and I could not move my head.

"Behold the Christmas criminals!" Sabine roared to the crowd. "This is what happens to traitors who plan riots on behalf of sinful holidays! These evildoers hoped to lead many of you into crime, but your mayor and Mr. Culmer have saved you! Look on them, and learn your lesson! There is no longer any Christmas in England, or in Canterbury!" Then Culmer directed the Trained Band soldiers to festoon the stocks with green boughs and holly, in a mockery of traditional Christmas decorations. There was nothing for Arthur, Elizabeth, Alan, and me to do but stand where we were locked in place as the sun traveled across the winter sky. All day, we were offered no food or water, and all of us were feeling weak when, in early evening, Culmer finally ordered us taken out of the stocks. Our legs were so stiff that we staggered as, at gunpoint, we were marched into the jail. Down stone steps we went, until, finally, we came to a heavy, barred door, which creaked ominously as it was opened and we were forced inside. The stone walls of this dungeon were damp and reeked of rot.

"There are empty buckets for you when you need to do the obvious," Culmer said. "Bread and water will be brought in the morning. By then you'll be so hungry, you'll think you're dining on fine holiday goose. In the meantime, why don't you pray to Father Christmas? Perhaps he'll come to save you." Then Culmer stepped back and nodded to a jailer, who grunted as he swung the heavy cell door shut. The single lantern lighting the hallway was extinguished, and we were prisoners in the dark.

We were brought outside in the cold morning light. Our appearances, I know, were appalling. Our clothes were nasty and torn, our exposed skin was filthy, and our legs so weak we could barely stand as we were locked into the stocks.

Twenty-one

e only knew it was morning when two jailers lumbered down the stone steps to our dungeon cell carrying a bucket of water and two loaves of stale bread. One stood outside with a musket and torch while the other unlocked the heavy door, growled "Breakfast," shoved the bucket and bread inside, then slammed the door shut and locked it again. The only light we had came from the torch, and it was a relief when the second jailer jammed it into a holder on the wall outside the cell and we could see a little by the flickers it cast through the barred window. As the jailers went back up the steps without another word, we took turns having long sips from the bucket—the water was sour tasting, and I tried not to think of where it might have come from—and then Arthur insisted we each eat some bread. None of us felt especially hungry, despite the fact we hadn't had a meal since noon the day before. Our troubles had overwhelmed our appetites. But Arthur pointed out we needed to keep up our strength, so we ate.

"I must know what's happened to Sara," Elizabeth moaned after she reluctantly gulped down a few mouthfuls of the awful loaf. "Surely someone has found her by now."

"I'm certain the Sabines have brought her to their home," Alan said reassuringly, though I could tell he was not as confident as he was trying to sound. "These people might have arrested us for trying to save Christmas, but they surely won't punish an innocent child." He chewed on his bread for a few moments and then asked, "What do you think they will do to us today?"

"Probably nothing," I said. "Culmer knows it is much more cruel to leave us here for a while wondering about his intentions before revealing them. Meanwhile, we'd better save what's left of the bread and water. It may be all we get for a while."

I was right. No one came down the stairs to our cell. Sometime during the day the torch went out, and we were plunged back into total darkness. The hours crawled by. I knew Alan and Elizabeth were tormented by their fear for Sara, and I felt the same. Arthur undoubtedly was devising escape plans, though nothing of the sort seemed possible. There was only the one door to our cell, and the narrow stone stairway leading up from it was undoubtedly guarded at the top. None of us speculated what Blue Richard Culmer and the Puritans might have in mind for our further punishment. Anything was possible. They could twist the laws in any way they pleased to suit themselves. We talked very little, because we were so discouraged and also because Arthur warned there might be some jailer perched on the stairs hoping to overhear information about the protest plan that he could report back to Culmer.

"We have to protect everyone else if we can," Arthur whispered. "I believe Janie only identified the four of us. With luck, all our captains and other supporters might be spared."

"Perhaps they'll march anyway, even though we've been taken prisoner," Alan said hopefully.

"That would surprise me," I replied. "You saw how everyone remained silent when we were pulled down High Street in chains. An effective protest needs leaders, so even if some of them do try to march without us on Christmas Day, they'll be confused and easily dispersed by Sabine and the Trained Band." As soon as I spoke these gloomy words, I regretted them. Our situation was bad enough without adding to it. So I didn't say anything more, and neither did the others. After a while I began thinking about my husband. I knew Nicholas was far across the ocean, preoccupied with bringing Christmas gifts to colonial children in the New World. How many more months would it take before he noticed there had been no letters from Arthur or me, and what would he do when he learned of our fate, whatever it might turn out to be?

I suppose all of us slept a little, though afterward it seemed to me I hadn't closed my eyes at all when the rattle of boots on stone steps indicated another day had passed. A new torch flared its light into our cell, and when the heavy door was unlocked and swung open, there stood Blue Richard Culmer.

"How are my guests this fine morning?" he jeered. "How wonderful you all look." This, of course, was sarcasm. All four of us were dirty from sprawling on the cell floor, and smelly from not bathing. After so many hours spent in darkness, even the feeble torchlight made us blink and rub our eyes.

"What do you mean to do with us, Culmer?" Arthur demanded. "You can't keep us prisoners without telling us what we're charged with and allowing us a fair trial on those charges."

Culmer emitted his usual odd cackle. "You don't understand our special new laws. In emergency situations dealing with obvious traitors, we can keep prisoners as long as we like without going through the usual motions of charges and trials. We decent English people are at war with sinners like you, and so you have no legal rights. But of this, you may be certain—for planning a violent riot in support of the illegal Christmas holiday, your punishment will be quite severe. Well, I'll leave you to wonder what will happen to you. Now that you're in custody, I'm off to London. We've heard rumors of Christmas plotters there. Please continue to make yourselves at home. Bread and water will be served soon."

As Culmer turned to go, Elizabeth cried, "What about my daughter? Where is Sara?"

He paused, then replied, "Someone mentioned that girl to me. You'll have to ask the Sabines about her."

"Then let me speak to the Sabines," Elizabeth pleaded. "She is only thirteen years old!"

"As far as I'm concerned, children of traitors should be treated like traitors as well," Culmer snarled. "I've got more important things to think about than your brat. Take it up with the Sabines, if they decide to waste time talking to you. And a Merry Christmas to all." He stalked out of the cell, the door was slammed shut and locked, and Elizabeth spent most of the next few hours sobbing uncontrollably.

Eventually there were more footsteps on the stone stairs. Unlike Culmer, Margaret Sabine did not come into our cell. Instead, she stayed outside the thick door, calling through the barred window for Elizabeth to stand up and speak to her.

"You, girl," she called. "Come over here at once! Are you ready to offer an apology?"

"What do you mean, an apology?" Elizabeth asked as she stumbled to her feet and over to our side of the door.

"You have betrayed my trust, and showed no gratitude for my years of kindness to you," Margaret Sabine declared. "I gave you work. My money, paid to you in salary, bought your family's food. In return, you planned to participate in, even help lead, a hateful, violent act that, had it been successful, would have destroyed my husband's career. Well, now you're caught, and I don't feel sorry for you. But I do expect you to at least ask my forgiveness."

"Mrs. Sabine, what about Sara?" Elizabeth pleaded. "Is she with you? Is she safe?"

"The apology first," Margaret Sabine demanded.

"I'll apologize for anything you like, but please tell me about my daughter!" Elizabeth cried.

"Well," the mayor's wife said, "I have very little to tell. When news reached me of your arrest, and that of your husband and this other woman, Layla, who also has repaid my kindness with betrayal, I sent some of my people to your cottage to fetch Sara. You are, of course, an unfit mother, since you recklessly threw in with these plotters without a care in the world about what might happen to your child. Angry as I am with you, I'm a Christian woman and would not let the girl suffer because of her parents' sinfulness. But they reported back to me that the cottage was empty. Sara was not there."

"Then, where is she?" Elizabeth asked in horror.

"I'm sure I don't know," Margaret Sabine replied. "It had been my intention all along to bring Sara with us when our family moved to London. You could not have objected. Being Sophia's lady-in-waiting would have been a far better life than you and your sailor husband could ever have given to her. But now that won't happen. Sara is gone, and I haven't time to spare seeking her further. After my husband makes clear on Christmas Day how he foiled your plot, Sophia and I are moving to our new London home, where Mr. Sabine will soon join us after a grateful Parliament names him to some very high government position."

"But Sara—" Elizabeth pleaded.

"Speak no more to me of her," Margaret Sabine said. "I was becoming somewhat annoyed with her, in fact. This is how people of my class are rewarded for trying to be generous to our inferiors. Your daughter, a peasant girl, too often seemed to think she was the equal of my little darling, a child of much higher breeding. Well, now I know where she got the idea. Her mother and father thought they could somehow challenge their social betters, and look where it got you!"

"Please find Sara," Elizabeth pleaded. "You're a mother, just like me."

"Oh, I'm nothing at all like you," the mayor's wife replied. She seemed about to say more when there was much thudding on the steps, and Mayor Avery Sabine stumbled outside the cell door.

"Come away, Margaret," he said impatiently. "Don't waste your time on these pathetic traitors."

"Mayor Sabine, please find my daughter!" Alan shouted from the back of the cell. "Sara can't be left out there all alone."

Sabine drew himself up and peered through the barred cell window. "You'd best worry about yourself, fellow. As for your daughter, well, there's always room on the streets for one more homeless girl."

Despite our rule against violence, Alan threw himself at the mayor. But his shoulder bounced off the locked, heavy door between them, and he sprawled on the cell floor. He lay there pounding his fist in frustration while Sabine, roaring with laughter, guided his stout wife back up the stairs and out into the sunlight it seemed that we four prisoners might never see again.

The last few days before Christmas passed in an agony of combined tedium and worry. Much of the time we had no light and had to sit in the dark. The hours crept by. Every so often, we'd be given bread and water. This poor diet sapped our strength. We worried about Sara, about the rest of the Christmas protestors, and, I admit, about what would finally happen to us. Culmer had made it clear we could be held without trial for as long as he wanted. We could be whipped, have our ears "notched," or even be executed. The longer we sat in the darkness, the more we couldn't help imagining various horrible fates. No one came to speak to us. Culmer had apparently gone back to London. Mayor Sabine had other things to do. By the third day, we'd mostly stopped talking among ourselves, because there was really nothing left to say. Sara might be anywhere. Every so often, I would think that it was my fault all this had happened to her, and to Elizabeth and Alan and Arthur. If I had just joined my husband in the New World, or if I had followed Arthur's advice and at least moved to the toy factory in Nuremberg instead of stubbornly insisting on staying in England and trying to save Christmas . . . I had never felt so terrible, or so helpless. And yet, deep inside I still believed that there was no coincidence in our Christmas mission and that I had remained in Canterbury for some great purpose.

On what we reckoned must be December 24, the day before Christmas, there were more footsteps on the stone. Two guards unlocked the door, and one called, "Layla Nicholas, come forward." I stood up with some difficulty. My legs were stiff from sitting on the floor for so long.

"What do you want with me?" I asked, trying to sound brave.

"I don't want anything," the guard said. "There's someone to see you, so come on up. I've been told not to tie your hands, but don't get any ideas about trying to escape. There are men with guns upstairs, and they wouldn't mind shooting a violent traitor like you."

"I'm not violent, and I'm not a traitor," I said.

"That's not how Mr. Culmer and the mayor tell it," he replied, and gestured for me to come out of the cell.

I slowly made my way up the stairs. When I reached the main floor I had to shield my face with my hands to block out the sunlight coming through the windows, because the glare hurt my eyes. When I lowered my hands again I saw someone familiar. Oliver Cromwell, dressed in plain Puritan black, looked at me sorrowfully.

"You can leave us alone," he told the guards. "Missus Nicholas will not attack me or attempt to escape."

"Our orders from the mayor are not to leave her," one of the guards said. "She's a nasty one, she is."

"My orders outrank the mayor's," Cromwell said. "Go." The guards did. He turned back to me and said, "I thought you'd be hungry, missus. There is cheese here on the table, and clean water in a cup. Refresh yourself."

It was a kind gesture, and I grabbed a hunk of cheese and began eating it. I was sorry I had to touch the food with my filthy hands; in the light of day I could see the dirt caked under my fingernails. I was sure I smelled very bad, but Cromwell was enough of a gentleman not to mention it or to wrinkle his nose at my odor.

"Missus Nicholas, I regret very much to find you in this situation," Cromwell said. "I did my best to warn you. Now, you must have the sense to cooperate fully with the mayor tomorrow on the so-called Christmas Day, so that we can end your suffering and all get on with our lives."

"What do you mean?" I asked suspiciously.

"Christmas is gone from England, and your plot to save it has failed," Cromwell said. "You must surely realize that. We can't have any more Christmas riots like the one you helped organize for the apprentices in London two years ago. If the people think they can have their holiday just by demanding it, then they next might decide to demand the restoration of the king. He, of course, has greatly disappointed me. He never intended to bargain in good faith, and give Parliament its proper influence. Well, a bad end is coming for him. But it doesn't have to be that way for you. Tomorrow, Mayor Sabine expects you and your three friends to stand up in front of this prison and call out to everyone that you renounce Christmas Day and all of its sinfulness. Do it, and afterward you'll be set free."

"Does Blue Richard Culmer know about this?" I asked. I knew there was no use trying to convince Cromwell I had nothing to do with the Apprentice Protest.

Cromwell sighed. "He didn't like it, but it was not his decision. I have consulted with Mayor Sabine. If Culmer had his way, the four of you would already have been executed. But the vast majority of us now in power are not bloodthirsty, missus. Be reasonable. You cannot save Christmas, so save yourself."

"And if I don't do as you and the mayor want?"

"Then you and your friends will be placed in the Canterbury stocks for all of Christmas Day, and afterward you will be taken to London for trial before Parliament. The charge will be treason. After you're found guilty, and of course you will be, all four of you will be thrown into the Tower of London and kept there forever. Don't let that happen. Speak against Christmas tomorrow, and I myself will take you to the London docks and pay your passage on a ship to the New World and your husband."

"I can't renounce Christmas," I said. "I love all the good things it stands for. I disagree with some of your beliefs, Mr. Cromwell, but I would never tell you to renounce them or be judged a traitor. That, I suppose, is the difference between us. And I promise you this: You will never successfully ban Christmas. You can't imprison everyone who supports the holiday. There wouldn't be a thousand people left free in England if you did. It may happen gradually rather than immediately, but all you believe you have accomplished—removing the king, giving full power to Parliament, creating a country that abides by your beliefs and no others—will be undone because you tried to take away the most wonderful celebration of the year. I don't want my freedom lost, but I want people to have Christmas more."

"So you refuse."

"I do."

Cromwell reached for his wide-brimmed black hat. "Then, Missus Layla Nicholas, I will see you next in the halls of Parliament, perhaps in a week. And I will take no pleasure in what happens to you there."

I was returned to the cell, where Arthur, Alan, and Elizabeth asked me what had happened. I told them, and added I thought they could each save themselves if they would stand up the next day and renounce Christmas as Cromwell and Sabine wanted.

"But you won't do that?" Alan asked.

"No," I said. "Perhaps outrage over what Parliament does to me will rouse public spirit and help save Christmas after all. There will be no disgrace if any of you makes a different choice."

But they didn't. I spent the rest of the day thinking about what I had told Sara—that great achievement always requires great sacrifice and how we each must decide how much we are willing to risk for our beliefs.

It was just dawn on December 25, 1647, when a troop of armed guards came to the cell and roughly pulled us up the steps. We were brought outside into the cold morning light. Our appearances, I knew, were appalling. Our clothes were nasty and torn, our exposed skin was filthy, and our legs were so weak we could barely stand as we were locked into the stocks. The guards hung holly and green boughs and signs saying "Christmas Criminals" in front of us. Town criers began to stroll up and down High Street, calling out that Mayor Sabine expected all shops to be open and business conducted as usual. Then they shouted that anyone defying these orders would join the Christmas criminals in the stocks. A dozen black-cloaked Puritans gathered in front of us and called out insults. A few tossed handfuls of dirt and pebbles in our faces, but we were already so grimy the added filth made little difference. The rest of the townspeople tried to hurry by without staring. After an hour the criers changed messages. Now they informed everyone that at high noon, Mayor Sabine would come to the stocks to make a public address.

Alan, Elizabeth, Arthur, and I remained hunched over in the stocks. We didn't talk. It took all our strength to keep our legs from collapsing, which would have been even more painful since we would then have hung from the stocks by our necks and wrists. About noon, as the winter sun shone weakly overhead, we sensed movement behind us, and Mayor Sabine appeared, surrounded by members of the Trained Band. He had a long, written speech in his hand and maneuvered in front of the stocks as a crowd began to gather. I waited almost numbly for him to begin what I knew would be a tirade against Christmas and a reminder to look hard at the traitors, because their fate would be shared by anyone who continued to support the sinful holiday.

Sabine turned and gave the four of us in stocks a long, disgusted look, turned back toward the crowd, held his speech in front of him, cleared his throat loudly, and proclaimed, "Good people of Canterbury, it is pleasant to see you going about an ordinary day instead of indulging in unlawful Christmas activities. As a sign of its love for godly people, your Parliament has condemned Christmas as illegal, and all those who continue to celebrate it are criminals. You see before you four evildoers who intended to terrorize you today at the head of a mob, burning shops and beating people in an attempt to force you to engage in drunken, evil acts that insult Jesus rather than indicate thanks for his birth. But we have saved you from them! I find great pleasure in announcing that tomorrow they will be taken in chains to London, where they will be tried by Parliament and—"

My head was held in place by the stocks, so I couldn't be sure what Mayor Sabine saw, only that, whatever it was, it caused him to stop talking, drop the pages of his speech, and motion for the dozen soldiers from the Trained Band to raise their muskets. Elizabeth, in stocks to my left, had a better view toward the West Gate and the beginning of High Street, and suddenly she gasped, "Is it really possible?" Then there was the thudding of footsteps from every direction, and a great procession swept in front of me, and I saw that, yes, it *was*.

Sara, John Mason, and the blacksmith named Clark made certain
they led the group at the West Gate, since it was their intention to rescue
the four "Christmas criminals" from the stocks. As the town bell tower
tolled noon, the marchers surged forward from six different directions.

Twenty-two

e learned later what happened to Sara after her parents and I were arrested. On the night that Culmer captured us, she sat up waiting for our return until well after midnight. Then, overcome with weariness and sure that our meeting at the barn was just taking longer than expected, she went up to her loft bed and slept.

But when Sara woke at dawn, the cottage was still empty and she knew something must be wrong. She got up and dressed, quickly ate a little fruit for breakfast, put on her warmest cloak, and went outside into the cold winter morning. She intended to walk from the cottage to the meeting barn atop the high hill, but she had only gone a few hundred yards when she noticed a commotion along the road toward Canterbury. Peeking around the adults lining the thoroughfare, she saw a horrifying sight—her parents, auntie, and Arthur chained together and being led toward town by blue-cloaked, leering Richard Culmer.

Sara's instinct was to scream and run to us, but my precious girl had enough sense to realize that would only make things worse. She might be arrested, too, and used as a bargaining chip to make her parents and me do whatever Culmer wanted. So she ran back to the cottage and raced up the ladder to her loft bed, where she lay shivering with fear—but only for a few moments.

As soon as Margaret Sabine heard of her parents' arrest, Sara guessed, she would send some of her servants to the cottage with instructions to bring her along to the mayor's house. That would still leave her at Culmer's mercy, so she had to run. The problem for the girl was that, because she had always been so shy, she had no friends other than Sophia whose family might take her in and hide her. So she had to make a decision, and quickly—would she stay cowering in bed until her parents' enemies came to get her or would she overcome her lifelong shyness and seek help from neighbors she'd never really gotten to know very well?

Sara chose not to wait for capture. She resolutely put some fruit and cheese and a small gourd of water in a pack and left the cottage, walking east away from Canterbury rather than west toward the city. She didn't know that she barely left in time—perhaps fifteen minutes after she shut the door behind her, Margaret Sabine's people arrived looking for her. But all they found was an empty cottage; Sara was out of sight in the nearby hills.

She knew that she should go to one of the other houses in the vicinity, identify herself to whoever lived there, and ask for shelter. Almost all the neighbors, she knew from overhearing conversations between her parents, Arthur, and me, opposed the banning of Christmas and were unlikely to turn a thirteen-year-old girl over to the nasty clutches of Blue Richard Culmer. But the thought of talking to someone she didn't know was almost as frightening as the sight of her loved ones as prisoners. Sara truly *was* shy, and the habits of a lifetime, even one that had so far lasted only thirteen years, were hard to overcome. So, that first awful day, she wandered and occasionally tried to find the nerve to ask for help, and always panicked at the last moment. Finally she found a small grove of trees in the space between two low hills. The spot was out of sight of the road, and Sara huddled there as the day dwindled into night, chilled by bitter December winds and petrified by the horrible turn her life had taken.

As she crouched for hours with her cloak pulled tight around her though, she began to think about overcoming fear, and about each person's responsibility, if something wrong is being done, to try and stop it. The three people she loved most in the world, the adults she looked to for guidance and protection, were undoubtedly in a Canterbury dungeon. There was nothing she could do about that. But she could, at least, do something about the Christmas protest they had so deeply believed in that they were willing to risk their freedom, even their lives, to help organize and lead it.

Just as the sun rose the next morning, December 20, a farmer named John Mason heard a knock on his cottage door. He opened it to find a young girl standing outside, shivering both with cold and nerves.

"My name is Sara, and I need to talk to you," she said, almost choking out the words because she so much wanted to turn and run instead. "You know my parents, Alan and Elizabeth Hayes, and my Auntie Layla. You've been meeting with them about the protest on Christmas."

"I'm afraid they've been arrested, child," Mason said, gesturing for his wife to come over and help him bring the shuddering girl inside. "It is a sad thing, indeed." The Masons fussed over Sara, putting extra wood on the fire to help her get warm, and insisting she eat some hot mush. Sara swallowed several spoonfuls before she felt strong enough to say anything more.

John Mason

"They trusted you very much," she finally said. "At night, they would talk about how brave you are, how they expected you, Mr. Mason, to be one of the best captains on Christmas Day."

Mason shrugged sadly. "I would have been proud to take part in any way I was needed. Now, of course, there will be no protest, since our leaders are captured and our plans are ruined. It would have been a good thing to save Christmas, but now all we can do is hope your parents and auntie don't give the rest of us away to Blue Richard Culmer."

Sara took a deep breath. "You're wrong, Mr. Mason."

He looked worried and asked, "You mean, you think your family will identify the rest of us in hopes of saving themselves?"

"No, not at all. My parents and auntie are very brave people. But now we have to be brave, too, and hold the protest that all of you have planned for so long."

"Our leaders are gone, child," Mason protested.

"Then *we* have to be the leaders, sir," Sara replied. "Those who stand by watching something wrong being done are as guilty as the people who do the bad thing. My auntie taught me that. Help me talk to all the people who were helping to plan the protest. We have to march on Christmas day. We have to."

For the next few days, Sara and John Mason walked dozens of miles, quietly visiting all the captains who'd been named by Arthur and convincing them that they still must march. A few could not be persuaded. Because of the arrests at the barn, they were now too afraid of Blue Richard Culmer, Avery Sabine, and the rest of the Puritans. Many were shocked to see a teenaged girl assuming leadership of such a complicated, important effort. No one realized how hard it was for that thirteen-year-old to overcome her bashfulness and talk to so many people. But Sara did this, and very effectively. She remembered all she had overheard from her loft bed when the adults downstairs were talking—how, above all, they wanted thousands of marchers, so sheer numbers would prevent arrests or other reprisals by Culmer, Sabine, and the Trained Band. So, when she had convinced most of the captains to continue the protest, she emphasized to them that they, in turn, must recruit as many other people as possible.

Then, leaving the adults to that task, Sara herself spent hours talking to other children. It was hard, at first. Besides her natural shyness, Sara also had a bad reputation among her peers to overcome. Boys and girls in Canterbury were all aware of her special friendship with Sophia, the richest child in town. While the rest of the working-class children had to help their parents in the fields or in shops, Sara had been enjoying private lessons and fine meals with Sophia, and so she was often resented. Her bashfulness was mistaken for snobbiness. But now, for the first time, she sought out other young people and talked to them about Christmas, how special it was, how it must somehow be saved. She explained the purpose of the march and its intended message to Parliament. Even more than the adults, the children understood: No one should have the right to force beliefs on others. And so a whole new youthful battalion of protestors was added to the demonstrators' ranks.

By the time of the final planning meeting, on the night of December 24 in the barn high atop the hill, the protestors accepted Sara as a leader. A week earlier, everyone would have considered such a thing impossible, particularly those who realized just how bashful she was. But, in times of emergency, intelligence, imagination, and courage are the most important traits, and no one had more of these than Sara. Mayor Sabine and the Trained Band assumed the plans for protest were dead, so Sara and the five dozen adults with her were able to meet in the barn without too much concern that soldiers might come for them. If they were still understandably nervous, they were excited, too.

"We have to remember tomorrow to approach all six gates at once," Sara cautioned. "One big crowd at one gate will just alert the guards. So let's gather everyone here just after dawn, then divide into six groups."

"How do you think of such things, young lady?" someone asked.

Sara smiled. "I heard Mr. Arthur say it to my parents and auntie." Here, she was displaying another sign of true leadership by not taking credit for someone else's good idea, even though she could have. Then, Sara and John Mason, who had also stepped forward to lead, reminded everyone that there was not to be any violence on the part of the protestors.

"The moment even one of us strikes a blow or throws a stone or breaks a shop window, that will give the mayor and Trained Band an excuse to claim we were rioting rather than protesting," Mason explained. "They'll use it as further evidence that Christmas is sinful and that those who support it are criminals. So we will march—"

"And sing," Sara added.

"And sing," Mason agreed, smiling fondly at the girl who he had come to admire very much. "We will have ourselves a very special Christmas celebration right on High Street, and when Sara gives the signal, waving her hands over her head, then we will all march back out of town to our homes. If we begin at noon, the whole business should take no more than an hour. This will be sufficient to make our message clear. Anything longer, and one of our people or one of the Trained Band might do something unfortunate. We want a brisk, peaceful protest."

Mason paused a moment, then said, "There is one thing more. We know, of course, that Sara's parents and auntie, along with their friend Arthur, are being held in the town jail. Certain information has reached us. By Mayor Sabine's order, tomorrow on Christmas Day they are to be taken out and put in the stocks as examples of how anyone who celebrates Christmas will be punished from now on. Those entering town from the West Gate must immediately get to the stocks and free them. Place them in the middle of the marchers, so that Sabine and his Trained Band can't recapture them. Clark, you are a blacksmith by trade." A massive man nodded. "Well, then, bring along a hammer and chisel for breaking the locks on the stocks. But use them only to strike the locks, no matter how tempted you might become to tap Mayor Sabine once or twice, as well."

Afterward, Mason and Sara walked back to his home, where she was staying with him and his wife. "We're going to save your parents and auntie," he promised.

"We're going to save Christmas, too," Sara replied.

She did not sleep that night. During the hours before dawn, she thought about many things—what if, for instance, the protest failed? It was possible Avery Sabine might be smart enough to order the city gates locked

Clark the Blacksmith

all Christmas Day long, to keep potential protestors out. Or what if not enough people showed up to march? Originally, her parents, Auntie Layla, and Arthur had hoped for a thousand marchers, perhaps two thousand. But if only a hundred or so actually participated, then the march would have no effect other than reassuring Mayor Sabine that few people really cared about saving Christmas after all.

Then Sara shed many tears, not from fear of failure, but because she missed her parents and auntie so much. She was being very brave by overcoming her shyness and stepping in to lead the protest, but she was still a thirteen-year-old girl who loved her family and was afraid for them. What if the marchers frightened the mayor and Trained Band so much that they turned their guns on the four Christmas prisoners?

Gradually, though, Sara calmed herself by realizing she had done all she could to prepare. She could not control the future. It had to be enough, just then, to know that she had tried to do the things she should. After a while, Sara slept, and she dreamed about a stout man with a white beard and warm smile, who patted her arm and told her that her courage was going to help save Christmas. When she woke, she remembered the man in her dream, and somehow this comforted her very much.

Christmas Day of 1647 in England dawned clear and cold. Fluffy white clouds decorated bright blue sky. Sara and John Mason gulped down porridge and hurried to the high hill where the protestors were to gather. As they walked, they talked quietly, mostly wondering how many people would come to join the march.

"Five hundred, at least," Mason guessed. "All our captains report they have met with enthusiastic response. Five hundred people gathered together on High Street will make for a very impressive demonstration, Sara."

"Five hundred won't be enough," she told him. "We must have a thousand or more. Only that kind of multitude will convince Parliament that Christmas can't be taken from us or intimidate Mayor Sabine and the Trained Band so none of us are arrested."

"Perhaps you shouldn't get your hopes up," Mason cautioned, and just then they passed a bend in the road and the steep hill with the barn on top sloped up before them. Usually, the barn looked quite striking, standing alone, silhouetted against the sky. But on this Christmas morning, there was a far more remarkable sight.

All up and down the hillside, a massive crowd of men, women, and children were waiting. They were wrapped in cloaks against the cold, and the raggedness of many of those cloaks indicated that the very poorest people of Canterbury and the surrounding area had come to march on behalf of Christmas. Though the morning was frosty and the act they were about to carry out was so risky, there was still about them a sort of excitement, even joy. As Sara and Mason approached, they were greeted with hearty shouts of "Merry Christmas." For the first time in her life, children her own age swarmed to Sara, greeting her like the special friend she had become to all of them, and this pleased her so much that she smiled despite the nervousness she still felt. And, even as those already there milled about, many more people kept coming to the hill, arriving from every direction.

"How many——" Sara began, awed by the crowd.

"Five, six, even seven thousand," John Mason gasped. "Who ever would have believed it? The love of Christmas truly runs deep in many hearts."

He and Sara called over their captains, who in turn gathered about them the people they had recruited for the march, and as they did, even more men, women, and children continued arriving, until finally about an hour before noon Mason estimated ten thousand were ready to march. He told the captains to get everyone's attention. It took several minutes. Someone had written a proclamation stating that the people of England would have Christmas back, even if it meant having the king back, too. He was asking everyone to sign, and the *X*s most of them made—few could actually write their names—took up many pages. Arthur would have forbidden the proclamation, because he wanted to keep the issue of celebrating the holiday separate from the fate of Charles I, but Mason and Sara didn't think of this and let the petition be passed around and signed. Finally, when the crowd was mostly silent, Mason and Sara stood before them. She was quaking inside. It had been one thing to talk in front of a few dozen people. Ten thousand seemed like too many, and for several panic-stricken moments she was sure she couldn't do it. But then she thought of Christmas, and her parents, and about what her Auntie Layla had taught her, and so she spoke. Her voice was still low rather than loud, but in a way that helped quiet the crowd, since they had to stop whispering among themselves to hear her.

"Merry Christmas to you all," she began, and ten thousand shouts of "Merry Christmas" came in response. "Today, we will march into Canterbury and save Christmas. There's really nothing left to say, except to remind you that we must enter all six gates at once, meet in the High Street market, and carry on from there."

"And no violence," John Mason added. "Any blow you strike will hurt Christmas more than it hurts the holiday-haters."

"Can we hit them back if they strike us first?" inquired a short, feisty man.

"As the Bible instructs us, turn the other cheek," Mason replied. "Remember this young lady's parents and aunt are Mayor Sabine's prisoners. We must not give him an excuse to do anything awful to them. All ready? Then let's march to Canterbury!"

The throng overflowed the road as they walked swiftly toward the town. Just before they came into sight of its walls, the march captains divided the marchers into six separate units. These half-dozen battalions of more than fifteen hundred each took different routes to Canterbury, arriving at the six town gates at approximately the same time. Sara, John Mason, and the blacksmith named Clark made certain they led the group at the West Gate, since it was their intention to rescue the four "Christmas criminals" from the stocks.

As the town bell tower tolled noon, the marchers surged forward from six different directions. The guards at the gates were simply overwhelmed. Even if they had thought of trying to slam the gates shut, all at once there were so many people surrounding them that they couldn't have done it anyway.

Down into the city swept the six groups of protestors, hustling past the few dozen armed Trained Band soldiers who, at any rate, had no idea of what to do. Coming through the West Gate, Sara and her group saw ahead of them the four sets of stocks, with Mayor Sabine standing in front preparing to address a crowd. They increased their pace, and the pounding of their feet on the street echoed off the buildings and alerted the mayor to their presence. He turned, saw them approaching, turned pale with fear, and dropped his written speech into the dirt. Then, in his heavy, graceless way, he ran for his home, more anxious to save himself from any possible danger than to confront the marchers.

It was only as the mayor turned to flee that first Elizabeth, then the other three of us in the stocks were able to see an apparent multitude of demonstrators spill into High Street, with a very familiar blonde-haired, blue-eyed thirteen-year-old girl in the lead. That sight caused her mother to gasp, "Is it really possible?" and then the burly black-smith was smashing the locks that held us in the stocks, and we were free to throw our arms around Sara and gaze in wonder at all the people who had come to protest on behalf of Christmas.

"Sara is responsible for this," John Mason shouted to us.

"So many people, Sara," I cried as I took my turn hugging her.

"Oh, there are many more, Auntie Layla," she replied, and as we hugged I saw over her shoulder that thousands of men, women, and children were pouring into the High Street marketplace from every direction. "I have to go do some things," Sara said, causing me to reluctantly let her out of my embrace. "We want our demonstration to be efficient as well as peaceful."

Her parents and I watched in wonder as this painfully shy child stood in front of ten thousand people and led them in singing "We Wish You a Merry Christmas" so loudly that the sound must have echoed inside the fine brick home where the mayor of Canterbury was cowering.

"It's a Christmas miracle!" Elizabeth Hayes exclaimed. "Everything is going to be perfect." But Arthur nudged me with his elbow and pointed. One of the Trained Band had mounted a horse and was galloping away through the West Gate.

"He's off for reinforcements, Layla," Arthur said. "The protest isn't successful yet." Everyone else, it seemed, was singing, and I wondered what would happen next.

Gradually, almost mechanically, Alan raised the club while the
mayor cringed at his feet. It was one of those terrible moments
when everything seems to happen in slow motion.

Twenty-three

or about an hour, everything went according to plan. Arthur suggested that we set our own sentries at each of the six city gates, so that reinforcements from the Trained Band couldn't storm in and take us by surprise. This was done—those few dozen Trained Band members already inside the walls of Canterbury were so overwhelmed by the number of demonstrators that they simply leaned on their muskets and watched as we marched and sang. Mayor Sabine, apparently, had no intention of coming back outside his house. Our thousands of protestors were behaving admirably. They sang Christmas carols, marched along all the main streets chanting "God bless Christmas," and courteously requested those merchants who had their shops open for business to please close their doors in honor of the birth of Jesus.

Most of the shopkeepers were happy to comply. They, too, loved Christmas, and only were working that day because Mayor Sabine had ordered them to do so. Perhaps a dozen others, mostly Puritans whose stores were owned by the mayor, haughtily refused to close. Because the purpose of our march was to support the right of anyone to believe as he or she wished, we took no further action. If they wanted to remain open for business on Christmas Day, this was their privilege—just as it was our privilege to celebrate the holiday we loved so much.

Initially, Arthur, Elizabeth, Alan, and I were kept in the middle of the protestors. Everyone was worried that the mayor and his soldiers would try to recapture us. But it soon became clear that we were in no immediate danger, and, besides, Arthur simply couldn't resist joining Sara and John Mason at the head of the marchers. I found myself there, too, with Alan and Elizabeth not far behind.

It was grand fun to go up and down Canterbury's streets, singing carols and seeing the smiling faces of city residents who suddenly realized that it might be possible to keep the holiday as an important part of their lives. The sun was shining, we were out of the dungeon, and it was Christmas! So an hour flew by, and Arthur whispered to me that it was now time to conclude.

"I'm rather surprised that more of the Trained Band hasn't arrived here already," he murmured in my ear. "I wonder what is keeping them." We didn't know until later that our Christmas protest wasn't the only one that day. In towns like Ipswich and Oxford, there were smaller but still effective demonstrations by working-class people who wanted their beloved holiday back. Some Trained Band troops were on their way to those places. In London, the Lord Mayor had another protest to quell. Canterbury's, though, dwarfed all the others, and it obviously was only a matter of time before more soldiers reached the city. Mayor Sabine had hopefully learned a permanent lesson, our protest had been potent but peaceful, and Arthur was right—we needed to go.

"I'm the one to give the signal, Auntie Layla," Sara called to me, and I was struck by how happy she looked, how excited. She raised her arms high in the air and waved. John Mason and our other captains all along the line of the march started shouting, "Disperse! Disperse!"

But then things began to go wrong. We'd set sentries at all six entrances to the city, and at this exact moment the ones at the North Gate shouted, "Soldiers coming! Maybe a thousand!" and that caused great concern among our number, though there was really no reason to panic. Even if a thousand Trained Band troops really were coming, we still outnumbered them ten to one. They could hardly arrest us all. But instead of filing quickly through the other five city gates and heading for their homes, almost everyone followed a natural instinct of gathering again as a large group in the town marketplace, while the North Gate sentries swung the heavy wooden doors closed and barred them from the inside. Arthur, Sara, Alan, Elizabeth, John Mason, and I tried to tell everyone to just remain calm and go home as we had planned, but instead thousands of voices suddenly raised again in "We Wish You a Merry Christmas," with the addition now of percussion—the soldiers were pounding on the North Gate and loudly demanding to be let in.

The man with the proclamation produced a hammer and nails. He ran to the mayor's house and tacked the thick packet of papers on its heavy wooden door. Then some of the teenaged marchers were overcome by youthful exuberance. Two footballs were produced, and a wild game broke out, with boys running and kicking the ball and shouting out friendly insults to one another. One of the footballs, kicked crookedly, bounced through the door of a dry goods shop that had remained open, and a dozen of the players charged in after it, accidentally knocking over some display shelves. Bolts of cloth rolled into the street, and the Puritan shopkeeper ran after them, shrieking that criminals were destroying his store. The crowd outside was between carols, and so his cries were clearly audible to the soldiers outside the North Gate, who understandably assumed that a mob was rioting inside the walls. They stopped banging on the gate, took up axes, and began knocking it down instead. Afterward, the Puritans would claim that pro-Christmas rioters not only broke down the gate, but burned it, too. Nothing was burned in Canterbury that day, but the rumor has persisted ever since.

The sounds of the wooden gate cracking apart frightened our demonstrators, who now expected to be attacked by the soldiers any minute. Despite instructions to remain calm from Arthur and me, some reached down for stones to throw or lengths of wood to use as clubs. Then the gate broke open and a long column of Trained Band forces marched in, all of them armed with muskets or heavy cudgels. The newly arrived soldiers seemed stunned at the vast number of demonstrators in the marketplace. Our ten thousand protestors were unnerved by the presence of the soldiers. An open space of about twenty yards separated the two groups, and, with tension mounting, Arthur and I knew something had to be done. We stepped in between. Sara tried to come with us, but her mother, reasserting parental authority, grasped her arm and firmly pulled her back.

The leader of the soldiers came forward to meet us, and identified himself as Colonel John Hewson. "What's the meaning of this unlawful gathering?" he demanded. "How dare you riot like this!" Our demonstrators had fallen silent. Everyone could hear what he said to us, and what we said to him.

"This is a demonstration, not a riot," Arthur corrected. "We have come to celebrate Christmas, which is our right."

"Parliament says different," Colonel Hewson replied. "We heard shouts from someone who'd been attacked. What's that all about?"

The owner of the dry goods shop scurried to the colonel's side. "These ruffians charged into my shop, breaking things and shouting they'd do the same to anyone who didn't join them in celebrating Christmas," he claimed. "I've been savagely beaten, and I demand that you arrest them all!"

"That's not true!" I shouted. "Some of the boys were playing football, and the ball was accidentally kicked through his open shop door, and there was some damage. But nobody did it on purpose, and certainly no one hit or threatened him. He's making that up."

"You'll have to tell it to the courts," Colonel Hewson said. "Quick, now, all those who broke things in this man's shop step forward and surrender." I had to admire the colonel. He was vastly outnumbered, and faced with a very difficult situation. But he was remaining calm, and that, at least, was reassuring.

"No one will come forward," Arthur said firmly. "Colonel, there are perhaps five hundred teenaged boys here today. I doubt this shopkeeper can specifically identify those who, for a few seconds, were inside his store. You know you can't arrest them all. Listen to me, please. I promise you that we will disperse now, and go back to our homes. A collection will be taken up to compensate this man for the goods that were lost, even though he lied about what happened. We'll also raise money to repair the gate your men broke down, if you like. So there will be no

Col. John Hewson

permanent loss or damage. You'll get credit for resolving such a potentially dangerous situation, which you would certainly deserve. We can all leave here in peace. What do you say?"

Colonel Hewson looked past us at the thousands of demonstrators milling nervously in the marketplace. He certainly noticed some had stones or sticks in their hands, obviously ready to fight if they thought it was necessary. The colonel was a soldier with enough experience to recognize a good offer when he heard one. He compressed his lips into a tight smile, and nodded.

"That seems like common sense," he said. "If you all go quickly; if, in twenty minutes' time, not one of you is still inside these city walls, then—"

Just as I allowed myself a sigh of relief, the front door to the mayor's fine brick home flew open, and clumsy, heavyset Avery Sabine once again lurched toward the marketplace. Colonel Hewson never finished agreeing to Arthur's proposal, because the mayor interrupted him.

"Colonel! Colonel, I say!" Sabine bellowed. "Shoot these Christmas rioters. Shoot every one!" He shoved his way through the line of Trained Band soldiers, and stood, snorting, by Hewson's shoulder, glaring at Arthur and me.

The colonel said reasonably, "Your honor, these people have just promised to disperse peacefully. They're going to pay for any damages. Let's leave it at that, and be glad we had no bloodshed."

"We *won't* leave it at that!" Sabine blustered. "I'm a man of great influence, and if you don't do your duty here, I'll see you reduced in rank and sent to serve in the loneliest outpost in England! Do what I say! Shoot them all, starting with these two! They were arrested by Blue Richard Culmer last week, along with another man and woman, for planning to incite this terrible riot!" He made a threatening gesture toward Arthur and me. Someone in the ranks of demonstrators behind us, panicking, launched a rock in the mayor's direction. It missed him, and bounced off the leg of a Trained Band soldier. He, in turn, raised his musket and pointed it at the crowd.

"Stop this at once," Arthur shouted. He turned toward our protestors and said, "There must be no violence. None!" Some of our people had their arms raised to throw rocks or swing sticks, but Arthur's air of command was sufficient to make them lower these weapons. Colonel Hewson did the same with his troops. "Muskets down!" he cried.

But Avery Sabine, his courage restored by the presence of armed soldiers, had no further interest in a peaceful conclusion. He snatched a stout club from one of the Trained Band troops, and, swinging it over his head, charged directly at me, probably because I, as a woman, seemed less formidable than Arthur. Alan jumped up in front of me and took Sabine's blow on his arm. The force of it knocked him down.

Seeing Alan on the ground, the mayor turned from me, stood over the fallen sailor, and raised his club again, ready to finish him off. Colonel Hewson and Arthur desperately shouted for their respective followers to stand back, and as they did Alan ducked away from the mayor's second blow and regained his feet. Moving nimbly, he yanked the club from Sabine's grasp. Suddenly unarmed, Sabine reverted to his natural cowardice and turned to run. But his clumsiness betrayed him. He tripped over his own feet and sprawled in the street.

Alan Hayes was a kind, decent man. From the day when we first began planning the Christmas Day protest, he had not only understood but insisted on a strict philosophy of nonviolence. But in the last week he had been arrested, along with his wife. He'd been frantic with worry about his daughter. He'd been held prisoner in a dark, smelly dungeon with only stale bread and dirty water for nourishment, and twice he'd been locked into public stocks. Now his arm ached terribly from the mayor's unprovoked attack, and Sabine, the one who'd laughed at the possibility Sara would have to live in the streets, lay fallen before him. Gradually, almost mechanically, Alan raised the club while the mayor cringed at his feet.

It was one of those terrible moments when everything seems to happen in slow motion. Arthur and I both began to rush to Alan's side, desperately wanting to prevent him from clubbing the mayor, which would certainly force Colonel Hewson to order his troops to shoot, which in turn would result in panic and more death when the demonstrators fought back against the soldiers. But Alan was too far away. I saw the club come up and knew we couldn't reach him in time.

But as the club rose, the door to the mayor's house swung open again. Thirteen-year-old Sophia Sabine raced out and threw herself over the prone form of her father. The sight of the child caused Alan to hesitate. As he stood there uncertainly, Sara pulled out of Elizabeth's grasp and ran to wrap her arms around him.

"No violence, Poppa," she reminded Alan.

Then everything was quiet for a long moment. I remember how, despite the throng all around me in the marketplace, I could hear birds chirping, and the rushing of the Stour River. The Trained Band soldiers shuffled in place, waiting for Colonel Hewson's instructions. Everyone stared at the four figures in front of them—Sophia shielding her father, Sara embracing hers.

Then, fearfully, Mayor Sabine stumbled to his feet. Alan lowered his club. They, too, seemed uncertain what to do next.

Sophia and Sara gazed at each other. Then they both took a step forward and hugged one another tight, tears streaming down their faces.

"Merry Christmas, Sophia," Sara said.

"Merry Christmas, Sara," Sophia replied. She reached out, took her father's arm, and gently led him back into their house. Sara stood looking after them as the door shut. Then she turned, took Alan's hand, and pulled him back toward the rest of the demonstrators. The club dropped at Alan's feet. There was no more anger left in him.

In moments, it seemed, the crowd began to melt away. The protestors quietly walked toward the various city gates that led to the right paths home. The Trained Band lowered their muskets. Colonel Hewson shook Arthur's hand and signaled for his soldiers to form a column.

"You'll see to raising the money for repairs?" he asked.

"I promise," Arthur said.

"That's enough for me," the colonel said. "I don't know what will happen next. You may be wanted in court. Do I have your word of honor you and the other three who were originally under arrest will stay in the area until everything is settled? Good. Then our work here is finished for today."

Arthur smiled and wished the colonel a Merry Christmas. The colonel wished him one back. "I hope your message gets to Parliament loud and clear," he said. "I love Christmas, too!"

Finally, only Arthur, Alan, Elizabeth, Sara, and I stood in the marketplace. All four of us adults looked like quite a sight, since we were all dirty and ragged from our week in prison.

"You need baths!" Sara suggested, reverting in that moment from a poised protest leader to a mischievous thirteen-year-old child. "The smell is making my eyes water!"

"I'll smell *you*, young lady!" her father joked, grabbing Sara and nuzzling her hair while she squealed with laughter. "Well, let's all go home. Arthur, I have no idea of what food we might still have left, but will you join us for Christmas dinner?"

"Please do, Mr. Arthur," Sara added. "It would be so nice if you did."

Arthur's eyes widened in surprise. "Are we friends, now, Sara?" he asked.

"I'm sorry if I seemed rude before, sir," she answered. "From now on, I'm going to try harder not to be so shy."

"Then you've just given us a fine Christmas present, my darling," I said to Sara, and held her hand as the five of us walked happily back to the cottage, singing Christmas carols and feeling thankful for our lives and all the blessings we enjoyed.

After scrubbing ourselves thoroughly with well water and changing into wonderfully clean clothes, we ransacked cupboards and finally assembled a Christmas dinner of dried fruit, potatoes, a few stringy winter vegetables, and fresh water. There was also bread, but Arthur, Alan, Elizabeth, and I had already consumed quite enough bread during our week in prison. We wouldn't want any more for quite a while. Afterward, I produced some candy canes for dessert, and we sang a few more carols. Almost as soon as it was dark, we all felt quite exhausted and were ready for bed. Arthur, who was staying with us for the night, paused as he prepared to go outside for a final washing-up at the well.

"Now, *that* was quite a Christmas!" he declared. By the time he came back inside, everyone else was already asleep.

I settled, over the next forty years, for watching her whenever I could.
I personally delivered Christmas presents to her son, Michael, and to
her daughters. The three youngest were Elizabeth, Gabriella, and Rose.
The oldest girl, the first child born to Sara, was named Layla.

Twenty-four

istory includes many great events, but very few neat, tidy endings. What happened in Canterbury on December 25, 1647, did save Christmas. It also contributed to the eventual fall of the Puritan government and the restoration of the monarchy in England. But all this took quite a long time. We didn't wake up on December 26 to find everything back the way it was before the king lost his throne and Christmas was abolished.

What we did find was that, sometime during the night, Margaret and Sophia Sabine were whisked off by carriage. Word reached Canterbury later that the mayor's wife and daughter had moved permanently into the family's house in London. Margaret Sabine informed all her new neighbors that Canterbury was no longer a fit place for godly people to live. Sophia Sabine, I suppose, soon did meet a suitable husband, and I hope she enjoyed a long, happy marriage. What a brave girl she was, rushing out to save her father from the clubbing he was about to receive! But I really don't know what happened to Sophia. I do know that she and Sara never saw each other again.

Mayor Sabine stayed behind in Canterbury. It quickly became clear that most of the people there now thought of him as a laughingstock. Whenever he would bellow out commands, nobody listened. His reputation among the Puritan leaders in London suffered, too—all of England heard about the Canterbury Christmas March, and how the city's mayor had acted like such a coward. Avery Sabine never did get the high position in government he had both coveted and expected. Instead, he had to keep operating his Canterbury businesses. Customers came into his mills and shops because it was convenient, not because they respected the owner.

In the spring of 1648, Sabine made one last attempt to regain his local influence. He formally charged Arthur, Alan, Elizabeth, and me with assault. Sabine also brought assault charges against a dozen or so other protestors who he had noticed during the demonstration, John Mason among them, and the man who had nailed the "Christmas and King" proclamation to the mayor's front door was accused by Sabine of treason. But this time, there was no Blue Richard Culmer swooping into Canterbury to arrest us. After our impressive Christmas march, Culmer never came to Canterbury again. He was a cruel man, but also a clever one. He realized his nasty tactics would not be effective anymore in a community where ten thousand people were ready to stand up against him. Instead, Colonel Hewson politely notified us all that we would be tried by a jury of our peers, as traditional English law required. He and his men escorted us—*not* in chains—to Leeds Castle, where we were kept in comfortable quarters rather than cells while the trial took place. Elizabeth arranged for Sara to stay with John Mason's wife. Mayor Sabine testified at the trial that he had been pulled down by Arthur, Elizabeth, Alan, and me and thoroughly beaten by our "hooligans" before he had been able to fight his way to freedom. His ability to make up stories was amazing, but in May the jury unanimously found us all not guilty, and we were free to get on with our lives.

And those lives were different. Elizabeth could no longer work for the Sabines. She had to take a job as a milkmaid on a local farm. She was paid much less, and the work was harder. But she gladly accepted this, saying it had been well worth the sacrifice to speak out on behalf of Christmas. Because his role in the protest had become well known and because Puritans still controlled most of England's shipping business, Alan could not find a place on any crews. So he had to start doing farmwork, too. At least he was no longer away from his wife and daughter on long voyages.

Sara, of course, had no more daily lessons with Sophia. But she did, finally, have lots of friends her own age and that helped ease her sense of losing someone who had been as close to her as a sister.

Just as soon as the jury set me free, I left Canterbury. I had to. I had been there almost six years and hadn't aged a bit. It was very hard to go. I told my friends there that I was going to briefly visit people I knew in Nuremberg, and then finally cross the Atlantic Ocean to reunite with my husband. Alan and Elizabeth told me I was always welcome in their home and that they would miss me very much. Sara cried, and begged me to never forget her. That was an easy promise to make. I had plans for my precious girl. As part of them, I did sail for Germany in the summer of 1648, but I had no intention of making the longer journey to America for some time yet.

Arthur guessed the reason. "You mean to ask Sara if she will become one of our gift-giving companions," he said one night in Nuremberg, where he and Leonardo were helping at the toy factory until they felt the time was right to reopen their factory in London. "That's why you've written to Nicholas that you can't come to the New World immediately."

"She is perfectly qualified to join our company," I replied. "You saw for yourself during the protest that she is brave and intelligent and completely dedicated to Christmas. I would reveal our mission to her now if she weren't still a child. I know if I did, she would come with me immediately, but it would break her parents' hearts to lose her. So I'm waiting until she is completely grown—twenty or twenty-five, let's say. Then she can come with me to America, and we'll join Nicholas and Felix in spreading Christmas joy there."

"What if she doesn't want to go?" Arthur asked. "I know she's told you she dreams of traveling to great cities, but young people do change their minds."

"Sara won't," I said confidently, and I waited. While I did, the events in Canterbury on Christmas Day 1647 had further effects on the future of England.

All over the country, people who were unhappy with heavy-handed Puritan rule took note of the march and how it intimidated their new, rigid rulers. They were also pleased when the grand jury refused to convict the march's leaders of any crimes. Support for King Charles spread to the point that, by the summer of 1648, there was civil war again. It was eventually put down by Oliver Cromwell, who led his army all the way into Scotland and Ireland, ruthlessly beating back opponents until, finally, England was really run by the military rather than Parliament—and Cromwell led the military. I hated the fighting, of course, and was especially grieved when King Charles I was executed in January 1649. It was Oliver Cromwell's idea, and I was so sorry that this essentially decent man had decided it was all right to use such awful tactics to achieve his purposes.

For Oliver Cromwell, afterward, things only got worse. Like King Charles before him, he became frustrated when Parliament wouldn't do exactly as he wanted. When its members voted to keep themselves in office rather than schedule elections, Cromwell dissolved Parliament and ended up creating a new one composed entirely of his own trusted supporters. These included the street preacher Praise-God Barebone, and the group became known as "Barebone's Parliament." They really had no power. Cromwell was named Lord Protector of England. He could have called himself the king, but that office had been legally abolished in 1649.

Oliver Cromwell tried hard to rule fairly, based on his religious and political beliefs. Non-Puritans like Catholics and Jews were allowed to quietly worship as they pleased, though they were given no power in Cromwell's government. Cromwell tried to establish schools for working-class children and to make laws based on the best interests of everyone instead of just the rich. He never wavered in his hatred of Christmas, and, while he reigned, celebrating it was still against the law. But, after what we did in Canterbury, there were no more threats of punishment for those who wanted to sing carols or feast on goose or exchange gifts in the privacy of their homes. Parliament couldn't risk more rebellion. The Puritans could, and did, pretend they had ended Christmas forever because there was no longer singing in the streets, and because many shops remained open on Christmas Day. But everyone knew better. Still, without public festivities there was a difference. We had managed to *save* Christmas, but it would be quite a long time before it was entirely restored as a wonderful holiday.

The anti-Christmas laws remained in partial effect until 1660. When Oliver Cromwell died in 1658, Puritan rule was highly unpopular with most of the English people. Cromwell was succeeded as Lord Protector by his son Richard, but Richard had little of his father's charisma and determination. Two years later, he stepped down and Parliament invited Prince Charles, the oldest son of the former king and queen, to come back to England and rule. King Charles II immediately announced "the Restoration," which effectively abolished all the laws passed by the Puritans.

So, celebrating Christmas, in private *and* in public, was once again perfectly legal. But, for more than another one hundred and fifty years the magic and wonder of the holiday didn't entirely return to England.

Many business owners *liked* the idea of their employees having to come to work on December 25, instead of enjoying a paid holiday. Working-class people still felt intimidated by the long years of holiday oppression. Arthur returned to London and reopened the toy factory there, since enough families once again allowed their children to receive gifts from Father Christmas. But no more happy crowds marched through cities singing and playing games and calling on their richest neighbors to share holiday snacks. Most people only dared to celebrate the holiday in their homes. And not all of Britain enjoyed even that limited pleasure. Christmas was not officially restored as a full holiday in Scotland until 1958. So, while Christmas flourished across the English Channel in Europe, it remained almost a half-hearted holiday for many in England until two important events.

First, in 1840, England's young queen Victoria married a German prince named Albert. Albert loved all Germany's wonderful Christmas traditions, including caroling in the streets, church services thanking God for sending his son, and even Christmas trees. With their queen encouraging Christmas celebrations, people in England began to openly enjoy the holiday. Then, in 1843, a fine British author named Charles Dickens published a short novel called *A Christmas Carol*. (I'm glad to say my husband and the rest of our company played a part in this; that story is included in Nicholas's book.) Mr. Dickens's amazing tale of an old miser named Scrooge and a crippled boy named Tiny Tim was a sensation all over the country. Between Prince Albert and *A Christmas Carol*, by 1844 Christmas in England was once again a time of great happiness, even for the poorest people.

By then, of course, I had been reunited with my husband for almost one and a half centuries. But Sara was not with us.

After I left Canterbury, I stayed with Attila and the others in Nuremberg. Several times each year, I would go back to England, and, from a distance, feel my heart swell with pride as I watched my beloved girl continue to grow up. Sara was so intelligent, so *good*!

Though, for the time being, I could not let her see me, I still could enjoy being near her. When she was sixteen, she started a free school for farm girls, teaching them to read and write and do sums. Only three or four came at first, for it was unusual for girls to learn these things. But they told their friends, and more girls came, until finally Sara was giving lessons to a hundred. This was, I knew, more proof that Sara not only deserved but needed to join our gift-giving mission. If she took so much pleasure in helping a hundred children, how much more delightful she would find bringing gifts and hope to hundreds of thousands! I decided I would reveal myself and our secrets to her when she was twenty. I was anxious to be with her again, and also anxious to join Nicholas in America. When I arrived with Sara, it would be like presenting my wonderful husband with a grown daughter! He would love her as much as I did, I knew.

But when Sara was nineteen, she met a farm boy named Robert. Suddenly, I could tell, she dreamed of something other than travel and adventure. A home and a family of her own became what Sara truly wanted. She married Robert, and they had five children, four daughters and a son. I knew then that I could never ask Sara to come join us. She would not want to be separated from her husband and children. I settled, over the next forty years, for watching her whenever I could. I personally delivered Christmas presents to her son, Michael, and to her daughters. The three youngest were Elizabeth, Gabriella, and Rose. The oldest girl, the first child born to Sara, was named Layla.

Sara lived a fine, full life, using her many talents to benefit others. She was a loving wife and mother, and a doting grandmother when her children married and had families of their own. As I watched her grow old, I couldn't help regretting what might have been. How I would have loved to have had my girl with me forever! But I had no right to force what I wanted on Sara, just as Oliver Cromwell and the Puritans had no right to force the abolition of Christmas on England. Instead, the most important thing was that Sara was happy. I reminded myself of this in late 1699, when she was buried in a Canterbury cemetery. More than a thousand people came to the service, many of them middle-aged women she had taught to read and write. After everyone else had left, I approached her grave and left on it a brightly colored candy cane. Then I booked passage on a ship to America, where I rejoined my husband, Nicholas, in 1700 after eighty years of separation. Until now, only he and Arthur knew about what really happened at the Canterbury March—and about Sara.

Now you have heard the story, too, and I want to ask you to do something. If you love Christmas, if you really cherish the hope and joy that the day can bring to everyone, spend just a moment each December 25 remembering those who made great sacrifices to preserve the holiday despite the efforts of its misguided enemies to destroy it. Instead of scorning someone who makes fun of Santa Claus and gifts and Christmas carols, invite him or her into your home to share genuine holiday happiness. Christmas will never be a perfect holiday, because people are not perfect. But, celebrated in the right spirit, it is as close to perfection as anything on this earth can ever be.

And, perhaps, when you see a candy cane, you will think of Sara and the Canterbury Christmas March. I always do.

Lars's Candy Cane Pie

This is a perfect holiday dessert, and everybody's favorite here at the North Pole. Besides being delicious, it's quick and very easy to fix.

1 8- or 9-inch pastry shell
12 candy canes
3 large eggs
1 14-ounce can sweetened condensed milk
1/4 teaspoon cream of tartar
1/3 cup sugar
1/2 teaspoon vanilla extract

1. Bake a pastry shell in an 8- or 9-inch pie plate. We use a refrigerated pie crust we pick up at the North Pole Grocery, and bake according to directions on its package. If you like, feel free to use your own favorite pie crust recipe. Place the cooked and

slightly browned pie shell on a cooling rack. Lower your oven temperature to 350° F.

2. While the pie crust is cooking, crush the candy canes into very, very small pieces and set aside for use later. We use a food processor so there's less mess, but you might have more fun placing them inside a strong, sealed food storage bag and crushing them with a rolling pin or even a small hammer.

3. Separate the eggs, placing the yolks in a small saucepan and the whites in a medium mixing bowl. Set both aside.

4. Add the sweetened condensed milk to the egg yolks in the saucepan. Stir the mixture over medium heat until it begins to thicken—which should happen before it boils! The longer you heat this mixture, the firmer your pie filling will be. Remove the mixture from the heat.

Lars

5. For the pie meringue, beat the egg whites in a bowl until soft peaks form. With your mixer still running, add the cream of tartar, then slowly add the sugar (about one tablespoon at a time). Now beat until stiff peaks form. Finally, beat in the vanilla extract.

6. Fold about two-thirds of the candy cane pieces into the egg yolk mixture in the saucepan. Don't overstir. If you do, the candy pieces will dissolve, which is all right, but the pie looks niftier when it's speckled throughout with little bits of candy cane. Now, pour this mixture into the baked pie crust.

7. Pile the meringue on top of the pie, being careful to seal the edges by spreading the meringue to the edges of the crust. Sprinkle the remaining candy cane bits on top of the meringue.

8. Bake the pie for 12 to 15 minutes, or until the top of the meringue is lightly browned. Let the pie cool before eating.

If you have extra candy canes, you can always serve this pie with a candy cane garnish! And here at the North Pole, we all agree it tastes best with a cup of coffee or a glass of very cold milk.

Merry Christmas!

Acknowledgments

THANKS ABOVE ALL, as usual, to Sara Carder, my editor. I'm also grateful to Andrea Ahles Koos, researcher *extraordinaire*; Jim Donovan, a fine literary agent; Joel Fotinos; Ken Siman; Katie Grinch; Robert I. Fernandez; Larry "Lars" Wilson; Carlton Stowers; Doug Perry; Felix Higgins; Charles Caple and Marcia Melton; Mary and Charles Rogers; Marilyn Ducksworth; Steve Oppenheim; Michael Barson; Elizabeth Hayes; Brian McLendon; Frank and Dot Lauden; Jim Firth; Del Hillen; Mary Arendes; Molly Frisinger; Sophia Choi for special inspiration, unintentional though it might have been; and Iris Chang, a brave, brilliant woman whose memory will always inspire those who were lucky enough to know her.

Everything I write is always for Nora, Adam, and Grant.

Let me offer my sincere thanks to everyone who read *The Autobiography of Santa Claus* and enjoyed it enough to also read this sequel. I wish you all a very Merry Christmas, this year and forever.

Further Reading

YOU CAN READ MORE about Oliver Cromwell, King Charles I, the British Civil War, Blue Richard Culmer, Avery Sabine, the London Apprentice Protest, and the Canterbury Christmas March in lots of history books, many of which should be available in your local library. Layla's story includes all the basic facts. Dates and the events taking place on them are accurate. You can get a good start by finding and reading *The British Civil War* by Trevor Royle (Palgrave/Macmillan, 2004); *Elizabeth's London* by Liza Picard (St. Martin's Press, 2003); *The Struggle for Christmas* by Stephen Nissenbaum (Vintage Books, 1996), and that favorite tool of so many historical novelists, Gorton Carruth's *The Encyclopedia of World Facts and Dates* (HarperCollins, 1993). If you don't own a copy, treat yourself to one. Every page is fascinating.